Timo G

Correlating Illustrations and Text through Interactive Annotation

Timo Götzelmann

Correlating Illustrations and Text through Interactive Annotation

Computer-aided Support for Textbooks

VDM Verlag Dr. Müller

Imprint

Bibliographic information by the German National Library: The German National Library lists this publication at the German National Bibliography; detailed bibliographic information is available on the Internet at http://dnb.d-nb.de.

Cover image: www.purestockx.com

Publisher:
VDM Verlag Dr. Müller Aktiengesellschaft & Co. KG , Dudweiler Landstr. 125 a, 66123 Saarbrücken, Germany,
Phone +49 681 9100-698, Fax +49 681 9100-988,
Email: info@vdm-verlag.de

Zugl.: Magdeburg, Universität, Dissertation, 2007.

Produced in USA and UK by:
Lightning Source Inc., La Vergne, Tennessee, USA
Lightning Source UK Ltd., Milton Keynes, UK
BookSurge LLC, 5341 Dorchester Road, Suite 16, North Charleston, SC 29418, USA

ISBN: 978-3-8364-6360-7

Zusammenfassung

Lehrbücher im Bereich der Anatomie, Naturwissenschaften und des Ingenieurwesens sind wichtige Hilfsmittel um Lernende zu unterstützen. In diesen Bereichen werden häufig die Struktur und die Zusammenhänge realer Objekte erklärt. Daher reichern Autoren die erläuternden Texte oftmals mit ergänzenden Illustrationen der erklärten Objekte an. Eine Schlüsselrolle spielen dabei Annotationen, welche Illustrationen und deren Teile mit ihren Bezeichnungen kennzeichnen und somit eine visuelle Verknüpfung zwischen textuellen Erklärungen und den abgebildeten Objekten zulassen. Illustratoren benutzen verschiedene Arten von Annotationen und eine Vielzahl von Annotationsstilen, um ein funktionales und ästhetisches Layout für die Annotationen in Hinsicht auf das illustrierte Objekt zu erstellen.

Da die Illustrationen in Büchern zwar dreidimensionale Objekte abbilden, jedoch nur eine bestimmte Sicht darauf zeigen können, kann dies zu Verständnisschwierigkeiten führen. Zudem können Illustratoren durch ökonomische Gesichtspunkte dazu gezwungen sein, eine Illustration passend zum Text, jedoch so allgemein wie möglich zu halten, was unter anderem zu einer nachteilig hohen Anzahl von Annotationen führen kann. Um dies zu kompensieren, können durch den Einsatz von modernen Computern angenäherte Modelle der realen Objekte interaktiv erkundet werden. Allerdings beachten viele bisherige interaktive Visualisierungen nicht die Wichtigkeit einer angemessenen Annotation der illustrierten Modelle. Durch die verschiedenen Annotationsarten und deren Stile gestaltet sich die Aufgabe der Berechnung eines Annotationslayouts zwar schwierig, allerdings eröffnet sich mit deren Lösung die Möglichkeit, 3D–Modelle interaktiv zu erkunden, ohne dabei auf die Annotationen nach Vorbild der Lehrbücher zu verzichten.

Eine weiterführende Zielstellung dieser Dissertation basiert auf der Schwierigkeit, dass sich beim Lesen traditioneller Lehrbücher durch die Kombination von erklärenden Texten mit ergänzenden Illustrationen oftmals wechselseitige Suchaufgaben ergeben. Beispielsweise müssen Lernende beim Lesen eines Textes eine Reihe der genannten Bezeichnungen in einer passenden Illustration finden, um die Teile der Illustration den Erklärungen im Text zuzuordnen. Wenn sie im umgekehrten Fall an einer Reihe von abgebildeten Teilen einer Illustration interessiert sind, müssen sie umständlich passende Textstellen suchen, welche genau diese Teile im Zusammenhang erklären. Die vorliegende Arbeit bietet eine Lösung dieser Suchaufgaben für elektronische Lehrtexte und 3D–Modelle an, welche zusätzlich interaktiv erkundet werden können. Durch die Lösung der automatisierten Ermittlung eines Annotationslayouts können zudem interaktiv Illustrationen erzeugt werden, deren Annotationen speziell auf beliebige Sachverhalte angepasst werden können. Damit ergeben sich intuitive Möglichkeiten, um die geschilderten Probleme als Ergänzung zu traditionellen Lehrbüchern zu lösen.

Abstract

Textbooks in the fields of anatomy, natural science and engineering are important resources to support learners. In these fields, the structures and relations of real existing
objects often have to be explained. Hence, expository texts are frequently complemented
by illustrations of the objects to be explained. A key role of this complement play annotations which identify illustrations and their parts by their technical terms and consequently may enable the establishment of a visual link between expository texts and
the depictions. Illustrators use different types of annotations and a variety of annotation
styles in order to design a functional and esthetic layout for annotations with respect to
the illustrations.

Since illustrations in educational books depict spatial objects, but only show a certain
view of them, this may lead to unintentional ambiguities. Additionally, due to economic constraints illustrators may be forced to design illustrations for expository texts
as general as possible, which amongst others may result in a large quantity of annotations. In order to compensate this, modern computers may be used to interactively
explore approximated models of real existing objects. However, many existing interactive visualizations neglect the importance of an adequate annotation of the models to be
illustrated. The usage of different annotation types and styles makes the computation
of annotation layouts a challenging task, but such a solution enables the interactive exploration of 3D models without forgoing annotations similar to those typically found in
educational books.

Another objective of this book is based on the difficulty that readers of traditional educational books often encounter mutual search tasks arising from the combined use of expository texts with complementary illustrations. For example, readers must find annotations in illustrations corresponding to technical terms in a text segment of their interest
in order to associate the illustrations' parts with their explanations in the continuous
text. In the opposite case, if they are interested in a set of depicted parts in an illustration, they have to laboriously find text segments which describe exactly this set of parts
in a context. This work introduces a solution to these search tasks for electronic versions
of educational texts and 3D models which may be interactively explored. Additionally,
through the solution of automated determination of annotation layouts, illustrations can
be generated which annotations can be adapted to individual contexts. Therefore, intuitive opportunities arise to address the characterized issues as addendum to traditional
educational textbooks.

Acknowledgment

In this section I would like to thank the persons who supported me. This book was written during my work as Ph.D. student at the Otto–von–Guericke University of Magdeburg and my research stay at the Technical University of Catalonia, Barcelona. I am particularly grateful to my adviser Prof. Thomas Strothotte who gave me the chance to work on such an interesting research topic and steered its progress by his valuable suggestions. Likewise, my special thanks go to my adviser Prof. Knut Hartmann, for the great collaboration and his constructive critics and discussions anytime during my work. Furthermore, for the very constructive support in special fields of my work I have to thank my advisers Prof. Andreas Nürnberger and Prof. Pere-Pau Vázquez. I would also like to thank my external reviewers Prof. Jürgen Döllner and Prof. Maneesh Agrawala for immediately agreeing to examine this Ph.D. thesis.

I also thank my team– and officemates Kamran Ali, Axel Berndt, Angela Brennecke, Rita Freudenberg, Tobias Germer, Dr. Marcel Götze, Niklas Röber, Prof. Stefan Schlechtweg, Dr. Henry Sonnet, Martin Spindler and the other persons who shared fruitful discussions and diverse leisure activities with me. My special thanks go to the secretariat, namely Stefanie Quade, Petra Schumann, Petra Specht and Beate Troré as well as the team for the technical support Thomas Rosenburg, Heiko Dorwarth, and Dr. Volkmar Hinz for helping me with various problems.

Further on, I have to thank Prof. Silvia Beck, Prof. Ingo Garschke, Prof. Uwe Göbel and Prof. Jochen Stücke for taking time for the expert survey and discussions on illustration and book design.

I wish to thank the German state of Saxony–Anhalt, the Otto–von–Guericke University of Magdeburg and its Faculty of Computer Science for the scholarships which allowed me to concentrate on my research for the past years.

Last but not least I would like to thank my sister and my parents for the support and encouragement they have always provided me. Likewise, all of those friends who supported me and reminded me from time to time, that there are more things in life than solely research.

Table of Contents

1 Introduction   1
   1.1 Motivation and Aims 4
   1.2 Results and Contributions 4
   1.3 Thesis Overview 5

2 Two Aspects of Annotations   9
   2.1 Introduction 9
   2.2 Annotations 12
     2.2.1 Disambiguation 12
     2.2.2 Differentiation of Annotations 13
     2.2.3 Storage of the 3D Models' Annotations 14
   2.3 Illustrations in Educational Books 15
     2.3.1 Usage in Educational Books 16
     2.3.2 Classification of Illustrations 17
     2.3.3 Computer–based Illustration 18
   2.4 Annotated Illustrations 21
     2.4.1 Functions of Annotations in Illustrations 21
     2.4.2 Illustration Layers 22
     2.4.3 Traditional Process of an Illustration's Annotation 23
     2.4.4 Annotation Layout for the Interactive Exploration of 3D Models . . 24
   2.5 Conclusion 24

PART I: ANNOTATION LAYOUT

3 Annotation Layout Foundations   25
   3.1 Introduction 25
   3.2 Analysis of Annotated Illustrations 26
     3.2.1 Corpus and Method 26
     3.2.2 Types of Annotations 26
     3.2.3 Categorization into Layout Containers 28
     3.2.4 Layout Styles of Containers 29
     3.2.5 Conclusion 32
   3.3 Existing Guidelines for Annotation 33
     3.3.1 Scientific and Technical Illustrations 33
     3.3.2 Annotation of Maps 36
     3.3.3 Conclusion 38

	3.4	Related Work	41
		3.4.1 Focus	41
		3.4.2 Existing Approaches	42
		3.4.3 Discussion	48
	3.5	Conclusion	49

4 Encapsulated Annotation Layout Approach — **51**

	4.1	Introduction	51
	4.2	Metrics for Layout Containers	52
		4.2.1 Legibility	53
		4.2.2 Unambiguity	54
		4.2.3 Visual Occlusion	55
		4.2.4 Frame Coherence	56
	4.3	An Encapsulated Annotation Layout Approach	57
	4.4	Algorithms for Annotation Layout	60
		4.4.1 Determination of Candidates	60
		4.4.2 Weighted Evaluation	62
		4.4.3 Initial Layout	63
		4.4.4 Coherence by Agents	66
		4.4.5 Adaptivity of styles	70
	4.5	Conclusion	71

5 Contextual Annotation — **73**

	5.1	Introduction	73
	5.2	Problem Analysis	74
	5.3	Approach	75
		5.3.1 Grouped Annotation Layout	76
		5.3.2 Exclusive Annotation	78
		5.3.3 Experimental Application	78
		5.3.4 Discussion	79
	5.4	User Study	80
		5.4.1 Method	81
		5.4.2 Results	83
		5.4.3 Discussion	84
	5.5	Conclusion	85

PART II: LINKING ILLUSTRATIONS AND TEXT BY ANNOTATIONS

6 Correlating Illustrations and Text — **87**

	6.1	Introduction	87
	6.2	Search Tasks	88
		6.2.1 Problem Statement	88
		6.2.2 Related Work	89
		6.2.3 A Concept for Correlating Illustrations and Text through Annotations	91
		6.2.4 Conclusion	96

6.3 Qualitative Descriptions of Views 97
    6.3.1 Specifications 97
    6.3.2 Related Work 98
    6.3.3 Approach 99
    6.3.4 Discussion 100
6.4 Searching Text Documents 100
    6.4.1 Specifications 100
    6.4.2 Retrieval Methods 101
    6.4.3 Information Retrieval Models 102
    6.4.4 Vector Space Model 105
    6.4.5 Interaction 106
    6.4.6 Necessary Adaptations 107
6.5 Conclusion 108

7 Application Scenario and Evaluation   109
7.1 Introduction 109
7.2 Experimental Application 110
    7.2.1 Framework 110
    7.2.2 Interactive Browser and Mutual Queries 111
    7.2.3 Interactive Query Refinement 113
7.3 User Study 116
    7.3.1 Method 116
    7.3.2 Results and Discussion 118
7.4 Discussion 120
7.5 Conclusion 121

8 Concluding Considerations   123
8.1 Theses 123
8.2 Critical remarks 128
8.3 Future Directions 128

A Annotation of Animated 3D Models   131
A.1 Introduction 131
A.2 Problem Analysis 131
A.3 Approach 132
    A.3.1 Necessary Adaptations to the Layout Approach 133
    A.3.2 Determination of Calm Regions 134
    A.3.3 Analysis of the 3D Parts' Movements 135
    A.3.4 Comparison 136
    A.3.5 Experimental Application 136
    A.3.6 Discussion 137
A.4 User Study 138
    A.4.1 Method 139
    A.4.2 Results 140
    A.4.3 Discussion 141
A.5 Conclusion 141

B   Investigated Corpus of Illustrations   143

C   Expert survey   149

D   Pseudocode Segments   153

E   Data Structures   157

F   Reference Systems   159

G   Video Scenes   161

Bibliography   163

List of Figures   177

List of Tables   181

Index   183

How to read the margin notes

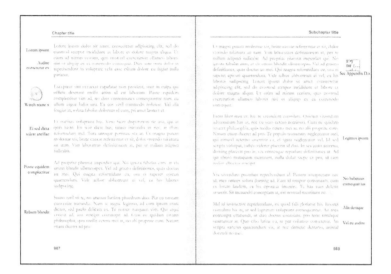

Type	Description
Text	In order to support skim reading over the text segments, several central statements and ideas of the continuous text are summarized.
  Watch scene x	In order to support the mediation of animated and interactive elements several video clips are additionally provided by the WWW. Note to watch video scene x according to Appendix G.x.
x:=y for (... See Appendix D.x	In order not to distract the continuity of the text, several pseudo-code segments were sourced out. The pseudocode is attached in Appendix D.x.

x

1 | Introduction

For generations, educational textbooks have been important tools to support learners in many fields of science such as anatomy, natural science and the technical domain. Authors aim at compiling comprehensive explanations in order to mediate complex subject matters in an effective way. For the explanation of real existing objects the exclusive use of text may be problematic. While text is superior in explaining the functioning of objects and their semantic relations, illustrations convey visual attributes and spatial relations [Bal97]. On this account, book authors often collaborate with illustrators who carefully adapt their depictions, in order to complement the explanations described in continuous text.

Textbooks as learning material

Text and illustrations

Automated Annotation Layout

In order to augment visual properties with additional information, several kinds of annotations can be integrated into the illustration and its parts. These annotations may particularly be used in order to establish the link between parts of the illustration and their technical terms. There are numerous publications recommending the combined use of depicted objects with annotations. Many of them base their arguments on the dual encoding theory introduced by PAIVIO [Pai71]. According to this theory, humans have two different and independent processing channels. While one of them processes visual elements, the other one is used for verbal elements. Thus, the conjunctive use of both channels significantly improves the mediation of information. Correspondingly, the psychologist MAYER showed that the combination of illustrations with annotations raises synergy effects in order to enhance the understanding of learners. He performed numerous user studies and argued that annotations without illustrations as well as illustrations without annotations 'did not allow students to build mental model of the system as indicated by problem-solving transfer' [May89].

Integration of annotations

Annotations are important

For centuries those illustrations are used as approved tools for educational purposes. However, their static depiction causes some problems. Since the spatial objects are depicted by *flat* images, problems may arise such as the occurrence of unintentional ambiguities as well as problems to depicting each of the important parts in the same illustration. The solution of illustrating an object from different viewpoints may only partially resolve all unwanted ambiguities and requires considerable cognitive capacities for the mental reconstruction of the object's spatial shape and arrangement of its parts [FMN+91].

Problem: spatial objects depicted by flat images

Ideally, one illustration could be generated for each thematic context described in an educational book, i.e., each aspect which describes a certain number of an object's parts (cf. Appendix C.8). Unfortunately, economic constraints force illustrators to merge multiple contexts into one illustration which manifests in a larger quantity of annotations. Addi-

Problem: economic constraints

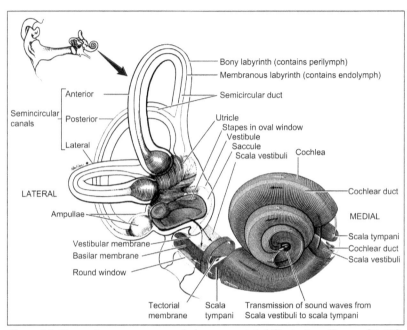

Figure 1.1: Human inner ear as example for an annotated illustration. (Source: [Tor97])

tionally, illustrators have to emphasize several parts in order to allow a differentiation of the contexts. However, this strategy may also spoil the constraints of human cognitive capacity. Very complex illustrations may overburden the viewer meaning that contexts cannot or only insufficiently be recognized [BY90]. The popular information designer TUFTE [Tuf97] even claims: 'If *everything* is emphasized, *nothing* is emphasized'. However, illustrators often cannot adapt illustrations to each single context described in the text, since the publishing costs of the books would exceed a bearable limit.

Exploration of spatial objects
In past decades the power of computers and their graphical abilities have progressed at a fast pace. Nowadays, 3D models, i.e., spatial approximations of real existing objects can be utilized to interactively explore their three dimensional shape and configuration. Through the dynamic nature of interactive visualizations it is even possible to explore animated 3D models, e.g., spatial and temporal approximations of a beating heart or a working combustion motor. Hence, the problem of the static nature of printed material can be addressed by interactive applications. Recently, such applications' benefits towards learning have been verified [NCFD06, LVK$^+$06].

Layout of annotations
As mentioned before, annotations are an important element of illustrations. Since the layout of annotations is an art whose basic principles are rarely discussed in literature (cf. Appendix C.4) and that comprises esthetic and functional constraints, it is a non–trivial task to compute a layout for annotations which resemble those of human illus-

trators. Unfortunately, there is no existing approach for the annotation of interactive visualizations of 3D models which explicitly considers the requirements of illustrations in traditional books. For example, annotations should be in the direct *spatial proximity* (see Figure 1.1) of the illustration's parts they denote [MA92a, BB98], but most of the approaches neglect this requirement. Other approaches are not able to annotate the visualizations in *real time*, so that they would not allow an interactive exploration of 3D models.

Special requirements for annotation

If the layout of annotations could be automated for the exploration of 3D models, it would be possible to address both problems induced by the static nature of books. Hence, interactive applications could aid learners to understand the configuration and shape of spatial objects. Additionally, it would be possible to generate various renditions of those 3D models, which are customized to specific contexts.

Automated annotation layout

Search Tasks

If illustrations are used in conjunction with continuous text, their annotations may help readers to associate textual descriptions and visual depictions. In other words, if the individual parts of the illustration are annotated with their technical terms, the descriptions in the continuous text can be bidirectionally linked with their depictions (see Figure 1.2). On the one hand, if learners read a certain text segment, they can locate the associated illustration and identify the parts of the illustration which are indicated in the text. On the other hand, they can study an illustration, in which case the annotations provide the technical denomination of the depicted parts which are required to locate appropriate descriptions in the continuous text. Hence, annotations are an important element for the complementary use of text and illustrations.

Annotations as bidirectional link

Furthermore, when user–defined contexts could be automatically depicted in annotated illustrations, another problem of books could be addressed: learners are confronted with search tasks. When they are reading a text segment, they have to search the corresponding illustration and identify the mentioned parts by their annotations. Conversely, if they are interested in explanations of specific parts of an illustration, they have to find the text segments which correlate with this information need. These search tasks could be supported by an interactive approach which determines correlating illustrations and texts.

Search tasks

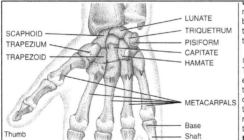

tuberosity that provides a point of attachment of the **biceps brachii muscle**. The body (**shaft**) of the **radius** articulates with two bones (**carpals**) of the wrist. Also at the distal end is a styloid process.

Carpals, Metacarpals, and Phalanges
The **carpus** (wrist) of the hand consists of eight small bones, the **carpals**, connected to each other by **ligaments** (Figure 6.24 on p. 127). The bones are arranged in two transverse rows, with four bones in each row, from the lateral to medial position, are the **scaphoid** or navicular, **lunate**, **triquetrum**, and **pisiform**. In about 70 percent of

Figure 1.2: Combination of continuous text and illustration. (Adapted from [Tor97])

3

1.1 Motivation and Aims

Inspired by the problems of traditional textbooks introduced above, two principal research goals can be identified. The *first objective* is to allow the computation of the manifold and complex annotation layouts similar to those used in illustrations of educational textbooks. Therefore, different types of annotations have to be determined. Based on their prevalent characteristics different layout styles have to be determined and formalized. Additionally, clear specifications for the computation of annotation layouts have to be deduced from the informal literature for the annotation of illustrated objects and the analysis results.

Objective: Annotation layout for 3D models

On the basis of 3D models consisting of multiple parts and their technical terms, an interactive approach has to be developed which computes annotation layouts for those models. It should consider the specifications and allow for defining individual preferences with respect to the type and layout styles of the annotations. This approach should not require extensive preprocessing and should be independent of specific types of 3D models and their application domain. Furthermore, this approach should incorporate methods which cope with the limited cognitive capacities of viewers. Hence, the annotation system should be able to guide the viewers' attention to specific contexts of the 3D model, but still leave the option to control the visualization.

Besides the annotation of interactive visualizations of 3D models the *second objective* copes with the challenge of search tasks which arise by the conjunctive use of continuous text and illustrations. The aim is to support learners when they are reading electronic versions of educational texts. Ideally, they should be able to select arbitrary parts of the text and obtain 3D models correlating with their selection. In the opposite case, they should be able to select arbitrary parts of a 3D model in order to obtain correlating explanations of the electronic educational texts. Finally, these results should be combined with the achievements of the first objective, in order to obtain an experimental application which can be used to support learners.

Objective: Support for search tasks

1.2 Results and Contributions

Based on the objectives described in the previous section, an approach was developed which enables the determination of annotation layouts that are similar to the archetypes in educational books whilst the user is able to interactively explore 3D models. This approach has been designed in an encapsulated manner in order to be independent of specific application domains and their 3D model types, which allows it to be embedded into existing rendering engines. Since the annotation layout can be controlled, it may be dynamically changed in order not to overburden the viewers' cognitive capacities and to use annotations to focus the viewers' attention to specific contexts.

Encapsulated annotation approach

These results are merged with a solution for the second objective: to intuitively support learners with their search tasks when reading educational material. This solution allows learners to add new educational material, i.e., 3D models and educational texts without the necessity of manual preprocessing. Hence, it can be applied towards many prospective approaches.

Correlating illustrations and text

These principal contributions were achieved:

- Analysis of different annotation types and their appearance in printed educational material.

- Deduction of specifications for a functional and esthetic annotation layout.

- Definition of metrics for the real–time evaluation of computed annotation layouts.

- Development of real–time annotation layout techniques which may be controlled by their parametrization.

- Development of a solution for adapting the annotation types and styles in accordance with user interaction.

- Development of methods to ensure the frame coherence of annotations during the interaction with 3D models.

- Development of an encapsulated annotation approach for the interactive exploration of 3D models independent of their type and target application.

- Development of context–driven annotation techniques such as exclusive annotation and grouped annotation.

- Development of techniques to annotate dynamic 3D visualizations in accordance with the annotation specifications.

- Development of intuitive methods to support the bidirectional search tasks with illustrations and texts.

1.3 Book Overview

This book consists of two parts which are organized in a consecutive manner. The first part (Chapters 3 to 5) addresses the first objective, i.e., the determination of annotation layout for the interactive exploration of 3D models. The second part (Chapters 6 and 7) addresses the second objective of this book in order to develop an approach to support the search tasks that occur when learners use educational textbooks that make complementary use of annotated illustrations and continuous text. Finally, to not distract the continuity of the text, several extensive elements and excursions were deferred to appendices.

Two consecutive parts

Postponed appendices

Chapter 2 introduces fundamental terms and motivates the necessity to subdivide the following chapters into two successive parts. First, it generally introduces annotations, followed by the basics of illustrations, and identifies the task of automated annotation. Finally, this chapter clarifies the function of annotations to bridge illustrations and text, and presents a layer model for illustrations that forms the basis for an automated annotation approach.

Terminology and basics

Part I – Annotation Layout for 3D Models

Analysis and formalization

Specifications and related work

Chapter 3 analyzes a corpus of educational books in order to derive and formalize a set of annotation types and their different styles. Next, it discusses guidelines of human illustrators and deduces a set of specifications for a prospective interactive annotation approach. Using these specifications, the existing approaches in the field of interactive annotation layout are assessed. As a result of this chapter, the annotation types can be described by only three different layout elements. The most common layout styles of each annotation type are formalized. The specifications derived can be used to assess existing automated annotation approaches and to define metrics for an automatic annotation layout.

Annotation metrics

Strategies and algorithms

Chapter 4 utilizes the layout styles and specifications derived in Chapter 3 in order to develop a flexible approach for the automatic annotation of 3D models. First, for each of the specifications, metrics are developed for the qualitative assessment of computed annotation layouts. Next, appropriate annotation algorithms are constructed on the basis of these metrics. The development of annotation algorithms supports that an annotation approach should to support multiple different annotation styles. In order to support a wide variety of styles by an interactive approach, heuristics must be employed. Furthermore, to allow different preferences of illustrators, the influence of each of the metrics may be weighted. Additionally, an annotation approach has to be adaptive, i.e., able to interchange the annotation types according to user interactions.

Contextual annotation

Chapter 5 extends the annotation approach developed in Chapter 4. It tackles the challenge of static illustrations that too many annotations might overburden the viewers' cognitive capacities. Two different concepts are proposed for the contextualized annotation of 3D models which are implemented in an experimental application and evaluated by a user study. The results of the approach and the evaluation lay the foundation for the second part of this thesis.

Part II – Correlating Illustrations and Text

Development of concept

Chapter 6 first motivates the challenge of mutual search tasks of educational textbooks, proposes a concept, and reviews the related work. Finally, two central elements of the proposed concept are contemplated concerning their applicability towards a practical solution. Through the equalization of media (i.e., illustrations and continuous text) by descriptive representations, similarities can be determined in order to allow mutual search queries. Users can be supported by reading educational material which uses both media complementary. A concept developed in this chapter forms the basis for domain specific applications.

Proof-of-concept

Chapter 7 picks up the concept introduced in Chapter 6 and applies it to the anatomic domain. Domain–specific adaptations are made in order to develop an experimental application. The annotation approach developed in the first part serves as an essential element to support the visual linkage between illustrations and text. The experimental application serves as proof of concept for the achievements of both parts of this thesis. The concept developed in Chapter 6 is evaluated by a user study, which not only validates the central statements of the concept and its applicability, but also grants additional insight into the practical use of the application.

Chapter 8 concludes this thesis, reviews the achieved results and gives some points of
criticism. Finally, this chapter summarizes central statements of the book and points out
its future directions of research.

Conclusion

Appendix A presents an optional extension based on the annotation approach developed in the first part of this book and proposes how to integrate this extension into the
concept of correlating illustrations and text developed in the second part of this thesis.
Since it is an optional extension, and so as not to disrupt the argumentative flow, it has
been postponed to the appendix. This extension addresses the usefulness of the interactive exploration of animated 3D models in combination with the advantage of annotated
illustrations. Consequently, animated 3D models such as a running motor or a beating
heart can be explored by users, while preserving the specifications for interactive annotation approaches.

*Annotation of
animated
3D models*

Appendix B covers statistics about investigated illustrations of the corpus of investigated books. This appendix has been postponed in order not to disrupt the text's continuity of Chapter 3. Initially, this appendix proposes an algorithm for the selection of the
books' illustrations. Accordingly, these illustrations are investigated so as to be able to
describe different phenomena of annotations.

*Investigation of
illustrations*

Appendix C reports an expert survey which addressed crucial questions of this book
that could not be answered by the review of literature. In order to obtain evidence,
multiple experts of the domain of illustration were consulted.

Expert survey

Finally, the remaining appendices briefly introduce additional information about a small
set of pseudocode segments (**Appendix D**), input data structures (**Appendix E**), the reference computer systems (**Appendix F**), and finally, the list of video scenes to this book
which can be found in the internet (**Appendix G**).

Two Aspects of Annotations

Outline

This chapter introduces fundamental terms and motivates the necessity to subdivide the following chapters into two successive parts. Since both parts spotlight annotations under different aspects, this chapter first introduces the usage of annotations in general, and finally in the special case of illustrations.

Achievements

For both problems addressed this chapter defines and focuses on required terms. It clarifies the function of annotations for bridging images and text and presents a layer model for illustrations which serves as a basis for a prospective automated annotation approach.

2.1   Introduction

Traditional educational textbooks are sophisticated resources to support learners in understanding complex subject matters. However, static paper documents have several disadvantages which can be improved by the purposive use of computers. This book addresses several issues of those textbooks, which are designed to explain complex spatial objects. Since books can only present static views of those objects, the communication of their spatial shape and arrangement may be ambiguous. This problem can be addressed by the use of computers, which allow to explore geometric models of the objects addressed in those books. A crucial task, normally performed by illustrators, is to augment the pictured object with additional data (i.e., textual terms and descriptions) and to focus on specific contexts. The first part of this book introduces novel approaches for the adaptation of this nontrivial *annotation* task for the exploration of geometric models by computer.

1st objective: Annotation layout

The conjoint usage of continuous text with illustrations may support the user during the learning process. Book authors often collaborate with illustrators in order to systematically complement the continuous text with depictions. By augmenting them with textual annotations, readers may link between the terms explained in the continuous text and their visual representations in the illustrations. However, in order to establish such a link from one medium, the readers have to search for the corresponding positions in the opposite medium. By the use of geometric objects which are augmented with additional electronic annotations identifying the parts of those objects, correlations may be found between electronic texts and 3D models. On this basis, the second part introduces a concept for the support of readers' search tasks by the help of computers.

2nd objective: Support of search tasks

As the starting point, based on both objectives initially described, fundamental terms have to be explicated and focused towards their use in this thesis. Next, because of the manifold usage of the term annotation, Section 2.2 addresses its disambiguation. Section 2.3 introduces and classifies illustrations used in books, and presents their automatic generation by computers. Subsequently, Section 2.4 explains the use of annotations in illustrations and presents a layer model in order to define a basis for both parts of this thesis. Finally, Section 2.5 concludes this chapter.

Media

According to WEIDENMANN [Wei95] media are objects, devices and configurations for the storage and communication of messages. Media can be designed to communicate messages for each of the human senses. Additionally, different codes can be used in order to mediate them. Utilizing adequate combinations of multiple codes this communication process may be supported, if they can complement each other and thus, aggregate their media specific communication capabilities by synergy effects. In this thesis, the term medium is used for two different media used in traditional educational books, i.e., images and continuous text.

Documents

In general language the term document is commonly used for handwritten or printed papers with an authoritative function (e.g., certificates, forms, letters). However, in the context of computers, this term covers a considerably wider range of representations. ENDRES AND FELLNER [EF00] introduce the term digital documents as self–contained data unit, which content is digitally encoded and stored on an electronic data carrier.[1] Thus, other types of data (e.g., images, 3D models, videos and audio files) can be seen as documents. Additionally, as long as they can be stored as a self–contained data unit these documents can even be subdivided into smaller units. In the case of text, even individual text segments such as sections, paragraphs and sentences may be considered as documents [SAB93].

Text Documents

A particular type of documents used in this book are documents containing continuous text. Since there are multiple types of texts, this book employs BALLSTEDT's [Bal97] differentiation between *expository texts*, *narrative texts*, and *instructive texts*:[2]

- **Expository texts.** Describe and explain characteristics of objects, states and processes. This type comprises all those texts which represent a domain of knowledge.

- **Narrative texts.** Report about situations, events, sequences of operations and their consequences. Those texts are predominantly used in the social sciences.

---

[1]Original text in German: 'Ein *digitales Dokument* ist eine in sich abgeschlossene Informationseinheit, deren Inhalt digital codiert und auf einem elektronischen Datenträger abgespeichert ist...'.

[2]Original terms in German: *Expositorische Texte, Narrative Texte,* and *Anleitende Texte.*

- **Instructive texts.** Are similar to expository texts, but do not extend the reader's conceptual, but procedural knowledge. This type of texts is used to support tasks which have to be guided by information about the sequence of actions, such as recipes or manuals for maintenance and repair.

Despite books of anatomy, natural sciences and technical documentation may also contain instructive texts and other types of media, the following of this book regards text documents as expository texts.

3D Models

Another type of documents used in this book are *3D models*. Of special interest are those 3D models, which are used to represent spatial approximations of real existing objects (e.g., anatomic or technical objects). They can be represented by multiple different electronic descriptions:

- **Surface models.** While *polygonal models* are sets of adjacent planar polygons, *free-form models* are sets of adjacent parametrized planes which are deformed by applying basis functions (e.g., splines) on a set of control points. Both of the models approximate the surfaces to describe the desired object.

- **Voxel models.** These models consist of a finite number of rasterized volume elements which are three dimensionally arranged.

- **Implicit models.** Consist of multiple mathematical equations which describe the surface as well as the volume of the spatial object.

- **Procedural models.** Use a set of parameterizable algorithms to generate spatial geometry.

Besides the spatial descriptions of the approximated object and its parts, additional information about the topology of 3D model's disjoint *3D parts* and their elementary components' connectivity (e.g., faces) as well as their appearance are usually stored along with the 3D model [FvDFH90].

Metadata

Metadata is often called data about data, and may be coupled with a document, a part of it, or a collection of documents [Nat04]. It can be used to describe documents in order to enhance their usefulness [Mar98] or to make them retrievable (e.g., for search engines). SCHMITT [Sch06] classifies three types of metadata according to their relation to the content of the documents:

- **Content independent.** These data do not describe the content of documents, but can be useful for administrative tasks and to ensure their correct interpretation. Other authors refer to that type of metadata with *Descriptive Metadata* [BYRN99, Mar95]. An example are the 15 basic metadata elements defined by the *Dublin Core* [WKLW98], including the documents author, creation date etc.

- **Content related.** These data relate to the document and describe it on a semantically low level, i.e., by information which can be automatically extracted from the document. This information can be used by search engines to find similar documents. Examples are histograms of images and information about video segments.

- **Content descriptive.** The data are used to semantically describe the document. Thus, search engines can facilitate text queries in order to search the documents. Since it is hardly possible to extract those data from the documents, they have often been manually added in a time consuming task. Another term for this class of metadata is *Semantic Metadata* [BYRN99]. Examples are names of persons on an image and captions.

This book concentrates on content descriptive metadata which can be used for the semantic description of text documents and 3D models, respectively their 3D parts.

Documents' Contexts

The word context is derived from the latin word *contextus*, which means *to weave together*: 'The part of a text or statement that surrounds a particular word or passage and determines its meaning' [Pic00]. This book considers text documents as a set of terms $d = \{term_1, \cdots, term_i\}$, whereas 3D models are assumed to consist of a set of 3D parts $m = \{part_1, \cdots, part_j\}$. Hence, in the following chapters contexts define a combination of multiple specific terms, respectively 3D parts.

Text context For educational purposes, text documents are usually divided into multiple text segments (e.g., sections, paragraphs) that contain a (sub–)set of terms and describe contexts semantically. By neglecting the semantical relations, in this book those *text contexts* are defined as $c_{text} \subseteq d$.

View context Analogously, the illustrations used in educational material constitute certain views of spatial objects to visually describe one or multiple contexts. In this thesis, a *view context* c_{view} is defined as a (sub–)set of a 3D models' parts, which are visible in a certain view.

3D context Furthermore, a *3D context* c_{3D} comprises a (sub–)set of 3D model parts, but without the condition that there exists a view which depicts each of them, so that $c_{view} \subseteq c_{3D} \subseteq m$.

2.2 Annotations

First, this section discusses definitions of the term annotation, shows that it is used for several applications and different aspects and states its use in this thesis. Finally, different possibilities of annotations' storage in relation to documents are discussed.

2.2.1 Disambiguation

Definitions The OXFORD ENGLISH DICTIONARY [Sim91] refers to the origin of the noun *annotation*, and its verb *to annotate* has its etymological roots in the Latin word *annotare*, which is derived from *nota* that means *mark* respectively *to mark*. Some sources only define the noun annotation only in the textual context: 'a note, added to anything written' [Sim91] respectively the verb annotate: 'add explanatory notes to a book, documents etc.' [Swa92]. Other dictionaries additionally consider diagrams [Pea99] and pictures [Dal97] as annotations. Furthermore, using the annotation as a verb–derived noun, it stands for:'the act of annotating' [Sin91].

In practical use the term annotation is utilized in multiple fields with different applications. As mentioned, textual documents may be annotated by adding notes and images [Pea99, Swa92, Dal97]. While annotations in biology are used to describe sequences of genes (e.g., [PPP⁺05]), in the context of software engineering it is used for a technique of program documentation in addition to textual comments (e.g., [KW03]). In linguistics, descriptions added to different levels of linguistic analysis, are referred to as annotations (e.g., [Wyn05]). For the world wide web, documents (e.g., hypertext, images) may be semantically annotated (i.e., with information about the content of the website, image or video) in order to make them automatically processable (e.g., [KPT⁺04]). Finally, in the visual context, annotation means the mapping of additional textual and graphical information into pictures [Tuf06].

Practical use

As shown, there is a wide variety of applications which associate the term annotation with completely different meanings. Since in this book this term is used differently for images and 3D models, the following section defines their individual characteristics.

2.2.2 Differentiation of Annotations

In general, annotations can be seen as metadata to documents. MARSHALL's [Mar98] research based on annotations of hypertext documents. She introduced multiple distinctive features in order to characterize different types of annotations, whereas most of them were hypertext–specific. However, she also differentiated between formal and informal annotations that can be applied to the focus of this thesis:

Annotations in hypertext

- **Formal annotations.** This type of annotation means content–descriptive metadata which are stored in addition to a document for improving its interoperability. Thus, computer programs such as search engines may process them in order to interpret the document's content.

- **Informal annotations.** These annotations are visualized along with the document (e.g., notes, marginalia) in order to inform the reader. Thus, humans may interpret them without additional tools, but it is more difficult to process them by computers.

This can be transferred to the annotations used in this thesis. Formal annotations are used with 3D models, which are referred to as *annotated 3D models*. Each geometric description of the 3D model parts is assigned to machine readable annotations, which help to identify each of those 3D parts. Using the annotations, computer programs may process these textual annotations, for example to make the 3D models retrievable by a search engine. Since the storage location of those formal annotations can be differentiated, Section 2.2.3 discusses three possibilities.

Machine readable annotations

On the contrary, informal annotations are visually attached to their documents. Hence, they are stored in combination with the documents according to their visual representa-tion. In this book illustrations in educational books are considered, which are annotated with different kinds of informal annotations. Section 2.3 introduces illustrations in gen-eral and Section 2.4 presents a layer model for *annotated illustrations*.

Visualized representations

To be briefly noticed at this point: formal annotations can be transformed to informal annotations by visualizing them by an applicable way to their referred document (see Section 2.4).

2.2.3 Storage of the 3D Models' Annotations

Multiple 3D parts Usually, 3D models consist of several 3D parts which may be annotated by a unique identifier (e.g., the technical term). Since there are multiple possibilities to store these annotations to their 3D parts, this section discusses alternatives and concludes with a problem–oriented solution.

Storage of metadata Sonnet [Son06] distinguishes between multiple types of metadata storage. He proposes techniques to integrate invisible metadata into images [SUS⁺06] and 3D models [SL05] in order to make them visible by a dedicated browser. For this type of application, he prefers the internal storage of the data. However, he also discusses the storage of the metadata which are separated from the document. This can be done by external individual storage (e.g., dedicated annotation files) or by external centralized storage (e.g., by a database management system).

Adaptation to annotations This differentiation can also be applied for the formal annotation of 3D models in the fo-cus of this thesis. Figure 2.1 abstracts three different types of the annotations' A storage in accordance to their documents D. In the following, their advantages and disadvan-tages are discussed.

- **Internal Storage.** For each of the 3D models the annotations are stored in the same files as the geometric descriptions (see Figure 2.1–left).

- **External Individual Storage.** For each 3D model there is a dedicated file AF that contains the annotations (see Figure 2.1–middle).

- **External Centralized Storage.** The annotations of all 3D models are stored in a central database of annotations ADB (see Figure 2.1–right).

Discussion. Internal storage has the advantage that the link between 3D model and annotations cannot get lost. Additionally, for external storage techniques, there is a necessity to define a convention to map the annotations to their dedicated parts. But external storage allows to be independent of the 3D model's format. Hence, for editing the annotation, it is not necessary to have an annotation authoring tool. However, when the annotations are centrally stored in a database, this implies additional administra-tive effort. A big advantage of storing the annotations externally in individual files is that they can easily be retrospectively edited without the necessity of additional tools.

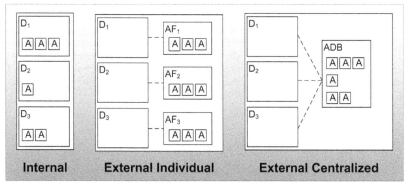

Figure 2.1: Three different options to store the annotations of 3D models.

Furthermore, they can also be exchanged by different annotation files stored in parallel, which allows to use annotations in multiple languages and adapt them to multiple text contexts.

Due to the independence of the 3D model's format and the simple management of the annotations, individual annotation files are used in this thesis. As a convention, their file names correspond with those of their 3D models, whereas the sequence of annotations corresponds with the sequence of defined 3D parts. In order to support the utilization of annotation authoring tools as well as manual editing, an XML structure is used as exemplified in Appendix E.

External individual preferred

2.3 Illustrations in Educational Books

This section discusses the term *illustration* and its usage in printed media (e.g., educational books, visual dictionaries, manuals). Those illustrations can also be automatically generated by the visualization of 3D models. Since illustrations often contain informal annotations, a model is introduced which describes annotated illustrations by different layers in order to form a basis for the following chapters.

The etymological roots of the word *illustration* are derived from the Latin word *lustrare* which means *to purify, brighten* [Sin91]. Other sources add the meaning to 'elucidate by using examples' [Pea99] as making clear by an example, or 'to provide visual features intended to explain or decorate (illustrate a book)' [MMW01]. Hence, complementing expository text with any type of image can be considered as an act of illustration. In this case the image irrespectively of its characteristics becomes an illustration. However, following the definitions (i.e., [MMW01]) above images can be termed illustration even without the act of adding images to expository text. If annotations are added to a normal photograph, this type of image automatically gets an illustration, since data was added in order to assist the communication process [Son06, p. 10].

Definitions

15

2.3.1 Usage in Educational Books

Types of usage

According to the illustrations' original definitions in dictionaries this term in general is not considered as an independent element, but in the juxtaposition with expository text in books. However, in modern use, there are also documents which predominantly consist of illustrations. Hence, the kinds of documents can coarsely be differentiated into two classes (see Figure 2.2).

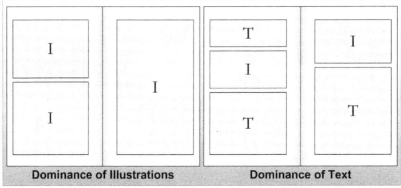

Figure 2.2: Abstracted examples of books predominantly consisting of illustrations I (left) and conjunctions of expository text T and illustrations (right).

- **Dominance of Expository Text.** Educational textbooks such as school books, scientific and anatomic textbooks usually complement extensive expository texts with illustrations. Especially to communicate visual attributes and spatial relations, this combination may have significant advantages over the solitary use of text [LL82]. Book authors try to situate the illustrations in spatial proximity to the text segments they are belonging to [Tuf06]. However, they are faced with the challenge to meet the often conflicting aim to design a good–looking page [Ran89] as well.

- **Dominance of Illustrations.** Visual dictionaries and anatomic atlases exhibit a different proportion of text and illustrations. They consist of a great amount of large illustrations which are augmented with textual (e.g., technical terms) and non–textual elements (e.g., lines). These illustrations serve to visually depict objects and to resolve their technical terms through the annotations, which are sometimes synchronously even provided in multiple languages. Since in medical education it is crucial to memorize each anatomic part of the human body with its specific terms and its visual appearance, in anatomy there is a prevalent use of atlases. Commonly, students use them in addition to educational textbooks.

However, this classification can only be seen as the end points of a spectrum (cf. also [SS99]). In practice, some documents (e.g., manuals) may completely differ in their proportion of text and images.

2.3.2 Classification of Illustrations

In printed media there is a wide variety of different types of illustrations. In order to define which type of illustration is to be addressed in this thesis, a classification has to be found. For the discussion of the classification of illustrations, this term is used in a synonymous manner with *image* and *picture*.

Manifold illustrations

LOHSE ET AL. [LBWR94] carried out a user study in order to obtain a classification of images (visual representations). They presented 60 different kinds of images to the subjects and instructed them to describe the images verbally. From the collected terms 10 different Likert scales (e.g., spatial–nonspatial, concrete–abstract) were derived, for which the subjects had to rate the images. Finally, the subjects had to cluster the images to self–defined groups which had to be hierarchically merged in the following. As a result, they derived 11 classes and a binary tree diagram. The class that corresponds to many illustrations found in educational textbooks is the structure diagram which 'expresses spatial data' by a 'static description of a physical object'.

WEIDENMANN [Wei94] distinguished three different types of illustrations. A depiction aims at showing an object as real as possible, while schematic images depict objects in an abstract way. In contrast, logical images represent the graphical presentation of artificial data. Further on, he characterized the intentions of illustrations as descriptive (describe the objects and parts of it) or instructive (instruct the user how to use the object).

BALLSTEDT's [Bal97] classification consisted of four classes and assessed the degree of reality of real existing object depictions. Realistic and schematic images corresponded to the definitions of Weidenmann. Furthermore, he introduced a class of images only consisting of contour lines, and a class that additionally had more realistic textures.

STROTHOTTE AND STROTHOTTE [SS97] classified images into three main classes with respect of the picture contents. Pictograms constituted a class of images that are strongly abstracted depictions, which do not show an individual object but are representative for groups of objects. The aim of those pictograms is to be commonly understood, since their meaning is well–defined. Abstract graphical pictures abstractly show 'properties of and relations in reality which are *invisible* to humans'. In order to allow this, graphical symbols (e.g., arrows or lines) are added. Presentational pictures show 'properties and relations in reality [...] which are *visible* to humans'. Thereby, the degree and technique of abstraction of the existing models may significantly differ from each other. Hence, photographs as well as line drawings are considered to this class.

TUFTE introduced the term 'information graphics' [Tuf97] which were images for mediating information in a sophisticated way. Those images can be built of artificial data (similar to abstract graphical pictures) or be made of graphical abstractions of reality (similar to abstract presentational pictures). In the latter case, 'mapped images' [Tuf06] mean to augment the depictions of real existing spatial objects with additional information.

Discussion. There are even more classifications of images, but these representatives show that images can be categorized by many different classifications. Even though, these classifications are just a rough instrument, since there can be fluent transitions

Definition image and illustration

17

between them. In this thesis, the term *image* is used for graphical documents in general. As one special type of images the term *illustration* refers to the depiction of a real existing object, which may be graphically abstracted in order to guide the viewer's attention.

2.3.3 Computer–based Illustration

During the last decades, the computational power of computers increased very fast. Especially the performance of graphics hardware progressed in a breathtaking speed, which enabled a wide range of new applications. Thus, it was possible to automatically generate visualizations of different types of data. In order to mediate an overview, this section first outlines several types of interactive 3D visualizations. After that, the computer–based illustration of 3D models will be focused on in order to discuss the graphical abstraction techniques adapted by computers.

Different 3D visualizations

Information Visualization

Information visualization means the process of transforming data into a visual rendition in order to help the viewer to understand the abstract information. CARD ET AL. [CMS99] state that information visualization is:'... the use of computer–supported, interactive, visual representations of abstract data to amplify cognition'. One of the main challenges in this field of research is to visualize large amounts of data, in order to allow the user to explore them and navigate through the information spaces as comprehensible as possible. Since these visualizations relate to abstract graphical pictures of [SS97], they are not addressed in this thesis.

Visualization of abstract data

Rendering of 3D Models

Modern computers may generate 3D visualizations which are similar to realistic photographs by performing several geometric transformations and computational operations onto 3D models (*rendering*). One of these transformations is the projection of the spatial primitives onto a 2D view plane V (see Figure 2.3). Those projections can be done in different ways by modifying the projection center. Perspective projections have a center of projection C that represents the position of the camera (or eye), while the parallel projection's center is located at the infinity. Thus, perspective projections approximate the actual visual perception of humans and appear more realistic. However, the component sizes of the 3D visualizations vary with their distance to the center of projection. The parallel projection appears less realistic, but does not perspectively distort the components of the 3D visualizations. Since these visualizations aim at generating images which appear to be made of real world objects, they can be classified as presentational pictures of [SS97].

Visualization of 3D models

Parallel and perspective projection

Exploration of 3D Models

The interactive visualizations can be explored by different techniques (cf. also [MD06a]). WARE ET AL. [WO90] distinguish between two different camera control paradigms which can be applied to meet different exploration goals:

18

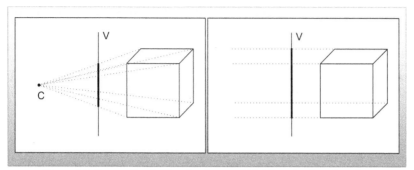

Figure 2.3: Perspective (left) and orthogonal (right) projection of a cube.

- **Eye–in–hand metaphor.** For spacious 3D models (e.g., rooms or virtual land-scapes) users may be surrounded by the spatial model. The users navigate (by walking or flying) through the virtual scene, whereas their interactions induce the 3D model to shift and rotate around them. These visualizations commonly use perspective projections in order to improve immersion and ease the users' orientation. *Feasible use for navigation*

- **World–in–hand metaphor.** For individual 3D models to be surveyed, a camera control may be advantageous, which can be compared to the examination of an atlas sphere. The user can explore this 3D model by zooming, translating and orbiting the camera around it. In order to give an impression about the actual spatial relations of the object, usually parallel projections are used. The images produced by these applications can be compared to the illustrations in educational material. *Feasible use for examination*

Hence, the applications for the interactive exploration of the 3D models in this book follow the world–in–hand metaphor, since it is likely not desirable to perambulate those objects. Like in many illustrations of educational textbooks, parallel projections are used.

Non–Photorealistic Rendering

Although scientific illustrations may depict real existing objects, this does not imply that the way of doing this is necessarily the most photorealistic one. According to FO-LEY ET AL. [FvDFH90], photorealistic depiction is not necessarily optimal for mediating information—if consciously unnecessary information is removed, this may be more ef-fective. SOUSA [Sou03] pointed out that although illustrations often look quite realistic, the primary motivation of illustrations is to communicate information. STROTHOTTE AND SCHLECHTWEG [SS02] even claim that the divergence from the photorealism may be the key to mediate information. *Photorealism is not always optimal*

Hence, illustrators consciously use a set of graphical abstraction techniques in order to focus the viewer's attention to relevant details, according to a specific view context. In educational books where illustrations are complementary used along expository texts, the text segments usually constitute such a context. However, it is also necessary to indicate the overall context of the illustrated object in order to support the viewer's understanding (e.g., [Mar89] or see Appendix C.10).

In the beginning of the visualization of virtual 3D scenes the aim was to generate images which appear as realistic as possible (*photorealistic rendering*). Later on, graphical abstraction techniques were used in order to guide the viewers attention (*non–photorealistic rendering* or NPR). Research in non–photorealistic rendering [SS02] aims at implementing graphical abstraction techniques used by human illustrators (e.g., [Hod03]). Thus, these methods transfer the benefits of consciously simplifying depictions and focusing the viewers attention to specific contexts in order to improve the effectiveness of computer–generated illustrations.

Focus viewer's attention

Applying a user study with rendered 3D models, SCHUMANN ET AL. [SSLR96] found out that for presenting drafts non–photorealistic illustrations may be even more appropriate than photorealistic ones. The subjects preferred sketched illustrations instead of those generated with a higher degree of realism.

NPR may be preferred

One of the most sophisticated classification schemes according to the scope of these techniques was introduced by PREIM ET AL. [PR02]. Relating to the emphasis of a specific 3D part three different classes can be defined:

- **Local techniques.** Are only applied to emphasize one specific part. Representative techniques for this class are the modification of the brightness, color or transparency (*ghosting*) of the related part. However, sometimes these techniques cannot be applied so that the presentation of the 3D parts' silhouette may be the better choice. Since the interactivity of computer generated illustrations, even for small objects blinking or movement may be an appropriate way to attract the viewer's attention [JRS02]. Additionally, the integration of other graphical elements like arrows pointing at the 3D part [Pre98] or shadows projected on a plane [RSHS03a] can be considered as local techniques.

- **Regional techniques.** Do not only affect a specific part, but also those which are in its proximity. Examples for this class are cutaway techniques [FS92, DWE03] which can be used to enable the visibility of covered parts. Depending on the depth of the used cutting planes, neighboring parts may even be eliminated.

- **Global techniques.** Affect the complete presentation of the 3D model in order to focus on a specific part of it. A technique called *3D Fisheye Zoom* [RR96] expands the size of the focused part, while the other sizes are reduced. Depending on the scope of the zooming function, this technique could also be considered as regional technique. A further representative of this class is the reduction of detail [Krü98] of those parts which are not in the focus by simplifying and combining them to one object.

This classification should be seen as rough schema and does not claim for completeness. For some of the techniques indirect emphasis [HP98] may be applied; for example, for the emphasis of a 3D part, a local technique can be applied to each of the remaining

Indirect emphasis

3D parts in order to deemphasize them. Hence, the scope of this technique is regional or global. Additionally, local techniques may not be sufficient for the emphasis of some 3D parts. This means, regional or global techniques may be necessary in order to guarantee the visibility of them, e.g., if they are hidden by other parts.

It depends on the individual task, which of those techniques have to be used in order to optimally focus the viewers attention. Although graphical abstraction techniques are not focus of this thesis, at a later date this work introduces the impact of annotations for focusing the viewers attention to certain contexts.

2.4 Annotated Illustrations

Illustrations in educational literature often use informal annotations in order to visualize textual metadata. They may help the user to understand the illustration and establish a link between terms used in the expository text and their visual complements depicted in illustrations.

In the specialized case, i.e., when metadata is visually added to the document, often the noun *label*, its verb *to label* and the verb–derived noun *labeling* are used. In terms of computer technology the COLLINS ENGLISH DICTIONARY [Sin91] describes a label as: 'a group of characters such as a number or a word, appended to a particular statement in a program to allow its unique identification'. Cartographers [Imh75] and illustrators [Hod03] use the word label for technical terms and signs for the identification of spatial contexts in their depictions. Other researchers both use the terms label and annotation (e.g., [Tuf06]), whereas the ladder term meaning is more general. Labels: graphical annotations

For the usage in this thesis, the term label is too restricted to serve as a substitute for the specialized type of graphically represented annotations. As an example, a short expository text or an image attached to a part of a picture is no label, but it is an annotation. Hence, in the following for the sake of consistency the term annotation is used instead of label. Annotation instead of label

2.4.1 Functions of Annotations in Illustrations

Expository text and illustrations in educational material are used in order to complement each other. Illustrators normally depict the objects according to the context which is given by the texts [Sou03]. Hence, their contexts correlate with each other to a certain degree. However, in order to allow appropriate linkage between the context described in the text and the context depicted in the illustration, referencing techniques have to be employed. These references may be established by non–verbal links, e.g., spatial proximity of the illustration to the text part which is describing the according context (see Figure 2.4–left). In most cases, however, figure captions are used to refer to the illustrations (see Figure 2.4–right). Illustration and text reference Reference to illustrations

For complex illustrations it is also necessary to refer to multiple parts of an illustration, e.g., in order to describe their interrelation. This may be done by textually explaining

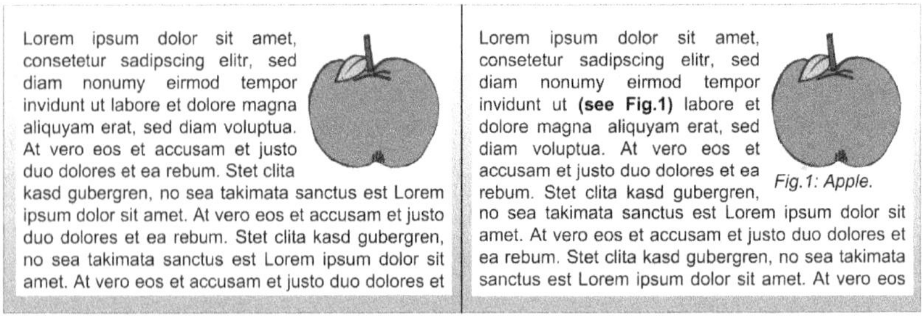

Lorem ipsum dolor sit amet, consetetur sadipscing elitr, sed diam nonumy eirmod tempor invidunt ut labore et dolore magna aliquyam erat, sed diam voluptua. At vero eos et accusam et justo duo dolores et ea rebum. Stet clita kasd gubergren, no sea takimata sanctus est Lorem ipsum dolor sit amet. At vero eos et accusam et justo duo dolores et ea rebum. Stet clita kasd gubergren, no sea takimata sanctus est Lorem ipsum dolor sit amet. At vero eos et accusam et justo duo dolores et

Lorem ipsum dolor sit amet, consetetur sadipscing elitr, sed diam nonumy eirmod tempor invidunt ut **(see Fig.1)** labore et dolore magna aliquyam erat, sed diam voluptua. At vero eos et accusam et justo duo dolores et ea rebum. Stet clita kasd gubergren, no sea takimata sanctus est Lorem ipsum dolor sit amet. At vero eos et accusam et justo duo dolores et ea rebum. Stet clita kasd gubergren, no sea takimata sanctus est Lorem ipsum dolor sit amet. At vero eos *Fig.1: Apple.*

Figure 2.4: Reference by spatial proximity (left) and reference by figure captions (right).

Reference to parts the visual characteristics of the mentioned illustration parts in the expository text, e.g., see the red part in the illustration (Figure 2.5–left). Conversely, illustrators may integrate annotations which allow the identification of parts of the depiction (see Figure 2.5–right).

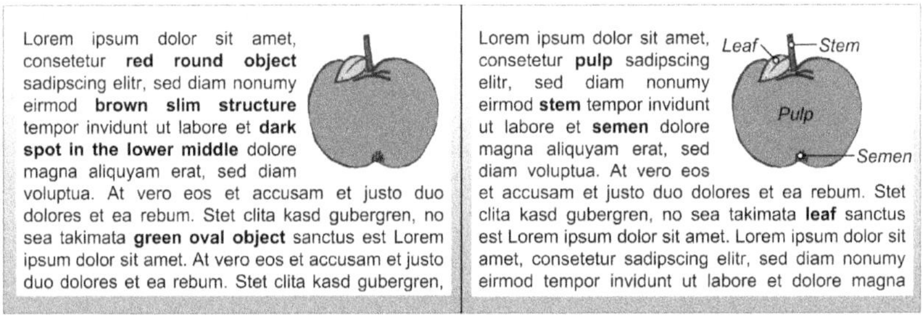

Lorem ipsum dolor sit amet, consetetur **red round object** sadipscing elitr, sed diam nonumy eirmod **brown slim structure** tempor invidunt ut labore et **dark spot in the lower middle** dolore magna aliquyam erat, sed diam voluptua. At vero eos et accusam et justo duo dolores et ea rebum. Stet clita kasd gubergren, no sea takimata **green oval object** sanctus est Lorem ipsum dolor sit amet. At vero eos et accusam et justo duo dolores et ea rebum. Stet clita kasd gubergren,

Lorem ipsum dolor sit amet, consetetur **pulp** sadipscing elitr, sed diam nonumy eirmod **stem** tempor invidunt ut labore et **semen** dolore magna aliquyam erat, sed diam voluptua. At vero eos et accusam et justo duo dolores et ea rebum. Stet clita kasd gubergren, no sea takimata **leaf** sanctus est Lorem ipsum dolor sit amet. Lorem ipsum dolor sit amet, consetetur sadipscing elitr, sed diam nonumy eirmod tempor invidunt ut labore et dolore magna

Figure 2.5: Reference to illustration parts by verbal description (left) and reference by annotations (right).

In both cases, for the figure captions as well as the annotations of the illustration parts, textual information may be used to establish the link between text and illustration. The textual information of both expository text and illustration correlates in order to establish a reference between both media. The textual annotations may establish the bidirectional visual link:

$$\text{Term} \leftrightarrow \text{Illustration's part}$$

2.4.2 Illustration Layers

The illustration and its informal annotations can be divided into different elements. *Elements of illustrations* Those elements can be described by layer models. Such layer models have been discussed by several researchers. In order to allow a differentiated view, SONNET [Son06] proposed a background layer which represents the whole illustration of the object and the illustration layer, which may contain metadata of any kind for illustrative purposes.

WU ET AL. [WKLH00] introduced a model for multimedia objects which comprises four different levels. The first level is the image level and corresponds to Sonnets background layer and solely contains the visual information. The second level represents the segmented image level which spatially subdivides the image and defines multiple regions of interests. These regions are annotated (e.g., textual annotations) in order to allow the link between segments and the following level. The third level contains measures and descriptions which were determined by image analysis functions that are assigned to the segments defined in the previous level. Finally, the interpretation level contains global information about the image as a whole.

This book adapts the layer concepts in order to build an adapted model which describes the layers of illustrations. The illustration model IM consists of four layers (see Figure 2.6), which can be described by $IM = \{B, O, S, SE\}$. SONNET's background layer is split into two parts. This means that in this book the background layer B represents the unoccupied space surrounding the illustrated object O. For this object, the logical layer S provides information about the illustrated object and its segmentation. Finally, the layer SE constitutes the informal annotations which are linked to the illustration's segments and the whole object. However, a deeper examination of this topic is postponed to Chapter 3.

Layer model

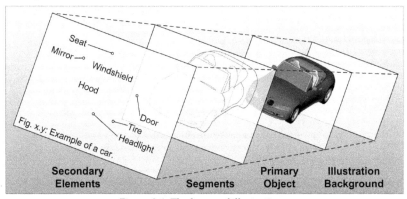

Figure 2.6: The layers of illustrations.

Henceforth, geared to TUFTE's terminology [Tuf97] the illustrated object O is called *primary object*. The remaining space on the background B constitutes the *illustration background*. The totality of the textual annotations as well as optional elements (e.g., lines, boxes) on layer SE are called *secondary elements*. By the logical layer S they are bidirectionally linked with corresponding image segment of the primary object. Thus, the image segments of the primary object are the *referred parts* of the corresponding secondary elements.

The layers' terminology

2.4.3 Traditional Process of an Illustration's Annotation

According to HODGES [Hod03], authors of educational textbooks have an initial meeting with the illustrators which serves as negotiation of the resulting illustrations' characteristics. Commonly, the text author defines how much space B the illustrator may use for

Consultation

the whole illustration. Furthermore, a discussion or a draft of the expository text clarifies which object O is to be illustrated, and the segments S which have to be augmented with the secondary elements SE.

Annotation process

The illustrator has to manage to design the object on the available background, while leaving sufficient space for the textual annotations. When the depiction process is finished [Sou03], the illustrator uses the visual information about the remaining background, the primary object and its segments as well as the textual annotations to determine an esthetic and functional *annotation layout* for the secondary element layer.

2.4.4 Annotation Layout for the Interactive Exploration of 3D Models

The objective of this book is to compute such a layout of secondary elements for an interactive application, in order to allow the annotated exploration of 3D models. This annotation layout adapts the manual process performed by human illustrators.

Adaption of layers to process

For computer generated illustrations, the extents of the background layer B can be derived from the size of the viewport. On this background, the 3D model is rendered onto the primary object layer O according to its geometric descriptions, materials and illumination parameters, while graphical abstraction techniques can be applied to certain parts of it. A special rendition of the rendered image serves as segmentation layer S. Using the elements B, O, S and the formal annotations stored for each part of the 3D model, an annotation layout can be computed.

2.5 Conclusion

This chapter investigated the use of annotations in illustrations and identified two challenges which are examined in two consecutive parts of this thesis. In the following their motivation is briefly concluded.

1st books part

The first part (Chapters 3 to 5) tackles the problem of automatically determining an annotation layout for the interactive exploration of 3D models. Chapter 3 introduces this topic, analyzes human illustrations, formalizes annotation styles and assesses the related work in that field. Chapter 4 makes use of these achievements and constructs an encapsulated approach for the annotation layout of 3D models. Finally, the first part concludes with Chapter 5 which applies the encapsulated approach and introduces contextual annotation styles. This extension is evaluated by a user study which effectuates novel interesting questions for the second part.

2nd books part

The second part (Chapters 6 and 7) addresses the complementary usage of expository text and illustrations in educational textbooks. Chapter 6 introduces this topic, identifies search tasks associated with the combined use of text and illustrations, and reviews the related work and points out the challenges in this area. Furthermore, an automated concept is proposed in order to support those search tasks by an interactive approach, which is implemented in Chapter 7 by an experimental application in the field of educational anatomy. Finally, this platform serves as the basis for a user study in order to evaluate central the statement of the concept and to give evidence about its applicability.

3 Annotation Layout Foundations

Outline

Chapter 2 motivated the problem of the annotation layout. This chapter analyzes a corpus of educational books in order to derive a set of annotation types and their different styles and formalizes them. Subsequently, it discusses guidelines of human illustrators and derives a set of specifications for a prospective interactive annotation approach. Based on these specifications, the existing approaches in the field of interactive annotation layout are assessed. Consecutively, Chapter 4 builds up on those specifications in order to realize the interactive annotation approach for 3D models.

Achievements

As a result of this chapter, the annotation types used in books can be realized with only three different layout elements. Possible layout styles of each annotation type are formalized. Next, guidelines of human illustrators are adapted to the interactive annotation of 3D models. These fundamental considerations are necessary to assess existing automated annotation approaches and to define metrics for an automatic annotation layout.

3.1 Introduction

Annotated illustrations in educational material use a variety of different informal annotations which have different appearings and functions. The layout of those secondary elements is not consistent and influenced by several considerations of human illustrators. In order to form a basis for the layout of secondary elements in interactive applications, beforehand their archetypes have to be investigated and categorized regarding their layout characteristics. Guidelines of human illustrators may serve as another source of information. Hence they have to be structured and assigned to the secondary element categories. Using these results, specifications have to be formulated in order to assess existing approaches and to develop a prospective annotation approach.

This chapter is organized as follows: First, Section 3.2 analyzes a corpus of educational books in order to derive a set of different types of annotations and their different annotation styles and to formalize them. In the following Section 3.3 guidelines of human illustrators and those which are stated in existing work are reviewed and summarized to a set of specifications for a prospective interactive annotation approach. These specifications are used in Section 3.4 to assess the existing approaches in the field of interactive annotation layout. Finally, Section 3.5 concludes this chapter.

3.2 Analysis of Annotated Illustrations

The archetypes of this book are annotated illustrations used in traditional textbooks in the fields of anatomy, natural science and the technical domain, which depict real existing objects. Since there exists neither literature (cf. Appendix C.3) nor a determinate style for the layout of secondary elements, an analysis of the corpus of illustrations had to be performed before any declarations could be made. In the following this corpus and the methodology of the analysis are introduced.

3.2.1 Corpus and Method

Corpus

The corpus consisted of 1253 illustrations used in 28 books mainly of the fields of human anatomy, natural science, and the technical domain. 21 books of the corpus were educational textbooks which utilized both expository text and illustrations, whereas seven books predominantly consisted of annotated illustrations (cf. Section 2.3.1).

These central questions were addressed during the corpus analysis:

- Which types of annotations are used in illustrations?
- Which layout requirements can be determined for each type?
- How can annotation types be classified concerning their requirements?
- Which annotation layouts are used for the annotations of those classes?
- How can a parametrization of annotation layout styles be realized?

Method

A first brief analysis pass served as an informal study in order to ascertain how many different *annotation types* had to be considered for a systematic analysis pass. Additionally, their most common representations were outlined (see Section 3.2.2). As a result of this first pass, the layout requirements of each annotation type had to be identified. The aim was to determine a set of layout element classes (*layout containers*) which comprise annotation types with identical layout requirements (see Section 3.2.3). Subsequently, the second analysis determined for each of those layout containers which *layout styles* are used in the illustrations. Section 3.2.4 parametrizes the most common styles for each of the layout containers.

For the sake of text continuity the details about the analysis including a more detailed description of an algorithm for the selection of a representative subset of the books' illustrations is sourced out to Appendix B.

3.2.2 Types of Annotations

This section reports general observations about the different annotation types which were found in the corpus of illustrations. This informal preparatory study was based on the central question how many heterogeneous types of annotations are present in the corpus. Therefore, for each observed illustration it was verified whether the annotations can be described by the already documented types. If this was not the case, the descriptions had to be adapted or even a new type had to be introduced. As the transitions between some of them were sometimes smooth, in the following they are briefly described by their most common representation. Note that in order enable a classification, rare phenomena were not considered for the description of the types.

- **Figure Captions** were the most common annotation type. They were commonly placed below the illustration, spanned over its complete width and referred to the whole illustration. Normally, they consisted of a figure number which had a referencing function and a short sentence. This sentence often summarized the semantic content of the image, but was also used to support the viewer's comprehension of the illustrations and how they had to be read regarding the utilized emphasis techniques (cf. also [Pre98]).

- **External Annotations** represented the most common type for the annotation of parts in an illustration. They commonly consisted of multiple elements. While the reference line established the visual link between textual information and the referred part, the anchor point marked the endpoint on it. This optional anchor point was located on salient regions of the illustration's part and the textual information was placed on the illustration background, but in a spatial relation of the referred part. They solely referred to specific parts of the illustrations and their textual information mostly consisted of a single line which represented a technical term or rarely its abbreviation.

- **Internal Annotations** were used less often than external annotations. Especially if a greater number of annotations was accommodated, they were used in conjunction with them. Usually, the text stroke of their textual information was horizontal, but in some illustrations it was also curved according to the shape of the part. Although internal annotations had the same referencing aims than external ones, their location was different. Since they directly overlaid their referred part, they did neither use reference lines nor anchor points. Some of the annotations were abbreviated or multi–lined, which predominantly manifested on very small sized parts.

- **Descriptions** were used as the rarest annotation type. They contained text, images and tables, which occupied a greater amount of space. If referred to the whole illustration, they were located on large free spaces at the illustration background. However, if they referred to a specific part, they were placed in an unambiguous spatial relation to it, while optionally using anchor points and reference lines. They included more extensive texts, images and tables in order to provide a more detailed description of the illustration.

- **Legends** were used in a very differing frequency. The most illustrators seemed to rein in their usage, while a few made numerous use of them when the space was limited, e.g., by a high number of parts to be annotated. Mostly they were used in conjunction with external and internal annotations which solely consisted of a key (i.e., number or letter). The collectivity of those keys was resolved in the figure legend in a tabular manner with the referred parts' actual technical terms. In most cases they were arranged to a rectangular box which was located alongside the illustration, where no important information had to be occluded. Similar to figure captions those types were used to support the comprehension of the illustration. Thus, they either referred to individual parts or to the whole illustration.

3.2.3 Categorization into Layout Containers

Aggregation

In order to develop methods for the layout of secondary elements, beforehand attributes had to be determined which are relevant for such an annotation layout. The aim was to aggregate similar annotation types into a set of layout elements which share their layout requirements. Hence, the preparatory study addressed a set of questions.

1. Does the content of the annotations usually reside on preferred *positions* relatively to the primary object? Does it overlay the primary object, or is it placed on the illustration background?

2. What is the *scope* of the annotations, i.e., do they refer to the whole illustration or only to a specific part of the primary object?

3. Which general statements can be made concerning the *extent* of the annotations? Regarding their area consumption and compared to the other types, do they either belong to the smaller or the larger annotation types?

4. Which differences in the type of *content* exist for the different annotations? Do they present single terms, symbols, more extensive text or even images and tables?

Similar layout necessities

The crucial question for the classification of the annotation types in books was which of them had similar layout necessities and thus can be treated by the same layout strategies. As the investigation of the corpus reveals, there are similarities between several layout specific attributes (see Table 3.1).

	Internal	External	Captions	Descriptions	Legends
Position	Overlay	Background	Background	Background	Background
	Inside Part	Near Part	Arbitrary	Arbitrary	Arbitrary
Scope	Part	Part	Illustration	Illustration	Illustration
Extent	Smaller	Smaller	Larger	Larger	Larger
Content	Term/Symbol	Term/Symbol	Text/Symbol	Arbitrary	Arbitrary
Container	**Internal Annotation**	**External Annotation**	**Annotation Box**		

Table 3.1: Layout containers share annotation types with equal layout requirements.

Only 3 containers

As a results of the analysis, only three layout elements are required. For each of those *layout containers* it was defined which one carries the annotations' content:

- **Internal Annotation Container.** In contrast to the other annotation types which are accommodated on the remaining illustration background, internal annotations are exclusively overlaying their referred parts of the primary object. Thus, a container for internal annotations has special layout necessities.

- **External Annotation Container.** Like internal annotations, the scope of external annotations is exclusively their referred parts of the primary object. However, they are placed on the illustration background in a spatial unambiguous relation to their referred parts. Hence, the container layout has to consider this requirement.

- **Annotation Box Container.** Whereas external and internal annotations consist of a single term or a symbol, the content of figure captions, descriptions and legends comprises texts, images, tables or combinations of them. Thus, these secondary elements are more extensive and their scope is the whole illustration, instead of being related to a specific part of the primary object. Since the transitions of those annotations are smooth and their layout necessities are similar, their layout is managed by one combined layout container.

Moreover, the analysis of the corpus of illustrations reveals that instead of a unitary layout style for each of the containers there are numerous differences among the illustrations. In order to parametrize the most common styles, the following section defines a set of container specific *layout styles* for each of the containers.

Multiple styles per container

3.2.4 Layout Styles of Containers

The analysis of the corpus of illustrations shows that there is a great variety of different layout styles and appearances for each container. This section formalizes those phenomena, in order to allow the parametrization of an illustration layout and in order to subsequently develop algorithmic solutions for the layout of the containers. The layout style of an illustration consists of up to three types of containers which share a set of features. The annotation style can be described by Equation 3.1.

Formalization of styles

$$Annotationstyle \subseteq \{Style_{Internal}, Style_{External}, Style_{Boxes}\} \qquad (3.1)$$

In the following, their individual components and specific features are addressed, followed by exemplary illustrations. These illustrations are augmented by numbered arrows ($\rightarrow$) in order to ease the assignment with the description of the examples. The original illustrations without those arrows can be found in Appendix G.

Additional arrows

Internal Annotation Styles

Internal annotations directly overlay their referred parts of the primary object, which usually makes their association unambiguous. They consist of a set of letters which are arranged in order to form a character string. Commonly, internal annotations are single–lined and their letters text stroke (*annotation path*) may be defined in different

Annotation path

ways. Internal annotation styles can be parametrized by two different main features, which are described by Equation 3.2.

$$Style_{Internal} = (c \in C, a \in A) \tag{3.2}$$

The elements of the individual features are parametrized as follows:

1. the *Contrast technique* $C \subseteq \{s, a, p\}$,

2. the *Alignment* of the textual annotations $A = \{h, n, c\}$.

Contrast techniques
In order to improve the legibility of the letters, *contrast techniques* can be used and even combined. Each of the letters can be surrounded by a white silhouette (s̲ilhouette), also called halo [HV96]. Another technique is to change the color of each letter (and silhouette) in the manner that a maximum contrast to the overlaid part of the primary object is obtained (cha̲nge). Optionally, the annotations can be placed in alternative regions where a good contrast to the annotations letters is given (p̲lacement).

Alignment
The *alignment* of internal annotations can be carried out in three different manners. The path of letters of the textual annotation can conform to a straight horizontal line (h̲orizontal), being straight but angled (an̲gled), or can have a curvature (c̲urved). Additional attributes like the font style, size and color can be changed individually for each annotation, but this does not influence the layout of the elements.

Example
As an example, Figure 3.1–left contains horizontal annotations (e.g., 1→Cuneus) as well as curved ones (e.g., 2→Gyros frontalis superior), while Figure 3.1–right shows a straight, but angled annotation (3→Cochlea). Figure 3.1–left does only influence the placement of annotations to preserve the contrast between annotation and primary object (e.g., 4→Precuneus), Figure 3.1–right uses multiple techniques: the annotations are surrounded by a white silhouette (e.g., 5→Posterior canal), some annotations have a changed font color (e.g., 6→Vestibular fenestra), or they are placed on a position of high contrast (e.g., 7→Vestibule).

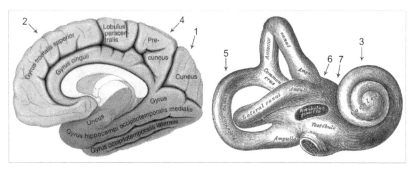

Figure 3.1: Internal annotation styles. (Source: [SPP01, p. 279] and [Gra18, p. 1328])

External Annotation Styles

External annotations refer to specific parts of the primary object. They either contain terms or symbols which extents are predominantly a single line. Unlike internal annotations, they reside on the illustration background and may consist of multiple parts. Besides their textual information (*textual annotation*), they optionally utilize additional secondary elements to prevent ambiguities in the assignment of textual annotation and primary object. *Reference lines* establish the visual link and *anchor points* denote the endpoint of the reference line on the assigned part of the primary object. External annotation styles can be parametrized by three different main features, which are described by Equation 3.3.

Textual annotation

$$Style_{External} = (p \in P, c \in C, a \in A) \tag{3.3}$$

The elements of the individual features are parametrized as follows:

1. the *Anchor Points* $P = \{v, i\}$,

2. the style of *Reference lines* $C = \{b, s, i\}$,

3. the *Alignment* of the textual annotations $A = \{r, r_v, r_h, s_u, s_c\}$.

Anchor points are utilized in the most cases (visible). However, some illustrators prefer to omit them (invisible). There are many slightly different styles of *Reference lines*, but in the most general cases they can either be bended (bended), or appear as straight lines (straight), or they can be omitted as well (invisible). Likewise, for the *alignment* of textual annotations, some illustrators define invisible rectangular areas around the illustrated object and place the textual annotations along the borders of that area (rectangular). These placements may be restricted to the vertical borders of the rectangles ($r_{vertical}$) or to the horizontal borders ($r_{horizontal}$). Another common possibility to align the textual annotations is to place them in a constant distance to the silhouette of the illustrated object. They are either uniformly distributed ($s_{uniform}$) or clustered to several groups ($s_{clustered}$). Additional attributes like the line style of reference lines or color and font of the textual annotations as well as an optional frame around them can be changed, but this does not affect the layout of the elements.

Anchor points

Reference lines

Alignment

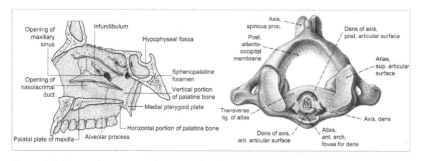

Figure 3.2: External annotation layout styles. (Source: [Rog92, p. 191] and [SPP97, p. 19])

Example

As an example, the annotation layout of Figure 3.2–left can be characterized as: no anchor points, orthogonally bended reference lines, and rectangular a annotation area, whereas the layout of Figure 3.2–right can be described as: visible anchor points, straight reference lines, and silhouette aligned annotations which are clustered.

Annotation Box Styles

Similar layout necessities

The three types of annotation boxes (figure captions, legends, descriptions) have several similarities. Thus, they can be grouped into one layout container. The transitions between them may be smooth. However, to determine the boxes' layout it is not crucial to distinguish between them, but to define a set of parameters which influence their layout. Annotation boxes are placed on the illustration background and are not essentially bound to specific parts of it. The annotation box styles can be parametrized by three different main features, which are described by Equation 3.4.

$$Style_{Boxes} = (c \in C, f \in F, a \in A) \tag{3.4}$$

The elements of the individual features are parametrized as follows:

1. the *Content* $C = \{t, r\}$,

2. the *Frame* style of the boxes $F = \{v, i\}$,

3. the *Alignment* of the boxes $A = \{t, b, l, s\}$.

Content

While figure captions only contain textual information (textual) which can be wrapped, legends and descriptions may contain critical *content* (i.e., images and tables) which have to maintain a minimum size to not become indistinct (critical). A *frame* of annotation boxes can either be existent (visible), which occupies additional space, or not existent (invisible). The *alignment* of annotation boxes is disparate. Figure captions are located above (top) or below (bottom) the illustration. However, legends and descriptions are located on free spaces on the background of the image (alongside). In special cases, annotation boxes can also be linked with a specific part of the primary object (assigned), whilst retaining the features of an annotation box. In this case they are located in a spatially unambiguous relation to the primary object's part.

Frame

Alignment

Example

Besides internal and external annotations, Figure 3.3–left shows both a figure caption (1→) and a description (2→). While the figure caption contains text and symbols and is located above the primary object, the description resides alongside it, and contains an image showing the context of the illustrated organ. In case of Figure 3.3–right the external annotations are encoded so that a legend is required to resolve the keys. The content of this legend (3→) is combined with the content usually carried in a figure caption (4→) into one single container and resides alongside the primary object.

3.2.5 Conclusion

This section derived three types of containers which have different layout necessities. Multiple styles of these containers were formalized in order to enable the definition of

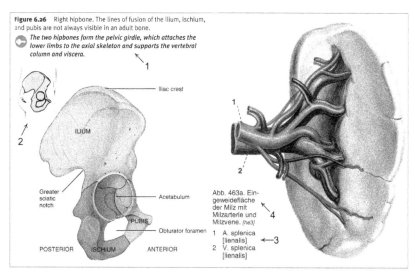

Figure 3.3: Annotation boxes styles. (Source: [Tor97, p. 129] and [Lip00, p. 310])

different layout styles. The defined styles only reflect a set of common layout phenomena and do not claim for completeness. In order to make declarations about specifications which have to be met by an interactive approach for the annotation of 3D models, the following section introduces guidelines of human illustrators.

3.3 Existing Guidelines for Annotation

In literature, there are a only few quite unstructured sources containing guidelines for the annotation of illustrations (cf. also Appendix C.3). First, this section introduces guidelines of different authors for the annotation in different fields like scientific and technical illustration, as well as the annotation of maps. Finally, these guidelines have to be summarized and adapted to the layout containers in order to define specifications as the basis for an interactive approach to annotate 3D models.

Illustrations and maps

3.3.1 Scientific and Technical Illustrations

Although annotated scientific illustrations exist for several hundred years, there are only a few available sources that describe guidelines for the annotation of those illustrations. This section introduces several important sources with declarations about the placement and appearance of the annotations used in illustrations.

TUFTE [Tuf97] introduced the term *smallest effective difference*, which means that secondary elements should be clearly identified as such, while not diverting the viewers

No dominant secondary elements

attention from the primary object. As an example, he showed an illustration of a human ear, which had very dominant secondary elements (see Figure 3.4–left). He created a redesigned version of the illustration (see Figure 3.4–right) by modifying the reference lines in their thickness, removing bends and minimizing the distance between parts and textual information by choosing a silhouette–aligned layout. BRISCOE [Bri96] agreed with TUFTE and suggested that legends should not have a surrounding frame, since it could divert the viewer from the primary object.

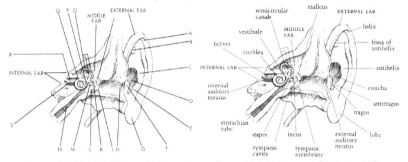

Figure 3.4: Original figure (left), redrawn figure (right). (Source: [Tuf97, p. 74])

Preference of direct annotation

Furthermore, TUFTE replaced the keys (letters) by direct annotations which were nearby their referred parts, and explained why legends, keys and codes (e.g., variation in text colors or sizes) should only be used for highly complex data like geological field maps. He stressed that images and text should not exist individually but in parallel, and mentioned: 'codes obstruct parallelism; replacing codes with direct annotations unifies the information.' [Tuf97, p. 98] and '...codes, keys, and legends are impediments to learning...' [Tuf06, p. 118]. PURNELL ET AL. [PSS91] showed that keys in illustrations induce tedious eye movements, which increase the cognitive effort. BALLSTEDT [Bal97] also recommended to use textual annotation instead of keys, because of those eye movements. BRISCOE [Bri96] agreed that direct annotations are faster to identify, but also noted that legends may be used to aggregate multiple annotations.

Internal annotation if advantageous

While BRISCOE [Bri96] and FEKETE ET AL. [FP99] agreed that annotations should not overlap the primary object, however, in specific cases (e.g., photographs) BRISCOE additionally suggested to directly overlay the image with the annotations. The illustrator has to estimate whether it is more advantageous to place the annotations in the surrounding area of the image.

Legibility

Consistent annotations

BRISCOE [Bri96] explained that annotations have to be of legible size, whereas the best legibility is given for horizontal annotations. However, in case of limited space, even vertical annotations could be used. Additionally, she affirmed TUFTE's [Tuf97, Tuf06] statement of preventing codes and clearly stressed to consistently use the same font, size and styles for all annotations in the illustration. However, for interactive environments, PREIM [Pre98] stated that annotations should change their style according to dynamic changes (e.g., spatial depth of parts) of the primary object. HODGES [Hod03] mentioned that in illustrations of printed material the most common fonts are from the *Helvetica* family and that their minimum size should be eight points in order to allow a good legibility.[1] BRISCOE [Bri96] augmented that the contrast of the annotation letters should be preserved. If the annotations overlay the primary object, she suggested to provide white letters with a black outline, and black letters with a white outline to establish a contrast to the overlaid image.

Preserve contrast

PREIM [Pre98] declared that crossing reference lines harden the assignment of text–image relations and should be prevented. HARTMANN ET AL. [HAS04] agreed and suggested that reference lines should be orthogonal to a main axis. Furthermore, anchor points should be placed in a position that eases the identification of the referred part.

Reference lines and anchors

CHIGONA ET AL. introduced a type of annotation boxes and propose a minimum width to preserve the readability since word breaks should be avoided. They agreed with PREIM [Pre98] that additional information to specific partss should be available on demand.

Annotation boxes

The interactive exploration of 3D models may require additional needs. BÉTRANCOURT & BISSERET [BB98] pointed out: 'text information should be close to the part of the picture to which it referred' for still images, which corresponds with the claims of TUFTE [Tuf97] and HARTMANN ET AL. [HAS04]. PREIM [Pre98] and FEKETE ET AL. [FP99] postulated an even more stringent condition saying that it is important that the assignment of the parts and their annotations is clearly visible all the time. This coincides with MORENO AND MAYER's [MM99] research which concluded that annotations should be near their referred parts—even in animations. Although PREIM agreed that annotations should be near to their referred parts, he also mentioned that minimizing the distance between annotations and their referred parts during user interactions induces frequent changes in the positions of annotations.

Interactive annotation

The *smallest effective difference* can be applied to more than just still images. TUFTE [Tuf97] stated: 'the strategy of the smallest effective difference applies to all display technologies', and thus, even to moving images. He gave an indication that frame coherence of a layout of secondary elements is as important as the layout itself. Small differences of the layout of annotations between the frames are important to not divert the viewer's attention. HARTMANN ET AL. [HAS04] agreed with the statement that annotations should move coherently.

Frame coherence

TUFTE introduced the term *Mapped Images* which means to annotate images with secondary elements. He used the map metaphor because in cartography maps are generated which sophisticatedly pinpoint the interplay of text and images: '...contradicting the methods of map design often causes trouble for any type of graphical display.' [Tuf06, p. 119]. HODGES [Hod03] gave guidelines for the illustration in many different scientific fields, just as maps. For the placement of annotations she referred to the work of IMHOF [Imh75], who set a milestone in cartography by publishing rules for the annotation of maps. He pointed out that the titles of maps are comparable with figure captions. For this reason, Section 3.3.2 subsequently covers IMHOF's suggestions about the annotation of maps.

Mapped images

Annotations in Cartography

---

[1]However, since the resolution of computer screens is much lower than for printed media, Section 3.3.3 addresses their special constraints.

3.3.2 Annotation of Maps

Maps do not illustrate spatial objects, but they represent strongly abstracted views of real existing geographic relations (see Figure 3.5). The annotations used in maps clearly differ from those of illustrated spatial objects. However, similarities can be found and might be partially adapted in order to form a basis of problem–oriented specifications.

Figure 3.5: Magnified excerpt of a map with different types of annotations. (Source: [Hir94])

Maps normally contain several hundreds or even thousands of annotations. For a long time suggestions and hints about the annotation of maps have only been taught among cartographers by word of mouth [Imh75]. IMHOF was one of the first cartographers who wrote down his experiences as suggestions and principles; nowadays, his work is numerously cited in the fields of topography and cartography. He pointed out: 'Poor, sloppy, amateurish type placement is irresponsible; it spoils even the best image and impedes reading'. The principles he defined were only of informal nature, as an advise for cartographers. However, as can be seen in the following, the field of the annotation of illustrated objects seems to make use of similar rules.

Informal guidelines for maps

He defined a set of general principles to achieve a functional and esthetic annotation placement in maps:

1. **Legibility.** The annotations should be easily readable and quickly located. The form, size, and color of the letters as well as their position and the position of other annotations influence this measure.

2. **Association.** The relationship of the annotations and their corresponding parts should be unambiguously recognized.

3. **Legibility of the Map.** The annotations should neither cover nor partially overlap any other map content or annotation.

4. **Form Integration.** The annotations should directly assist in revealing the designated part's position and shape.

5. **Classification.** The size and style of annotations should be used to mediate the classification and hierarchy of parts in the map.

6. **Distribution.** The distribution of annotations in the map should neither be too even nor too dense.

IMHOF pointed out that these principles are conflicting with each other and accentuated that it is a very complex task to determine a good annotation layout. Furthermore, something special about maps is that regions to be annotated are sometimes overlapping, which dramatically increases the complexity of an annotation layout. COOK AND JONES [CJ90] discovered that cartographers spent between 20 and 50 per cent of working time on the annotation placement.

Complex annotation task

In order to explain special necessities of different features, IMHOF defined three different types of map annotations (see Table 3.2) for which he made different suggestions in the manner of illustrating both a good and a poor example.

Type	Exemplary Usage
Point designations	Cities, summits, small area features.
Linear designations	Rivers, streets, borders.
Areal designations	Mountains, isles, countries, lakes.

Table 3.2: Imhof's types of annotations in maps.

Besides the informal rules, which were considered for the global annotation task, he made suggestions for the handling of each individual annotation type. For each of the three types of annotations both horizontal text strokes as well as curved text strokes are possible. However, he mentioned that horizontal annotations are to be preferred because of their optimal legibility.

Legibility

Point designations curvature should only be used, if the annotation layout benefits from it, or if overlaps with other features can be prevented. The usage of curved text strokes with linear and especially areal designations along the axial lines of the referred part has the advantage that it can help to disambiguate the spatial shape. The axial lines can be described by the medial axis for closed areas introduced by BLUM [Blu67]. It represents a graph structure $M = (V, E)$ where the edges E connect the vertices V determined by the centers of maximal inscribed circular disks within the area (see Figure 3.6). Vertices and junctions of the graph M may be considered as salient points of the area [Pre98]. However IMHOF argued that the curvature of the text strokes should not be too high and, if possible, doubly curved lines should not appear either. He also proposes that the cartographer should care about a visually equal spacing of the text stroke.

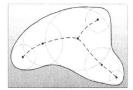

Figure 3.6: Simplified medial axis (dashed line) according Blum [Blu67].

Unambiguity
Medial axis
Salient points

Another type of annotation which is not mentioned in IMHOF's work are *map legends* which are an essential component of maps. They contain multiple elements and associate the codes, used by the remaining secondary elements of the map, with nominal information (e.g., city annotations, river annotations, area annotations etc.), ordinal information (e.g., number of citizens) as well as numerical information (e.g., scales). These elements are arranged in a box which is situated alongside the map, where it does not occlude important map features.

Essential use of legends

3.3.3 Conclusion

Summary and specifications
Different informal guidelines were found in literature, observing the annotation process from different points of view. This section summarizes and discusses these guidelines from the view of an interactive application which has to annotate 3D models in the way it is done in the investigated corpus of books. Finally, to form a basis for a problem–oriented approach, a set of specifications for an interactive annotation of 3D models has to be defined.

Adaptivity to illustrations
Maps can be partially adapted to the layer model of illustrations (cf. Section 2.4). The depiction of the geographic features can be compared with the primary object of illustrations. Since it spans the whole image, each of its annotation types is overlaying a part of it and there would be no remaining space for the background layer. However, maps would additionally require multiple segment layers in order to allow the placement of the annotations. As already mentioned [Tuf97, Hod03], IMHOF's principles for the annotation of maps can partially be applied to the annotation of spatial objects. He also classified different types of annotations according to the differing features of the referred parts.

Annotation types are different
If areal designations are extensive enough to accommodate annotations, they can be compared to internal annotations. Point and line designations do not have an area to accommodate annotations, their annotations are placed alongside the referred part. However, they are neither placed in a certain distance on the border of the map, nor they have secondary elements like reference lines which could overlap. Hence, they are only partially related to external annotations. Unfortunately, there is no literature for integrating annotation boxes as well as their individual types into the layout of annotations. Additionally, those layout elements are usually covering the primary objects, which clearly differ from illustrations. Another difference to the illustration of 3D models is that the annotation of 2D maps has not to consider visibility problems of 3D parts induced by the 3D interaction with the primary object.

Annotation problem is different

Guidelines are partially different
Many of the guidelines defined for the annotations of illustrations and maps are similar. However, there are a few clear differences between them. While BRISCOE claims for a consistent annotation appearance, the annotation of maps means to consciously encode extra information into annotations by using such different annotation appearances. TUFTE also clarifies that the use of legends and codes in illustrations should be limited to the use in justified cases. Hence, in the following, the focus is on consistent annotation while offering the flexibility to alter the appearance of annotations.

Global and individual specifications
Adapted from IMHOF's practice, the remainder of this section defines *container intrinsic specifications* which take into account the special requirements of each container as well as *global specifications* which address to the overall layout.

Container Intrinsic Specifications

- **Legibility.** In order to obtain an optimal legibility, typographic factors have to be considered. Because of their limited resolution, for computer monitors a font size of at least 10 to 12 points without serifs should be used (e.g., Arial, Helvetica) [Bol01, Kön04, Bal97]. Additionally, the font styles of the annotations should be consistent.

- The text stroke of *internal annotations* should be controllable in their steepness and curvature. In terms of ensuring maximum legibility, they should even be horizontal [Imh75]. Unlike the other annotations, internal annotations overlay their referred parts. Especially, if the spatial structure of the underlying illustrations is indicated by color gradients or shades, the low contrast to the letter color negatively influences the legibility of the annotation. Thus, contrast preserving techniques should be employed.

- *External annotations* and *annotation boxes* should neither overlay other annotations nor the primary object. Moreover, their optional reference lines should not cross each other.

- **Unambiguity.** The association between the textual annotation and its referred part should be intuitive.

  - *Internal annotations* should not overlap segments of the illustration. In terms of supporting unambiguity, their annotation path should be aligned to the medial axis of the reference part (cf. [Imh75]).

  - In order to improve the unambiguity of *external annotations*, their anchor points should be placed on salient positions of the referred part, their reference lines should not cross and their textual annotations should reside in a minimum distance to their referred parts.

  - *Annotation boxes* which refer to a specific part have the same specifications for unambiguity as external annotations.

- **Visual Occlusion.** The presentation space of the primary object and the annotations is shared. Thus, the occlusion of visual information by annotations should be minimized.

  - The occlusion of important parts of the illustration by *internal annotation* letters should be minimized. Since internal annotations share their presentation space with reference lines they should not occlude them.

  - Anchor points and sections of reference lines of *external annotations* overlay the primary object and their placement should consider that the occlusion of important visual information should be minimized. Additionally, reference lines should not overlay internal annotations.

  - *Annotation boxes* share their presentation space with external annotations and should not cover those textual annotations or reference lines. In case that an annotation box is referring to a specific part of the primary object it has the same specifications like external annotations.

- **Frame Coherence.** An unsteady annotation layout diverts the viewer's attention from the primary object. In order to preserve the smallest effective difference, visual discontinuities of the layout elements should be minimized and the extent of their movement should be as marginal as possible.

- The individual letters of *internal annotations* should only change their position only if necessary. When the text stroke changes its position this change should be minimal and continuous. The annotation style should also only change if necessary.

- The anchor points and the annotation text of *external annotations* should only move if necessary, and if so, they should move minimally and continuously.

- *Annotation boxes* as the largest layout elements should only change their position and size if necessary. If so, this change should be continuous and minimal.

Global Specifications

- **Coverage.** The annotation layout approach should manage the layout of all defined containers and their styles in one combined framework.

- **Flexibility.** Besides functional aspects, illustrators seem to select the annotation types and styles by esthetic and personal preferences. Hence, individual preferences should be definable. Additionally, in order to meet special necessities of applications, the approach should allow to define different font attributes of the annotations.

- **Applicability.** The approach should address the annotation of visualizations of multiple different 3D model types (cf. Chapter 2).

- **Scalability.** Illustrations in textbooks may contain up to 80 annotations [Pre98]. However, this number of annotations may produce visual clutter and can induce tedious search tasks [RT92, p. 606]. Hence, as a compromise the approach should be designed to be able to accommodate about 20 to 30 annotations.

- **Selectiveness.** The approach should either allow to annotate a maximum number of visible parts, or to define importance values for each of the 3D parts which is considered by the computation of the layout approach.

- **Media capabilities.** To guarantee a smooth interaction with the 3D model, the approach has to be designed to compute the annotation layout on a modern system with at least 15 frames per second (cf. [FvDFH90, p. 3]).

Conflicts In case of the annotation of maps, some of these specifications conflict with each other. As an example, to guarantee a maximum of frame coherence the positions of the layout elements should not change. However, this behavior would spoil many other specifications. Thus, the annotation approach should allow to define preferences for different applications.[2]

For an interactive approach for the annotation of 3D models, these specifications should be fulfilled. The next section introduces existing approaches in the field of interactive annotation of 3D models and reflects about the necessity of novel approaches.

---

[2]The strategies implementing those preferences will be discussed in Chapter 4

3.4 Related Work

In order to review the related work done in the field of a 3D model's annotation lay-out a problem–oriented focus has to be defined. Next, existing approaches have to be discussed in respect of the specifications defined in Section 3.3.3.

3.4.1 Focus

There are numerous works on computing annotation placements for static (e.g [CMS95]) and interactive (e.g., [PGP03]) 2D maps. However, since the annotation of maps uses dif-ferent annotation types and specifications (see Section 3.3.3), this section focuses on in-teractive applications which augment 3D models of real existing objects with secondary elements at interactive rates. Many applications concentrate on the visualization task, while neglecting the annotation layout. However, this section focuses on applications, which explicitly manage the layout of secondary elements. This implies that the aim of these applications is to interact with a *primary object*, while the layout of the secondary elements has to be found *automatically* and at *interactive rates*.

3.4.2 Existing Approaches

This section presents the existing approaches using the eye–in–hand and the world–in–hand metaphor (see Section 2.3.3) in the defined focus and briefly introduces their setting and specifies their layout constraints. A successive discussion rates those con-straints according to their appropriateness to the specifications.

Eye–in–hand Metaphor

① BELL ET AL. [BF00] introduced the term *view management* for the integration of additional 2D information into the view plane of virtual and augmented 3D environ-ments (see Figure 3.7). The approach supported each of the annotation types, which

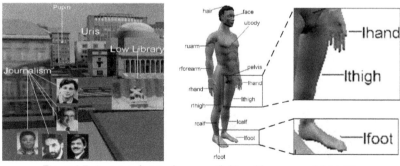

Figure 3.7: Annotated virtual campus (left) and human model (right).

were coherently moving whilst the user interacted with the scene. The biggest disadvantage of this approach was that it suffered from the rough approximation of 3D parts via bounding boxes. Consequently, visible 3D parts might be accidentally considered as invisible because of too large bounding boxes of surrounding 3D parts. Furthermore, anchor points and internal annotations might be situated on incorrect placements outside of the referred part (see Figure 3.7–right). Additionally, external textual annotations might cover the primary object (see Figure 3.7–left) while the amount of occluded information was not considered. Different annotation styles were not considered, since the annotations adapted their size according to the available space of the projected 3D parts, which affected the legibility. The approach processed polygonal models, whereas it did not selectively annotate each visible part. Due to of possible overlaps with 3D parts, the screen might get cluttered in case of many accommodated annotations.

② MAASS&DÖLLNER [MD06a] used billboarding techniques to integrate secondary elements into visualizations of 3D city models. The exploration of the 3D models was primarily designed for the eye–in–hand metaphor. In order to enhance the immersive sensation the internal annotations were directly attached to the geometry of their assigned 3D parts (i.e., buildings) (see Figure 3.8). The approach approximated the hulls of the buildings in order to attach the billboards to the nearest point on the 3D parts, whereas the billboards orientation was adapted to the geometry of the hull. During the interaction the billboards coherently transited to adjacent positions on this hull while collisions between the billboards and the hull were resolved. The amount of annotated parts could be adjusted to the distance from the viewer. By attaching the annotations to the hulls in object space, the annotations on the billboards were perspectively distorted. This allowed a more realistic annotation of 3D city models while the user perambulated the 3D model. However, the legibility was massively suffering from this distortion (see Figure 3.8–right)—especially if many annotations had to be accommodated in small 3D parts. Additionally, by using billboards the internal annotations were not used to adapt different styles and thus, a layout parametrization was not considered. Since the approach worked with the geometry of polygonal 3D models its applicability was restricted. Finally, occlusion of important visual information was not considered by the approach.

Figure 3.8: Multiple annotated buildings with billboarded annotations.

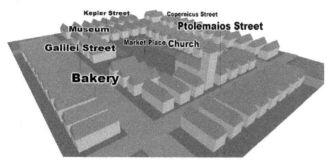

Figure 3.9: Virtual landscape with annotations communicating depth by font size.

③ Another approach of MAASS&DÖLLNER [MD06b] presented a dynamic placement technique for annotations in polygonal 3D landscapes. This technique used external annotations to augment visible and invisible 3D parts (see Figure 3.9). The approach selectively annotated the 3D model, while closer 3D parts were considered to be more important and were favored in order to avoid overlaps with other annotations. The external annotations were connected to their referred parts by vertical lines. The placement algorithm checked the visibility of the 3D parts, sorted the annotations by their depth, detected their position, and rendered them accordingly. To improve the legibility, the black letters of the annotations were surrounded by a white silhouette. Two approaches were presented which resolve an overlapping of the annotations. Although the annotations might overlap several 3D parts, the layout algorithm did not consider which amount of important information is occluded by the annotations. In order to improve immersion, the annotation fonts adapted their size to allow a better impression of spatial depth of the referred 3D parts. However, it did not guarantee an optimal legibility for distant annotations and spoiled the specification of illustrations for consistent font styles.

World–in–hand Metaphor

④ The Zoom Illustrator approach, developed by PREIM ET AL. [PRS97], aimed at the interactive exploration of polygonal 3D models (see Figure 3.10). The approach arranged external annotations which were placed in designated areas on the left and right border of the screen and established the link between the textual annotation and its referred parts by multiple reference lines. The approach supported interaction with both annotations and 3D model. For the textual annotations a fisheye zoom expanded annotations of high interest, whereas those of low interest were shrunk. Additionally, the approach allowed to generate descriptions of the visible 3D parts in a figure caption below the primary object, but this was not handled by the annotation layout algorithm. The approach was designed for polygonal 3D models and used one style for both external annotations in order to annotate each of the visible 3D parts. The interaction with the 3D model caused numerous crossings of the reference lines, which negatively influenced the legibility and unambiguity. The scalability of annotations was sufficient, but suffered from the visual clutter induced by crossing reference lines with an increasing number of an-

43

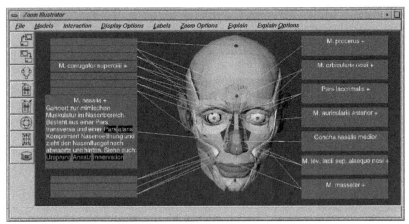

Figure 3.10: Zoom Illustrator interface with annotations in designated areas.

notations. Frame coherence was not explicitly considered, but via keyboard interaction the user was able to rearrange the annotations in order to reduce the crossings. Finally, occlusions of the reference lines with important visible parts of the 3D model were not considered.

⑤ CHIGONA ET AL. introduced a work about the dual use of image space [CS02]. They pointed out that the visualization of text can either be used for reading textual information or shading information. Initially, the letter sizes of the texts were just one pixel wide and used as shading information. By clicking on an image part, the user was able to increase the text size until its legibility was sufficient. Since this approach was only used for images, another approach of CHIGONA ET AL. [CSRS03] adapted this integration of text to annotate shadows of polygonal 3D models like the approach of RITTER ET AL. [RSHS03b] does. These shadows were used as annotation boxes which established the link between primary object and textual information. The presentation of the annotation could not be adjusted to task–specific preferences. However, the approach of RITTER ET

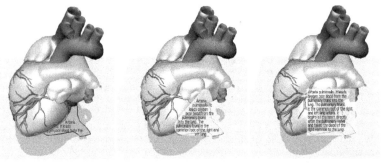

Figure 3.11: Morphing from internally annotated shadows external annotation.

AL. required a manual layout of the annotations. The approach of CHIGONA ET AL. provided two styles of annotation boxes (see Figure 3.11): the annotations were either integrated into the shadow projections or they were expanded to a rectangular external annotation which overlayed a certain part of the primary object while the occlusion of important visual information was not considered. If an annotation was expanded, the assignment to the referred 3D part was ambiguous, because multiple 3D parts were overlaid (see Figure 3.11). Both styles did not take into account to preserve the contrast between text and background and, thus, lacked of legibility. Since the textual information automatically adapted to the shape of its referred part on the shadow, the approach coped with coherent transitions of the annotations did not consider to annotate multiple parts simultaneously. However, it was possible to select the 3D parts which had to be annotated.

⑥ SONNET ET AL. [SCS04] described an interactive technique to explore annotated polygonal 3D models by a probe for explosion diagrams. On demand, the user was able to request annotations, which were placed in an annotation box outside of the primary object, towards the nearest boundary of the view plane. This container was clearly linked with the 3D part by a polygonal connector which origin were two edges of the bounding box of the 3D part. There were three different styles of those external annotations (see Figure 3.12) which contained the text the user was able to scroll through. However, the approach did not allow for different preferences of the annotations' texts presentation. The transitions of the annotations were smooth, and although the intrinsic legibility of the annotations was good, they might overlay the primary object and even other annotations, which negatively affected the legibility. The overlaps with other annotations impeded the annotation of numerous 3D parts. Furthermore, the approach did not consider whether the annotations occluded important parts of the primary object.

⑦ GÖTZELMANN [Göt04] introduced an interactive approach to augment polygonal 3D models with internal annotations as depicted in the illustrations (see Figure 3.13). The approach applied several algorithms on the color–coded projection of the 3D model in order to determine the medial axis of the projected 3D parts of the primary object. A scanline algorithm determined the medial axis efficiently but imprecisely, while a second determined the medial axis by voronoï graphs which was computationally more complex but also more precise. Internal annotations could only be placed, if the projections

Figure 3.12: Annotated explosion diagrams: different external annotation styles.

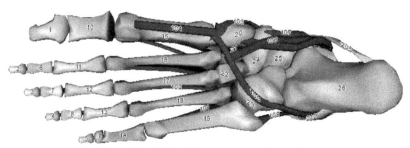

Figure 3.13: Multiple internal annotation styles.

of the 3D parts were extensive enough. The algorithm accomplished three different layout styles. For a good legibility the annotation stroke was placed horizontally in a salient position, if there was enough space. For a better integration into the shape of the 3D part, the annotation stroke might also be aligned according to the medial axis, or alternatively slanted. Additionally, different fonts could be used for the annotations. To preserve the contrast between the letters and the ground, the black letters were either surrounded by a white halo, or their color was inverted, depending on the brightness of the underlying part of the object. Since the approach only needed rendered renditions of the 3D models, it was independent of their specific type. However, this work was not explicitly prepared for the use of arbitrary 3D model types. It was not considered, if important parts of the primary object were overlaid by the letters, but their transparency might have been adjusted. However, this solution also negatively influenced the legibility. Both algorithms for the determination of the medial axis might have produced annotation paths which contained unsteady parts or caused a high curvature, which negatively influenced the legibility. During the user interactions, the annotations smoothly interpolated their positions. However, distant jumps might have induced drastic changes of the medial axis of referred 3D parts.

⑧ ALI ET AL. [AHS05] implemented a layout system to integrate external annotations into visualizations of polygonal 3D models. It supported six different layout styles and was applied in several applications (i.e., [BG05, LRA$^+$07]) (see Figure 3.14). In order to reduce computational complexity, the textual annotations were considered as zero–sized points. This restricted the flexibility of the layout to single–line external annotations with constant height, but the approach handled various font attributes. Legends and descriptions were used as well, but not integrated into the layout approach. Although the approach did not explicitly address the application for other 3D model types as the internal approach [Göt04], it worked on the color–coded projection of the 3D model, which allowed to transfer this method. Using this projection, the positions of the anchor points were situated on the medial axis. Subsequently, positions alongside the anchor points were allocated for the annotations, an initial annotation layout was determined which eliminated overlaps of the textual annotations, and finally, line intersections were resolved. Additionally, the annotations moved from the bounding box pixelwise horizontally or vertically towards their associated part to reduce the length of the reference line. However, the textual annotations were placed at a rough approximation of the

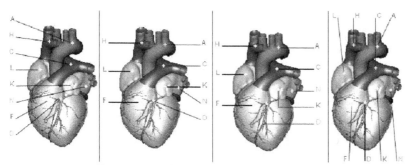

Figure 3.14: Multiple external annotation styles.

3D model silhouette; for complex shaped primary objects (i.e., hollow) this did not ensure the minimum distance. To enhance the frame coherence of the annotations, the approach kept previous positions of anchor points as long as possible. If the position of the annotation was changed, their movement was smoothly interpolated to the new position. However, this position might be distant to the old position. Finally, the algorithm did not consider if important parts of the primary object were covered by the reference lines of the annotations and it did not handle the individual annotation of a specified set of annotated 3D parts.

⑨ The work of OLBRICH [Olb06] addressed the external annotation for polygonal 3D models in an interactive application (see Figure 3.15). Using the z–buffer of the rendered scene, the approach determined if the fixed anchor points on the 3D parts were visible. The approach managed to visualize a large amount of annotations at interactive rates but the initial placement and interaction with the 3D model caused overlaps among them. Olbrich introduced a metric, which calculated displacement vectors in order to shift overlapping annotations. However, this strategy did not rule out overlaps of annotations, which caused legibility problems. If annotations could not be shifted, they disappeared, which resulted in an unsteady layout. Three different annotation

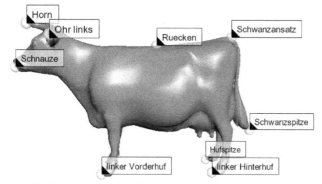

Figure 3.15: External annotation by allowing overlaps with primary object.

styles were supported. The first style placed the annotations directly besides the anchor points, which unfortunately occluded parts of the primary object. The approach did not consider if important parts of the 3D model were occluded. Additionally the legibility suffered from these overlaps, since no contrast preserving techniques were used. The second style placed the annotations' text strokes on the left and right screen border, while the third style placed them onto a ring that subscribed the primary object. Since the anchor points were directly fixated to the 3D model, it could be ensured that the annotations were visible. However, the silhouette of the object was not considered. Thus, in the ladder two cases a minimal distance to the referred part could be established. The approach allowed to freely adjust the font attributes and to display spatial depth or importance values of certain 3D parts by different font sizes. The importance values could also be used to define the priority of the annotation layout.

3.4.3 Discussion

Using the same specifications derived from the guidelines of human illustrators (cf. Section 3.3.3), this section rates the introduced existing approaches. The results of the assessment in the previous section are summarized in Table 3.3.

First, the container intrinsic specifications for *int*ernal and *ext*ernal annotations as well as annotation *box*es are listed, followed by the global specifications. The existing approaches are discretized into different levels of fulfillment. Since not all approaches handle the layout of each container type some attributes are marked as *not applicable*. If an approach handles the layout for a container type but does not address certain specifications, it is marked as *not considered*. In case a criterion defined in the specification is considered but only partially met, it is noted as *not sufficient*, if only some points are not addressed, it is marked as *good with constraints*. Finally, if specifications are met well, the approach is considered as *good*.

Interpretation of table

	[BF00] ①	[MD06a] ②	[MD06b] ③	[PRS97] ④	[CSRS03] ⑤	[SCS04] ⑥	[Göt04] ⑦	[AHS05] ⑧	[Olb06] ⑨
Container (int./ext./box.)									
Legibility	o/o/o	●/■/■	■/o/■	■/●/■	■/●/■	■/●/■	o/■/■	■/oo/■	■/●/■
Unambiguity	●/●/●	oo/■/■	■/oo/■	■/o/■	■/o/■	■/oo/■	oo/■/■	■/o/■	■/●/■
Occlusion	●●/●●/●●	●●/■/■	■/●●/■	■/●●/■	■/●●/■	■/●●/■	●/■/■	■/●●/■	■/●●/■
Frame Coherency	oo/oo/oo	oo/■/■	■/oo/■	■/●/■	■/oo/■	■/oo/■	o/■/■	■/o/■	■/o/■
Global									
Coverage	oo	●	●	●	o	o	o	o	o
Flexibility	●	●	●	●	●	●	o	o	oo
Applicability	●●	●●	●●	●●	●●	●●	●	●	●●
Scalability	o	o	oo	o	●	●	o	oo	oo
Selectiveness	●	oo	oo	oo	o	●	●	o	o
Media Capabilities	oo	oo	oo	oo	oo	oo	oo	oo	oo

■ *not applicable* ●● *not considered* ● *not sufficient* o *good with constraints* oo *good*

Table 3.3: Evaluation of the related work according to the specifications.

The existing approaches tackle various problems in different fields. For applications using the eye–in–hand metaphor, methods improving the navigation and immersion seem to outweigh other specifications such as legibility. Hence, those approaches are based on different specifications than those using the world–in–hand metaphor. However, most of the approaches do not explicitly address the annotation of different 3D model types' visualizations by a unified method. Additionally, as it can be seen in the table, the existing approaches have strengths in some of the specifications, but none of the approaches can be applied to adequately annotate interactive 3D models.

Differing specifications

3.5 Conclusion

This section analyzed illustrations in books and determined that three layout containers are sufficient for the annotation of illustrations. For each of these containers the most common layout styles were formalized, followed by an investigation of guidelines of human illustrators for the annotation of illustrations. These guidelines served as a basis to formulate specifications for a system which interactively annotates illustrations the way human illustrators do. Using these specifications, the existing approaches were assessed and it was revealed that none of them meets all of the specifications properly. The following Chapter 4 develops a problem–oriented approach which addresses each of these specifications.

4 | Encapsulated Annotation Layout Approach

Outline

This chapter utilizes the layout styles and specifications which were derived in Chapter 3 in order to develop a flexible approach to automatically annotate 3D models. Additionally, it addresses novel questions arising through the acquired ability to interact with those annotated 3D models. First, for each of the specifications, metrics are developed to assess the quality of annotation layouts. Subsequently, these metrics are used for the construction of an encapsulated annotation approach as well as appropriate algorithms.

Achievements

The introduced metrics allow to compare the suitability of multiple alternative annotation layouts. It manifests that only two renditions of the rendered 3D model are necessary to compute the secondary elements' layout for 3D models of any type. In order to offer a wide variety of styles, heuristics have to be employed to evaluate annotation layouts at interactive rates. The influence of each of the metrics has to be weighted in order to enable different preferences of illustrators. Finally, it becomes clear that annotation styles have to be adaptive; an annotation layout approach has to be able to interchange the styles of annotations.

4.1 Introduction

The last chapter formalized layout styles and derived specifications in order to allow the development of a problem–oriented solution. In this chapter these specifications serve as the basis for the development of a problem–oriented approach. For the illustration of several algorithms, a 3D model of a human heart is used as a running example. It is a complex shaped object (see Appendix C.13), which supports the claim for the need of an interactive 3D exploration. In most anatomic books there is the necessity for multiple different views of it to clarify its components, spatial shape and configuration.

Specifications as basis

Running example

In order to enable the determination of the quality of annotation layouts, Section 4.2 transfers the container intrinsic specifications into metrics for the evaluation of each secondary element's placements. To realize the global specifications, the following sections introduce numerous novel techniques. For the *applicability*, Section 4.3 describes an annotation approach for the interactive exploration of 3D models, independent of their type and their target application. Section 4.4 specifies efficient annotation algorithms for the *coverage* of the previously defined annotation styles, which enable the use of the metrics while meeting the *media capabilities*. In order to make the layout *flexible*, Section 4.4.2

Container specifications

Global specifications

proposes the use of weights for the evaluation of the layout configuration, according to the individual preferences and the necessities of target applications.

Layout whilst interaction

Some of the specifications address issues arising by the interactive exploration of 3D models whilst computing an annotation layout. In order to reduce the flow of secondary elements, Section 4.4.4 explains a technique for the improvement of the *frame coherence*. To allow interaction with the annotated primary objects whilst preserving the layout pre–settings, Section 4.4.5 explains the necessity of an *adaptive* annotation layout. Section 4.5 concludes the achievements of this chapter.

4.2 Metrics for Layout Containers

Need of metrics

To obtain an appealing annotation layout, alternative annotation placements must be assessable. The popular software engineer DEMARCO pointed out: 'You cannot control what you cannot measure' [DeM82]. Thus, this section introduces metrics for the evaluation of an annotation layout. Subsequently, these metrics are used to assess which of the multiple alternative annotation placements is optimal.

Distance functions

As multiple annotation metrics use *distance functions*, Table 4.1 gives a brief overview of the most common distance metrics. The *Euclidean* metric is preferred, because it computes the distances in Euclidean space (see graphical representation of Equation 4.1.1). However, its computation requires floating point variables and more complex computational operations than other distance measures. Hence, for time critical procedures, e.g., the *Manhattan* metric and the *Maximum* metric may be used for a faster approximation of the spatial distance.

Name	Function		Graphical
Euclidean	$\text{dist}_1\left(\vec{a}, \vec{b}\right) = \sqrt{\sum_{i=1}^{n}\left(a_i - b_i\right)^2}$	(4.1.1)	
Manhattan	$\text{dist}_2\left(\vec{a}, \vec{b}\right) = \sum_{i=1}^{n}\left|a_i - b_i\right|$	(4.1.2)	
Maximum	$\text{dist}_3\left(\vec{a}, \vec{b}\right) = \max\left\{\left|a_i - b_i\right|, 1 \le i \le n\right\}$	(4.1.3)	

Table 4.1: Distance functions with their graphical representation ($a, b \in \mathbb{N}^2, n = 2$).

The following sections deduce metrics M from each of the specifications legibility sl, unambiguity su, visual occlusion so, and frame coherence sc, which are designed to reach their optimum at minimum values. Each section starts with a short introduction of the specification. Subsequently, the metrics of all three containers internal ci, external ce, and boxes cb are defined.

4.2.1 Legibility

In literature the terms legibility and readability are not used unambiguously. Their usage in this book accords to a discussion [Kön04] about their different meanings. The
term *legibility* refers to the ability to easily recognize single annotations. Hence, if the
letters of a term can only be recognized with considerable effort they lack of legibility.
On the contrary, *readability* is affected by visual clutter. Thus, if the reader is diverted
from secondary elements or if the esthetics of the annotation layout is bad, this means a
bad readability. In order to summarize them in one metric, both terms are addressed in
this section.

- **Internal.** Optimal legibility is given for horizontal text strokes. However, slanted
  and curved text strokes are necessary to meet different specifications. Hence,
  Equation 4.2 determines the angle between the horizontal axis and the positions
  of the first letter $\vec{L}_1 \in \mathbb{N}^2$, and the last letter $\vec{L}_n \in \mathbb{N}^2$ while Equation 4.3 computes
  the average sum of angles between the letters $\vec{L} \in \mathbb{N}^2$ of the text stroke.

$$\alpha\left(\vec{a}, \vec{b}\right) = \arctan\left(\frac{|a_2 - b_2|}{|a_1 - b_1|}\right)$$

$$\text{m1}_{sl}^{ci} = \alpha(\vec{L}_1, \vec{L}_n) \tag{4.2}$$

$$\text{m2}_{sl}^{ci} = \frac{1}{n-2} \sum_{i=2}^{n-1} \left| \alpha(\vec{L}_{i-1}, \vec{L}_i) - \alpha(\vec{L}_i, \vec{L}_{i+1}) \right| \tag{4.3}$$

- **External.** The readability of the annotated illustration suffers from reference lines
  which are crossing each other and those reference lines which are crossing different internal and external annotations.[1] Equation 4.4 sums up the number of
  line–line crossings, while Equation 4.5 counts the overlaps of textual annotations
  with reference lines.

$$\text{m1}_{sl}^{ce} = \sum \text{line–line overlaps} \tag{4.4}$$

$$\text{m2}_{sl}^{ce} = \sum \text{annotation–line overlaps} \tag{4.5}$$

- **Boxes.** The legibility of annotation boxes is dependent on their content and not
  affected by the annotation layout. To preserve the readability of annotation boxes
  they have a minimum size. If annotation boxes are assigned to a specific 3D part,
  a metric $\text{m1}_{sl}^{cb} \equiv \text{m1}_{sl}^{ce}$ as well as $\text{m2}_{sl}^{cb} \equiv \text{m2}_{sl}^{ce}$ is used to consider their reference
  lines.

The method used for the determination of the average curvature of the text stroke of
internal annotations is only a rough measure. In future approaches more sophisticated
methods could be tested in terms of their potential improvement on the reliability of the
metrics.

Curvature approximation

---

[1]Internal and external text strokes are approximated by a line connecting their first and last letters.

As mentioned in Chapter 3 illustrators may add a white silhouette (halo) to the black letters or invert the color of internal text strokes or even single letters in dark regions.[2] Additionally, the visual characteristics of the primary object parts surrounding the letters influences their legibility. Optimal legibility can be considered when the ground is uniformly colored [SH00]. Since the visual occlusion metric copes with the contrast of the primary object parts, this topic is deferred to Section 4.2.3.

Contrast techniques

4.2.2 Unambiguity

The specification of unambiguity means that secondary elements should clearly mediate the assignment to their referred parts. External annotations are placed on the exterior of the primary object, but should reside in a minimum distance to their referred part [MA92a, BB98]. Internal annotations directly overlay their referred 3D parts and should be placed at salient points of them (cf. Chapter 3). However, to meet different metrics, a displacement from salient points cannot be avoided.

- **Internal.** This metric (see Equation 4.6) determines the sum of distances between the n letter centers $\vec{L} \in \mathbb{N}^2$ of the text stroke and the salient point $\vec{S} \in \mathbb{N}^2$ (see Figure 4.1). Additionally, the algorithm explained in Section 4.4 manages the alignment of the text stroke to the medial axis of the referred part of the primary object.

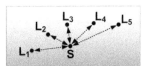

Figure 4.1: Salient point S and $n = 5$ letter centers L.

$$m_{su}^{ci} = \frac{1}{n} \sum_{i=1}^{n} \mathrm{dist}\left(\vec{L}_i, \vec{S}\right) \qquad (4.6)$$

- **External.** This metric (see Equation 4.7) measures the distance between the anchor point $\vec{A} \in \mathbb{N}^2$ on the referred part of the primary object and the n connection points $\vec{T} \in \mathbb{N}^2$ of the textual annotation (see Figure 4.2).

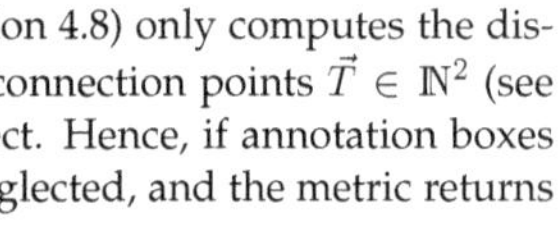

Figure 4.2: Anchor A and $n = 4$ connection points T.

$$m_{su}^{ce} = \min(\mathrm{dist}\left(\vec{A}, \vec{T}_i\right), 1 \leq i \leq n) \qquad (4.7)$$

- **Boxes.** The metric for annotation boxes (see Equation 4.8) only computes the distance of the anchor point $\vec{A} \in \mathbb{N}^2$ to the boxes' n connection points $\vec{T} \in \mathbb{N}^2$ (see Figure 4.2), if it refers to a part of the primary object. Hence, if annotation boxes are not assigned to specific 3D parts they can be neglected, and the metric returns to a minimum distance.

$$m_{su}^{cb} = \begin{cases} 0 : & \text{if not assigned;} \\ \min(\mathrm{dist}\left(\vec{A}, \vec{T}_i\right), 1 \leq i \leq n) : & \text{if assigned.} \end{cases} \qquad (4.8)$$

---

[2]There is even a US Patent [Ade99] which describes a method to automatically attach halos to letters.

Introducing this second metric points out, that different specifications can be mutually contradictory. As an example for an internal annotation, optimal legibility can only be considered for straight and horizontal text strokes. However, the medial axis of an part only appears like this in a few cases. Thus, the demand for optimal readability induces to have no optimal unambiguity and vice versa. To cope with contradicting metrics, Section 4.4.2 introduces application–dependent weights.

Mutually contradictory metrics

4.2.3 Visual Occlusion

In order to establish the links between textual annotation and the referred part, some of the secondary elements are overlaying the primary object. While internal annotations partially cover the primary object with their letters, the anchor points and reference lines of external annotations occlude visual information (see Figure 4.3). The aim is to prefer placements of the secondary elements at uniform shaded parts of the primary object.

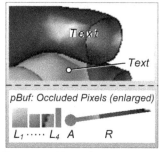

Figure 4.3: Exemplary pixels covered by secondary elements.

In order to measure the uniformity of overlaid parts of the primary object, the following metrics use the standard deviation that can be computed time efficiently. Equation 4.9 assumes the array of m occluded pixels of secondary elements rendered into the buffer *pBuf* as brightness values. First, the mean brightness value of the sampled pixels $\overline{pBuf} = \frac{1}{m}\sum_{i=1}^{m} pBuf_i$ is computed in order to sum up the differences between this value and each sampled pixel.

$$\text{info(pBuf)} = \sqrt{\frac{1}{m}\sum_{i=1}^{m}(\text{pBuf}_i - \overline{\text{pBuf}})^2} \tag{4.9}$$

- **Internal.** Internal annotations cover their referred parts by their n letters L. Thus, this metric determines the visual occlusion by the rectangular approximation of the individual letters. Equation 4.10 incorporates the total visual information occluded by the letters.

$$m_{so}^{ci} = \sum_{i=1}^{n} \text{info}(L_i) \tag{4.10}$$

- **External.** External annotations cover the primary object by their reference line R and optionally by their anchor point A. Hence, this metric (see Equation 4.11) determines the total information occluded by both R and A.

$$m_{so}^{ce} = \text{info}(A) + \text{info}(R) \tag{4.11}$$

- **Boxes.** If an annotation box is assigned to a part of the primary object, the sum of the information occluded by the anchor point A and the reference line R is computed, otherwise the metric (see Equation 4.12) returns that no information is occluded by the box.

$$m_{so}^{cb} = \begin{cases} 0: & \text{if not assigned;} \\ \text{info}\,(A) + \text{info}\,(R): & \text{if assigned.} \end{cases} \quad (4.12)$$

Alternative techniques An alternative way to compute the amount of information is to determine its information theoretic entropy. However, a low number of sampled values may result in unreliable estimates [HO97]. An approach for placing text in augmented reality systems [LT04] determines the contrast features by methods considering the spatial frequency of the overlaid parts. However, these methods can be less efficient in terms of computational costs. Nevertheless, future studies could analyze the appropriateness of those metrics for this approach.

Contrast estimation Minimizing the visual occlusion has another positive effect. If the parts of the primary object surrounding the secondary elements are uniform, a higher contrast can be achieved that may result in a better legibility [SH00].

4.2.4 Frame Coherence

An unsteady layout of secondary layout elements during user interaction may disturb viewers. Hence, the layout elements should only slightly change their position and appearance (cf. Chapter 3).

- **Internal.** This metric (see Equation 4.13) computes the sum of the distances of the positions of n letters $\vec{L} \in \mathbb{N}^2$ between their old and their new position.

$$m_{sc}^{ci} = \sum_{i=1}^{n} \text{dist}(\vec{L}_{i_{old}}, \vec{L}_{i_{new}}) \quad (4.13)$$

- **External.** Changes in the positions of anchor points $\vec{A} \in \mathbb{N}^2$ are determined by Equation 4.14, while changes of the textual annotations $\vec{T} \in \mathbb{N}^2$ are computed by Equation 4.15.

$$m1_{sc}^{ce} = \text{dist}(\vec{A}_{old}, \vec{A}_{new}) \quad (4.14)$$

$$m2_{sc}^{ce} = \text{dist}(\vec{T}_{old}, \vec{T}_{new}) \quad (4.15)$$

- **Boxes.** The metrics determine the changes of the position of the center point of annotation boxes $\vec{B} \in \mathbb{N}^2$ (see Equation 4.16), as well as their change in their width B_w, respectively height B_h (Equation 4.17).

$$m1_{sc}^{cb} = \text{dist}(\vec{B}_{old}, \vec{B}_{new}) \quad (4.16)$$

$$m2_{sc}^{cb} = \max(|\Delta B_w|, |\Delta B_h|) \quad (4.17)$$

Disappearing annotations Another strategy to prevent the user from getting diverted by moving layout elements could be to fade them out during the user interaction and fade them in when the user has stopped. However, this would force the user to do each assignment between annotations and referred parts after each interaction. Hence, further studies would be necessary to evaluate if this strategy impedes the *smallest effective difference* [Tuf97].

In this case, only the movement of layout elements of a certain annotation type is considered. However, annotations should be able to even adapt their annotation type. Hence, Section 4.4.5 covers this subject matter and presents a strategy for an annotation container spanning kind of frame coherence.

Extended consideration

4.3 An Encapsulated Annotation Layout Approach

Each of the 3D models mentioned in Chapter 2 are usually rendered with different operations. In order to determine a flexible annotation layout for these 3D models, algorithms have to be applied which meet the specifications derived in Chapter 3. Since the approach should be flexible and reusable, it has to be encapsulated. In terms of encapsulation, it has to be ensured that the approach has narrow interfaces, in order to apply it easily to different interactive visualizations of 3D models. Hence, an approach has to be developed which can be simply plugged onto existing applications, without constraining the visualization and interaction with the models.

Heterogeneous 3D models and applications

Interfaces

In order to be independent of both the type of 3D model and its visualization and not to influence the interaction with the model, the *input* interface can use the projection of the model. Besides a G–buffer of the 3D model's shaded projection (*frame–buffer*), another G–buffer has to be additionally provided, which represents the segmented view of the visible areas of the frame–buffer. Hence, as the second G–buffer, the color–coded projection of the 3D model (*ID–buffer*) assigns each pixel of the frame–buffer a unique color–ID value. Each single 3D part is assigned to a set of annotations. The translation between color–ID of the ID–buffer and textual annotation is carried out by an annotation table as outlined in Figure 4.4.

Input: Frame– and ID–buffer

To decouple the annotation layout from the visualization of the annotations, the *encapsulated annotation approach* provides two alternative output interfaces. In the *layout only mode* solely the layout specific parameters (visible annotations, position, angle, sizes of the set of annotations) are offered. Since in this mode the individual application has to handle the rendering of the secondary elements, it provides the possibility to apply this approach independent of the visualization rendering system. However, in the *rendering mode*, the approach additionally visualizes the secondary elements. This may constrain the applicability of the approach, but also simplifies its use.

Output: Layout configuration or Annotated scene

Distance–buffer

The arrangements of all three types of annotations heavily rely on shapes and silhouettes of each part of the primary object. For each of the annotation types, the distance between annotation and assigned part is important. Hence, the determination of distances is use-

57

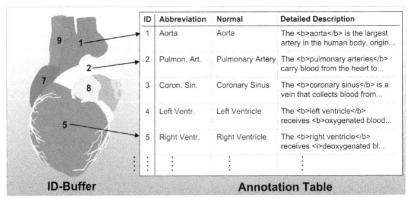

	ID	Abbreviation	Normal	Detailed Description
	1	Aorta	Aorta	The \<b>aorta\</b> is the largest artery in the human body, origin...
	2	Pulmon. Art.	Pulmonary Artery	The \<b>pulmonary arteries\</b> carry blood from the heart to...
	3	Coron. Sin.	Coronary Sinus	The \<b>coronary sinus\</b> is a vein that collects blood from...
	4	Left Ventr.	Left Ventricle	The \<b>left ventricle\</b> receives \<b>oxygenated blood...
	5	Right Ventr.	Right Ventricle	The \<b>right ventricle\</b> receives \<i>deoxygenated bl...

ID-Buffer   **Annotation Table**

Figure 4.4: Translation between color-ID (shades of gray) and textual annotation.

Important: Distances for annotations

ful for the layout task. Within the encapsulated annotation approach, prior the layout task a distance field is computed which constitutes a third G–buffer (*Distance–buffer*). This distance field assigns each pixel of the ID–buffer its minimal distance to the boundaries of each projected 3D part (see Figure 4.5). An adequate method for determining such a distance field has to perform very time efficiently in order to meet real–time constraints, and should be capable of handling multiple segments denoted by color–IDs.

Figure 4.5: Exemplary distance field: banana shaped object with color–ID 1 on its background with color–ID 0 (left) and its distance field (right).

Distance transformation

There are numerous approaches for distance transformations. In his survey paper MOORE [Moo02] compares different techniques and algorithms in terms of time efficiency and quality of the resulting distance fields. He concludes that the algorithm from CUISE-NAIRE AND MACQ [CM99] is the most time efficient one, albeit other approaches may yield more exact results. This algorithm uses a technique called *vector propagation*, to transform a binary image into a distance field in linear time for n pixels. In the first pass, the algorithm starts from the upper left corner and sweeps over each pixel of the image until the lower right corner is reached. If the current pixel belongs to the object, a morphological operator detects if there are already computed propagation vectors in its direct neighborhood. Next, for the current pixel it generates a propagation vector computed of those in its neighborhood. The second pass performs in the same manner in reverse order with a different neighborhood operator.

Propagation of distance vectors

Since the approach of this book has to meet real–time constraints and uses large input images, multiple optimizations have to be considered to determine the distance field.

58

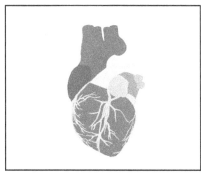 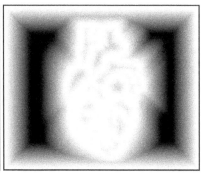

Figure 4.6: Color–coded heart indicated by differing shades of gray (left) and its distance field (right). The darker the pixels, the higher the distance values.

First, instead of the Euclidean metric the algorithm uses the Maximum metric (see Table 4.1), which is less accurate, but can be computed more time efficiently. Secondly, a smaller rendition of the input image is used, hence only $\frac{1}{4}$, $\frac{1}{8}$, or $\frac{1}{16}$ of the original resolution is considered. Finally, a further modification of the algorithm treats each color–ID as well as the background and the view plane borders as separate parts to be transformed. As an example of the resulting distance field, see Figure 4.6.

Problem related optimizations

Recent approaches even support the computation of the distance buffer by the graphics hardware (e.g., [ST04]). However, additional preprocessing steps necessary for this approach would impede the advantage of these techniques. Furthermore, they could involve additional dependencies between the encapsulated approach and the application respectively the graphics hardware.

Hardware acceleration

Architecture

In order to unify the interface to the encapsulated annotation approach, the *application* visualizes the 3D models of a certain type of *3D description* and handles the user interaction (see Figure 4.7). Besides the shaded version, likewise a color–coded rendition has to be provided. Via layout *parameters* the application can control the encapsulated annotation approach. The *encapsulated annotation approach* reads the annotation table and uses the ID–buffer to compute the distance–buffer. Subsequently, the annotation layout is determined. As mentioned, the output interface offers two different modes. ① If the application is considered to render the annotations, the approach offers an interface with the layout configuration. ② However, the encapsulated annotation approach may also render and project the annotations with built–in functionality.

Integration of the encapsulated approach

The annotation's font attributes could be used to encode additional information (e.g., importance) of 3D parts. Especially, the z–buffer values of the annotated parts could influence the font sizes of their annotations. This could be done by offering an additional input interface for the z–buffer. However, since several illustrators clearly claim to annotate illustrations consistently, this task is not considered for the annotation layout, but as an application dependent task. Hence, the application can influence the layout para-

Consistency of font attributes

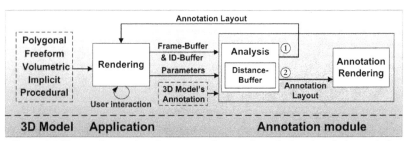

Figure 4.7: The application's architecture in *layout only mode* ① and *rendering mode* ②.

meters of the encapsulated annotation approach to achieve a less consistent, but flexible appearance of the annotations.

4.4   Algorithms for Annotation Layout

This section introduces parameterizable algorithms used for the determination of the annotation layout by using the input data. First, the search space is reduced in order to determine candidate positions for the annotation placements. Next, the need of heuristics for the evaluation of possible annotation placements is motivated—followed by the algorithms using them to determine an initial layout. Finally, the coherence of the annotation layout during user interaction is addressed.

4.4.1   Determination of Candidates

Reduction of search space   In order to compute an annotation layout at interactive rates, the search space of the potential candidates has to be drastically reduced. The layout constraints for each of the containers differ from each other. Thus, this section develops particular strategies for the determination of potential candidates of each container.

Internal Annotations and Annotation Boxes

Disjoint layout space   The search space of internal annotations and annotation boxes are designated areas, where the layout elements have to be accommodated. Both types of containers have to be placed on salient areas of their referred part respectively the illustration background. In order to determine a set of potentially good container placement candidates at interactive rates, a fast greedy method is applied for both of them.

Squared tilings   This method is based on squared tilings of the primary objects part's area or the illustration background. It uses the distance buffer to determine the salient positions for the candidates for both annotation types. Due to the use of the Maximum metrics, for any location with a distance value d, it is possible to allocate a square with an edge length $2d$ centered on this position.

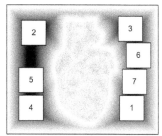 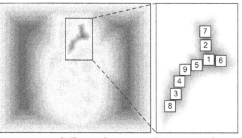

Watch scene
2–1

Figure 4.8: The numbers refer to the sequence of allocated squares of annotation boxes (left) and internal annotation candidates (right). Hatched parts denote another color–ID.

In order to obtain candidates for an internal placement respectively annotation boxes, local maxima are determined within the distance field masked with the color–coded region of the referred parts of the primary object or the background code in the ID–buffer (see Figure 4.8). In order to reduce the number of convenient annotation placement candidates, a minimal annotation extent d_{min} is considered. For internal annotations d_{min} represents the size of the tallest letter, and for annotation boxes the size of the smallest reasonable annotation box.

Local maxima of distance field

Initially, all the space is unallocated. Then, the maximum distance value of the unallocated space is determined. If this value d is greater than d_{min}, its position and the distance value is stored in a result list. Subsequently, an area of the size d_{min} around that maximum is allocated. This process is continued until no more maximum greater than d_{min} can be found in the distance field of the remaining unallocated space. As a result, disjoint salient points were located and serve as foundation for the evaluation of possible annotation placements (see Section 4.4.3).

See Appendix D.1

External Annotations

For parts of the primary object which are neither internally annotated nor expanded to annotation boxes, external annotations are placed on the remaining background space. This approach implements an annotation layout style with a defined distance between the object's shape and external annotations (see Figure 4.9). Violating this *annotation orbit* may disturb the viewer by visual clutter and mean an additional cognitive load to interpret this differentiation. The annotation orbit can be computed very efficiently on the distance field masked with the background code in the ID–buffer. The candidates for the placement of external annotations are extracted in a single pass by detecting positions with the correct distance. The resulting set of external annotation candidates constitutes the foundation to evaluate possible annotation placements (see Section 4.4.3).

Shared layout space with annotation boxes

Equidistant annotation orbit

In order to obtain multiple annotation layout styles, the annotation orbit approach allows two different alignment modes. If a circular layout is preferred, a defined distance to the objects silhouette is determined (see Figure 4.9–left). If, however, a rectangular layout is desired, the bounding box of the primary object may be used to arrange the candidates (see Figure 4.9–right).

Circular or rectangular alignment

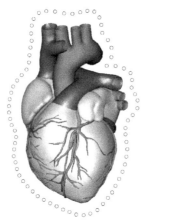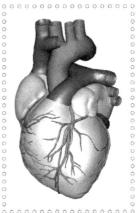

Figure 4.9: Orbit: constant distance to the 3D model's silhouette (left) or bounding box (right).

4.4.2 Weighted Evaluation

The last step drastically reduced the search space to a number of possible annotation placements for each of the container types. For the subset of possible placements, each of the remaining *candidate* positions is evaluated, according to the *metrics* defined in Section 4.2. For each of the individual annotations a matrix $n \times m$ is obtained with their individual values v (see Equation 4.18).

Layout evaluation

$$
\begin{array}{c@{\qquad}ccc}
 & candidate_1 & \cdots & candidate_m \\
metric_1 & v_{11} & \cdots & v_{1m} \\
\vdots & \vdots & & \vdots \\
metric_n & v_{n1} & \cdots & v_{nm}
\end{array}
\tag{4.18}
$$

Based on subjective and application–dependent preferences, each of the metrics may be differently weighted. In an optimal layout configuration the combination of candidates of all annotations are chosen for the annotation which minimizes each of the values determined by the (weighted) metrics. However, because of the complexity of the search space (annotation × candidates × metrics) an optimum cannot be analytically determined.[3]

No analytic solution

Greedy layout

Human illustrators place the annotations sequentially (see Appendix C.11), by starting with the most difficult or most important ones (see Appendix C.12). This sequential proceeding is adapted by a greedy method in order to obtain sufficiently appealing an-

---

[3]Even a simpler problem, the placement of one annotation type in maps, has been proven to be NP–hard [CMS95].

notation layouts. First, the determined values for each of the metrics are normalized, i.e., linear scaled to the consistent range $v \in \{0.0, 1.0\}$. For each of the individual annotations the candidate is determined that minimizes the weighted sum of the determined values (see Equation 4.19).

```
x:=y
for (...
  if /
```
See Appendix
D.2

$$\text{choice} = \min \left\{ \sum_{i=1}^{n} w_{ij} * v_{ij}, 1 \leq j \leq m \right\} \tag{4.19}$$

Furthermore, the handling of the containers follows a specified sequence. Due to space limitations of the referred parts, internal placement of annotations cannot be ensured. Thus, the possibility of their accommodation has to be considered first. External annotations and annotation boxes share their layout space on the illustration background. However, since the space consumption of annotation boxes is superior to those of external annotations, their layout is determined prior to the external annotations. Finally, external annotations can be placed on the candidate positions, which are not already accommodated by annotation boxes to ensure a compact and non–overlapping layout.

Layout sequence

4.4.3 Initial Layout

This step determines the initial layout of the annotations. In the sequence described in section 4.4.2 each of the candidates are evaluated using the placement algorithms described in the following.

Internal Annotations

To meet the unambiguity specification, internal annotations have to be placed on salient positions on the referred part of the primary object. Based on the salient points determined by the candidate positions, the n letters L of the text strokes have to be arranged.

Arrangement of letters

For the arrangement of the letters of internal annotations there are three different styles. The most common style is to arrange the letters of the text stroke horizontally, in order to allow an optimal legibility. However, the limited space of the referred parts may require to angle the stroke of the letters. When neglecting the declined legibility it additionally has the advantage that the text stroke supports the unambiguity measure by disambiguating the spatial shape of the part. This unambiguity can even be maximized if the text stroke adapts to the medial axis of the referred part, as suggested by Imhof [Imh75]. Using a distance field, the parts' medial axis can be extracted in order to accommodate each of the letters on it. However, it was shown [GAHS05] that the strict use of the medial axis has several disadvantages. The high curvatures and numerous bendings (see Figure 3.6) are inadequate for text strokes because they impair the legibility. Additionally, even small changes to the part's silhouette (e.g., induced by user interaction) may induce enormous changes in the medial axis which negatively affects the frame coherence.

Horizontal stroke

Straight, but slanted stroke

Curved stroke

In order to allow for each of the internal styles and to control the angle and curvature of the text stroke which orients to an underlying distance field, a problem–oriented algorithm had to be developed. The algorithm uses individual layout elements for each letter of the text stroke which are placed on the referred part in sequential order.

Sequentially placed letters

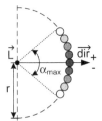

Annotation Path Appearance	α_{init}	α_{max}	dir
Straight horizontal	$= 0°$	$= 0°$	
Straight angled	$> 0°$	$= 0°$	
Curved upwards	$> 0°$	$> 0°$	+
Curved downwards	$> 0°$	$> 0°$	-
Curved	$> 0°$	$> 0°$	

Figure 4.10: Internal letter layout element (left) and its parameters for different text strokes (right).

Layout elements

These layout elements consist of several parts (see Figure 4.10–left). The rectangle carrying the letter's visual representation is centered over point $\vec{L}$. Since mono–spaced internal text stokes do not look appealing, the radius r serves as a spacer between a letter and its subsequently placed letter. In order to control the sequential placement of the letters, the maximum angle of curvature α_{max} can be defined which must not exceeded when placing a subsequent letter. Additionally, the text stroke should orient at the medial axis of the referred part. In the defined segment of a circle α_{max} with the radius r there are multiple pixels on the underlying distance field. Hence, the algorithm places the subsequent letter on the maximum value. Another vector $\vec{dir}$ points from $\vec{L}$ to the placement of the subsequent letter element. Finally, the direction $\vec{dir}$ may be restricted to be positive or negative.

Parametrization

When using these layout elements multiple annotation layout styles can be determined by only three parameters (see Figure 4.10–right). As stated before the maximum angle of curvature is defined by α_{max}. Setting this parameter to zero, *straight horizontal* text strokes are determined. The letter which is initially placed plays a special role, i.e., it uses α_{init} instead of α_{max} because it may control the angle of the text stroke. That means, if α_{max} is set to zero, α_{init} can generate *straight angled* text strokes. By setting a desired maximum angle $\alpha_{max} > 0$, *curved* text strokes are generated. Finally, using this setting, additionally text strokes can be determined which are *curved upwards* and *curved downwards* by restricting the direction parameter $\vec{dir}$ to a negative or positive value.

Example

In the following, the sequence of the letter's placement is explained by the exemplary text stroke 'Labelpath' (see Figure 4.11). Initially, the layout element $\vec{L}_{mid}$ of the midst letter ('l') is placed on the center point of a candidates square, i.e., salient points of the referred part of the primary object. Then, within the circle segment defined by the initial angle α_{init} on the radius r_{mid} each value of the distance field is evaluated. The layout element for the next letter $\vec{L}_{mid+1}$ ('p') is placed on the maximum value of the distance field, whereas it is orthogonally aligned to the direction vector dir_{mid}. For the subsequent letters, the algorithm processes in the same fashion, until L_n is processed. However, the subsequent letters use α_{max} instead of α_{init} . After the algorithm reached the end of the text stroke, it continues in the same fashion, but in reverse order from $\vec{L}_{mid}$ to $\vec{L}_1$ by rotating α_{max} by 180°.

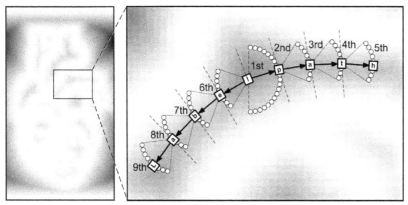

Figure 4.11: Sequential placement of the letters on the distance field. First, the midst element is placed on a candidate with an initial angle of $\alpha_{init} = 180°$. Subsequent letters (see ordinal numbers) are placed by $\alpha_{max} = 75°$.

For performance purposes, a set of rasterized concentric circles with differing r is precomputed. Therefore, the determination of maxima of the distance field within a segment of a circle is very time efficient. Furthermore, by adding weights (intensities in Figure 4.10–left) to the elements of the circle's sector, low angles can be preferred. **Extensions**

For each candidate, this analysis is done with several variations of the starting angle and the maximal angle, in order to get horizontal, straight and curved samples of annotation paths. If a placement of a text stroke is not possible (i.e., at least one letter is outside the part's designated area), this alternative is rejected. Next, these path candidates are evaluated and scored using the metrics described in Section 4.2. The winning candidate is chosen while the others are discarded. If none of the alternative placements were successful, the part of the primary object is marked to be externally annotated.

Watch scene 2–2

Annotation Boxes

External annotations and annotation boxes share the same resource—the illustration background. Their initial annotation layout is done in a greedy manner: whenever annotation boxes or external annotations are placed, they allocate their display area. Since annotation boxes consume significantly more space on the background than external annotations they are placed prior them. **Greedy allocation** **Hard cases first**

The accommodation of annotation boxes is carried out in a greedy manner, while a priori relevance values may be used to define priorities. Initially, annotation boxes of minimal size are evaluated (see Figure 4.12). After the selection procedure, the borders of all annotation boxes are simultaneously expanded until they reach the borders of other annotation boxes or until they reach their maximal size (according to the distance field value).

65

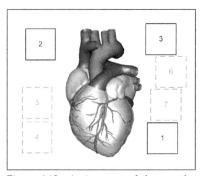 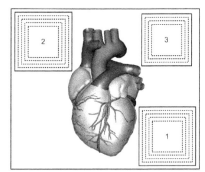

Figure 4.12: Assignment of the top three candidates (left), simultaneous expansion (right).

External Annotations

The referred part's maximum value of distance buffer determined for internal annotations serves as initial anchor point of the external annotation. The annotation texts of external annotations are sequentially placed on the remaining background space of the primary object with a greedy method. Because each accommodated annotation lowers the chance to obtain an optimal placement for succeeding annotations, it is important to place the most relevant or critical annotations first (see Appendix C.12).

Annotate from inside out Hence, the layout sequence adapts a strategy of experienced human illustrators: annotate complicated areas from inside out. Therefore, the convex hull of the set of anchor points is determined (see points in Figure 4.13–left). Referred parts, which anchor points are located within a big distance to the nearest point on the convex hull (yellow points) are annotated first, while those which define the knots of the convex hull (white points) are considered at the end. However, the layout sequence can alternatively be controlled by application–dependent a priori relevance values.

Optional a priori relevance

Before an alternative placement is evaluated, its feasibility is tested. First, it is verified whether these candidates are inside the view–port. Overlaps with other parts, annotation boxes, and already placed annotations are prohibited as well. All validity checks are based on point–area tests and on rectangle–rectangle tests on the ID–buffer. In order to determine the alignment of the annotation text, the algorithm tests both a left– and right–aligned annotation placement as well as a top– and bottom–aligned placement according to each connection point.

For all external annotations each of the candidates are evaluated according to the weighted metrics. The annotations are placed at the positions with the highest score and allocate rectangular areas corresponding to their bounding boxes (see Figure 4.13–right).

4.4.4 Coherence by Agents

The previous section determined an initial layout for the secondary elements. Though, while the user is interactively exploring a 3D model, an adapted annotation configu-

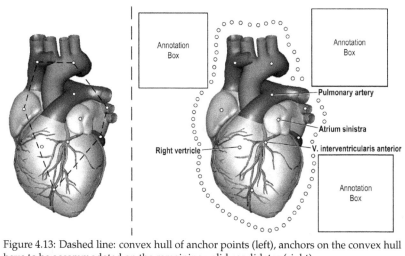

Figure 4.13: Dashed line: convex hull of anchor points (left), anchors on the convex hull have to be accommodated on the remaining valid candidates (right).

ration may be determined. However, this can induce drastic changes to the layout of each of the layout containers and may accidentally attract the user's attention. This conflicts with TUFTE's [Tuf97] claim that not the secondary elements but the primary object must have the focus of the illustration. In order to pay attention to this claim, the *smallest effective difference* can be applied to an annotation layout for interactive applications. Therefore, this section addresses the frame coherent transitions of the secondary elements.

No drastic changes in the layout

Since big changes of the layout elements may attract the attention of the user, it is crucial to reduce their flow. Unlike the initial layout, the strategies presented in this section do not consider the whole set of candidates for each container type, but the local neighborhood of the individual annotations.

Local strategies

The *annotation agents* are autonomous entities that are assigned to individual annotations. They evaluate the annotation's local neighborhood, in order to determine local optimizations. When these agents have discovered an improvement, they may shift the annotation in discrete steps towards the more optimal position. Additionally, those agents have a limited *lifetime*, i.e., they may perform a defined number of steps to determine local improvements to the layout of their assigned annotation. A longer lifetime means that they are more flexible and it is more likely that the agents determine local maxima of their metrics. However, a shorter lifetime results in slighter changes of the annotation's positions. In practical use, a compromise for this parameter has to be found.

Agents

Watch scene 2–3

Types of agents

There are two types of agents which control the positions of different secondary elements. In the following, both types are briefly introduced:

67

Evaluate
8–neighborhood

- **Pixel–neighborhood agents.** These agents evaluate their direct neighborhood of pixels. Hence, they consider all alternative placements in the 8–neighborhood of the illustration's pixels (see Figure 4.14) and evaluate them according to the underlying distance field values. If they detect a higher value, they adapt the *hill–climbing* behavior, i.e., the associated annotation changes its position towards this location. This class of agents is used in each of the three container types.

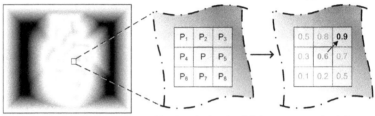

Figure 4.14: Agent evaluating neighborhood of P (middle), movement (right).

Evaluate
neighborhood
on orbit

- **Annotation–neighborhood agents.** This type of agents is used to evaluate the direct neighborhood of external annotation's candidates according to the metrics defined in Section 4.2 and to shift external annotation's texts. Based on their current position, they request the scores of the nearest external annotation candidates on the primary object's orbit. Accordingly, the agent moves the external annotation's text to the alternative with the highest score. In order to ensure the ideal distance of annotations to the silhouette, the agents are only allowed to move along the previously computed orbit.

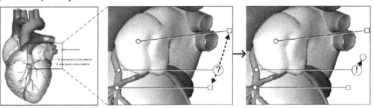

Figure 4.15: Annotation–Agents request (middle), and response (right).

Additionally, different behaviors of external annotation's text can be achieved by this type of agents. By extending the scope of these agents to the n nearest candidates on the orbit the presence of neighboring annotations can be considered. This allows to adapt the *flocking behavior* introduced by REYNOLDS [Rey87]. Hence, the agents of neighboring annotations can exert forces towards the position of the current agent. On the one hand, by using repulsive forces from the neighboring agents an equal distribution of the annotations on the orbit can be obtained (see Figure 4.15). On the other hand, attracting forces support a *cohesion* behavior in order to form clusters of external annotation texts.[4]

---

[4]The concept of using separation and cohesion behavior also seemed to be intuitive in order to achieve esthetic internal text strokes. Individual letter agents aimed at preserving an ideal distance while being

Coherence Strategies of Containers

Each of the containers applies agents in order to support the layout coherence. In the following their layout strategies are introduced which have to be considered for each frame.

- **Internal Annotations.** In order to support the frame coherence, internal annotations should preserve the arrangement of all letters of the internal text stroke. This means that the text stroke should remain in its previous configuration as long as each of their letters reside completely on their referred part of the primary object. For that reason, the ID–buffer can be checked on the letter's positions. If one of the letters is situated outside of its referred part, a re–layout of the annotation path has to be initiated.

  If possible preserve old configuration

  Additionally, each internal annotation uses a pixel–neighborhood agent which is located at the center of the midst letter. In order to evaluate local improvements of their placement the agent determines if there is a better alternative concerning the unambiguity in the neighborhood and shifts the entire text stroke. Hence, smoothly moving the text stroke towards the center of the referred part of the primary object minimizes the necessity for frequent re–layouts.

  Pixel–neighborhood agents

- **Annotation Boxes.** Since annotation boxes are extensive containers, their position and size should change smoothly and only if necessary. As stated before, the distance value at the central point of an annotation box reveals the maximum extent of the box. However, overlaps with other annotation boxes have to be prevented by intersection checks of their borders. On the one hand, the annotation box can be extended if there is more available space. On the other hand, if an annotation box is slightly too large, it can also be smoothly shrunk. In the worst case it has to collapse and fade in on a new position if its minimal size cannot be maintained.

  The annotation boxes also utilize a pixel–neighborhood agent, which is located at its center. If the distance field of the neighboring pixels is higher, it shifts the whole annotation box towards this position. This strategy supports the box to reside on local maxima and thus, reduces the risk to shrink below its minimum size.

  Pixel–neighborhood agents

- **External Annotations.** External annotations use both types of agents. The position of the anchor point is managed by a pixel–neighborhood agent, whereas an annotation–neighborhood agent handles the coherence of external annotation texts.

  Anchor points should be placed on salient points of an illustration's part. Therefore, they are initially placed on the global maximum of the distance field masked with the referred part's ID–buffer. This might imply drastic jumps between subsequent frames during user interactions. Thus, a pixel–neighborhood agent considers the neighboring pixels of the distance field and changes the position of the anchor point stepwise towards a local maximum.

  Pixel–neighborhood agents

---

homogeneously oriented. However, the chain–like text stroke layout outperformed this approach both in terms of efficiency and quality.

Annotation–
neighborhood
agents

External annotation texts have to reside on a point of the objects orbit. To ensure a clustered or evenly distributed layout, annotation–neighborhood agents are used to determine better placement alternatives in the direct neighborhood on the primary object's orbit. If an improvement of the metrics' score is found, the annotation text smoothly transits to a new point of the primary object's orbit.

Interactive Layout versus Static Layout

Static without
coherence

For the interactive exploration of 3D models it is important to reduce the flow of layout elements. However, utilizing frame coherence techniques may contradict with the presentation of an optimal annotation layout. For static applications it is more advantageous to simply compute the initial layout. Hence, functions for the capturing of still images should consider this fact by previously computing the initial layout.

4.4.5 Adaptivity of styles

Need for
adaptation

In an application which allows to interactively manipulate the 3D scene, the annotation layout should be computed in real time. Thus, according to the changed view on the 3D model, for each frame a new annotation layout has to be computed. However, not only the positions and appearances of the annotations should change, but also their annotation style and type. Internal and external annotations use disjoint areas of illustrations. While internal annotations directly overlay their referred parts, external annotations occupy the illustrations background. Due to user interactions with the 3D model it cannot be ensured that there is sufficient space in frame n to repeatedly accommodate each internal and external annotation again with the same annotation type which was used in the previous frame $n - 1$.

Space restrictions

Watch scene 1–2

As a simple example, Figure 4.16 shows a sequence of images where the user is zooming into the 3D model. Initially, there is not much space to accommodate internal annotations, but the annotations of the visible parts can be placed externally. In the process of zooming into the model, the illustration background decreases significantly, while the area of the illustration's parts is increasing. Thus, external annotations change their type to internal annotations in order to handle the changed space constraints.

Cutoff
parameters

Adaptation
hysteresis

See Appendix
D.3

To allow this adaptation for each annotation alternative internal and external placements can be evaluated. If the evaluated score of an internal annotation is worse than the score of an external alternative it can be placed externally. The opposite case occurs, if the best external placement is scored worse than a possible internal placement. For this reason, a cutoff parameter for both internal and external annotations can be applied to define if a placement score is considered as not sufficient. However, even for minimal user interactions the annotations might adapt their type between internal and external annotation. In order to reduce the visual flow of elements, these adaptations should be minimized. To avoid frequent changes of the types of an annotation and thus to improve their frame coherence, a simple hysteresis algorithm can be utilized to control the sensitivity of the adaptation. An additional parameter for the hysteresis can be used to define which difference of the evaluated internal and external scores has to exist to permit a change of the annotation type.

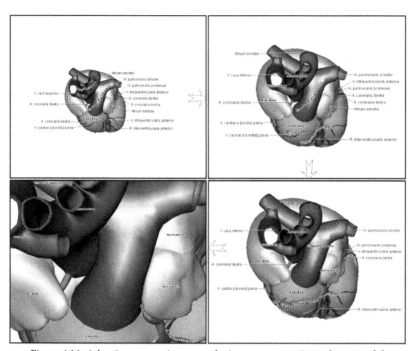

Figure 4.16: Adapting annotation types during user zooms into a heart model.

Annotation boxes usually refer to the whole illustration and thus cannot be adapted to internal and external annotations. Those annotation types can be integrated into the global annotation layout or be defined as pinned by the layout parameters (see Section 4.3), i.e., they do not change their size and position. Hence, if there is no available space on the illustration background they are hidden, or when they are pinned, they occlude the primary object. Even if an annotation box refers to a part of the primary object, it should be excluded from the adaptation, because adaptation of those extensive layout elements would induce immense changes to the annotation layout.

4.5 Conclusion

The metrics introduced in this chapter allow multiple annotation styles and assessment of alternatives for a good annotation layout. Due to multiple optimizations, the determination of the annotation layout may be computed at interactive rates, copes with user preferences and tackles problems induced by the user interaction. The result is an encapsulated and flexible approach, that can be used in many fields of applications. However, there are some concluding remarks on the approach.

As can be seen in the supplemental videos, the legibility of the rendered internal an-notations is not optimal when using the approaches' *rendering mode*. This problem is mainly caused by aliasing effects which occur when the annotation's individual letters are rotated. However, this is a technical problem that does not depend on the layout approach. Using the approaches *layout only mode* prospective applications which re-quire a more sophisticated font rendering, may utilize dedicated approaches such as the *FreeType* library [Tur].

Legibility may be improved

If the primary object covers the whole illustration (e.g., by extensive zooming), there is no space to accommodate external annotations. However, in order to maximize the number of external annotations several unimportant 3D parts could be rendered semi–transparently in order to allow the external annotations to overlay them. This could be consistently done with the encapsulated annotation approach by assigning the color–ID of the illustration background to those 3D parts. Hence, the approach would determine the external annotation's orbit by treating the unimportant 3D parts as background. However, this method induces legibility problems and additional visual occlusion by the external annotation's texts and should only be used for well–founded exemptions.

Conscious overlay

Finally, this approach is designed to annotate each of the visible parts of the primary object. However, to cope with the selectiveness specification, only a subset of 3D parts could be annotated. Hence, the focus of the following Chapter 5 is to adapt annotation layouts to defined 3D contexts.

5

Contextual Annotation

Outline

This chapter extends the encapsulated annotation approach developed in Chapter 4. It presents the advantage of the ability to generate annotated illustrations during user interaction. Unlike illustrations in textbooks, interactive 3D visualizations are not static and can be individually adapted to generate annotated illustrations focusing on different contexts interactively chosen by the user.

Achievements

For the contextualized annotation of 3D models this chapter presents two different concepts. An experimental application is developed in accordance to this approach and a user study evaluates the central statements. As another result, it becomes clear that annotations may be used to focus the viewers attention to specific image contexts. The results of the approach and the evaluation lay the foundation for the second part of this thesis.

5.1 Introduction

The previous Chapter 4 addressed the general technical problem of determining an annotation layout for 3D models that the user interacts with. The encapsulated approach is designed to be independent from different 3D models and their interactive visualizations but is flexible enough to enable application dependent preferences. This chapter introduces a problem–orientated extension of the encapsulated annotation approach. Traditional textbooks are static media that may only include a limited number of illustrations. In order to accord with economic constraints human illustrators are often confronted with the challenge to design illustrations that cover multiple text contexts, which may be not the optimal strategy when considering human cognitive limits. However, these space and cost restrictions are not given for an interactive application, so that more efficient illustrations for specified contexts can be generated. *Extension of encapsulated approach* *Context–driven annotation*

Whereas the initial goal of annotating 3D models was a good *scalability*, Section 5.2 introduces the advantage of *grouped* and *exclusive* annotation of 3D parts according to given contexts. Correspondingly, Section 5.3 introduces two different techniques for the contextual annotation of 3D models. An experimental application serves as proof of concept and realizes both techniques whereas users are able to interactively define and select contexts of interest. Section 5.4 evaluates the central statements of these techniques by an user study. Finally, Section 5.5 discusses the achievements and the novel ideas arisen from this chapter which lead over to the second part main of this thesis. *Chapter overview*

5.2   Problem Analysis

Illustrator's dilemma

The expository texts used in educational books are usually structured into multiple text contexts (cf. Chapter 2). Human illustrators carefully depict the objects described in the expository texts in order to adapt the illustrations to the parts mentioned in text contexts. Ideally, there would be one dedicated illustration for each text context (cf. Appendix C.7). However, as BRISCOE [Bri90] stated: '...the printed figure is limited by space and money considerations' they are forced to combine multiple text contexts within one illustration (cf. also Appendix C.6).

Emphasis techniques

In order to cope with these constraints, illustrators often utilize graphical emphasis techniques in order to guide the viewers attention to different contexts. There are several works (e.g., [KR95]) which successfully transfer the use of emphasis techniques to automated approaches. However, according to the declaration of TUFTE [Tuf97, p. 74]: '...when *everything* [...] is emphasized, *nothing* is emphasized...' these techniques have to be applied with prudence. Hence, the effectiveness of graphical emphasis techniques may also be affected by the number of emphasized parts.

Limited capacity

When multiple contexts are depicted, besides the number of emphasized parts, illustrators also have to insert many annotations into a single illustration. But this strategy often spoils the learning efficiency. In order to improve the learning efficiency, the number of annotations should also be limited. Psychological experiments point out that the number of parameters of a single cognitive process or cognitive representation is limited to seven plus or minus two [Mil56], five [Sim74], or only four [HBMB05]. To cope with these limitations, the primary object as well as its secondary elements can be adapted to one context (see Figure 5.1).

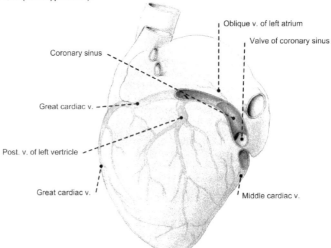

Figure 5.1: Only veins are annotated, whilst other parts are deemphasized by semi–transparency (Source: [SPP01, p. 89]).

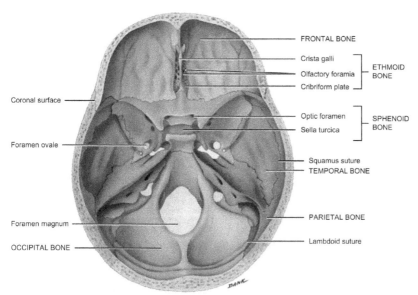

Figure 5.2: Illustration with grouped annotations and colored (shaded) parts (Source: [Tor97, p. 113]).

If multiple contexts have to be illustrated, a contextual layout of the annotations should support the viewer. According to the *chunking principle* cognitive psychologists suggest to hierarchically reorganize unstructured data. However, the number of individual representation units (*chunks*) should not exceed the cognitive capacities. In order to indicate semantically related contexts their parts belonging together may be indicated by colors or grouping of the annotations (see Figure 5.2).

Unfortunately, current interactive annotation approaches neither consider the limitation of the human cognitive system nor apply the chunking technique. Only the *excentric* annotation approach [FP99] in the field of information visualization aims at minimizing the number of additional layout elements by an exclusive annotation of merely the members of the cluster in focus. However, there are no existing approaches coping with the *contextual annotation* of 3D models.

5.3 Approach

For interactive applications the limitations of static media are not given. This means, by adapting the encapsulated annotation approach described in Chapter 4, individual annotation layouts for illustrations can be computed in real time. In order to formally approximate contexts explained in text segments of textbooks, in this approach human experts can define a *taxonomy* in advance to the user's exploration task. The grouped

Adaptive annotation layout

75

organization of annotations should reflect semantic considerations. Hence, the experts can interactively select 3D parts and group their related annotations into clusters which represent text contexts and may be arranged to a hierarchical structure.

Modern 3D modeling software employs hierarchical structures (*scene graphs*) in order to segment complex models into their components. However, the individual external storage of the taxonomy in XML structures (see Appendix E.2) assigned to the 3D models offers several advantages (cf. Chapter 2). It allows to store multiple contexts, which are independent of the type of 3D model and can be easily be edited.

Advantages of external storage

During the interactive exploration the user may utilize the domain taxonomies in order to select groups of interest. By selecting one of the contextual groups, each of its members is selected in order to form a text context. For each of the text contexts a corresponding 3D context can be generated, i.e., this selection influences the annotation layout and the application of graphical emphasis techniques. The encapsulated annotation approach is extended in order to adapt the contextual techniques. Adapting *Gestalt principles*, in the application all annotations of a selected text context are merged in an annotation box (proximity), are aligned with respect to the annotation box (alignment), and share the same background color (similarity). Additionally, the user can request contextualized visualizations of the illustrated object, which merely comprise the annotations relevant to the defined text context.

Applying both techniques

The following sections introduce a technique to form groups of annotations as well as the exclusive annotation technique in order to focus the viewers attention and to clarify semantical contexts. As a proof of concept, an experimental application is briefly introduced, and finally this section critically discusses the achievements.

5.3.1 Grouped Annotation Layout

This approach is based on the encapsulated annotation approach developed in Chapter 4. Grouped annotations can be considered as multiple external annotations which annotation texts are arranged to one cluster. Thus, annotation boxes can be used to aggregate these clusters of external annotation texts. However, despite being arranged to a cluster, the external annotations should be near to their referred 3D parts. In order to establish the spatial proximity of those annotation boxes and the referred 3D parts, a shared anchor point can be calculated (see Figure 5.3–left).

Initial layout of groups

Shared anchor point

Thus, the encapsulated annotation approach provides all anchor points of the visible 3D parts belonging to the individual groups. Next, for each of those groups the centroid C of all anchor points belonging to it is calculated. Finally, this centroid is used to determine the annotation boxes' candidate with the minimum distance to it. This candidate serves for the initial placement of the annotation box, which accommodates the annotations belonging to the group (see Figure 5.3–right).

```
x:=y
for (...
  if (
```

See Appendix D.4

After the initial assignment of the external annotations to their related annotation box, their placement sequence has to be determined. To resolve their reference lines' intersections, the positions of the annotation texts can simply be switched. Although the brute force approach is of squared computational complexity, the optimal sequence can

Layout inside groups

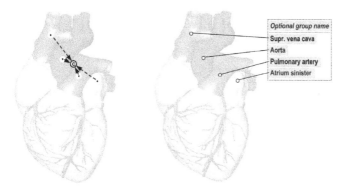

Figure 5.3: Determination of centroid (left), accommodation of external annotations in the nearest annotation box candidate (right).

be determined algorithmically, since there should not be more than seven elements in one group.

During user interaction with the 3D model, the layout of the annotation boxes is managed by the encapsulated annotation approach. However, there is a small set of annotation groups which represent one context. Thus, in order to improve the frame coherence, those annotation boxes could also remain on their position until they overlap the projection of the 3D model. Resolving reference line intersections of the annotation group allows an esthetic presentation of them, but negatively affects the frame coherence. Hence, the user should specify whether legibility (few intersections) or frame coherence (few annotation text swappings) is more important to the current task.

Frame coherence

     (a) Focus on the red group   (b) Focus on the green group

Figure 5.4: Changing between groups (without transparency).

In the experimental system only one contextual group obtains the focus. The 3D parts and annotations of this *active group* are emphasized. Therefore, 3D parts, reference lines, and annotation boxes are drawn opaque, whereas the components of unfocused groups are rendered semitransparently (*indirect emphasis*). This strategy also reduces the impact of intersections between reference lines of different annotation groups. To focus on another contextual group, the user has to click on the specific 3D part or its annotation (see Figure 5.4).

Watch scene 3–1

5.3.2 Exclusive Annotation

While the general annotation approach follows the specification: 'if possible, annotate all of the visible 3D parts', this section clarifies the surplus of selective annotation, i.e., in visualizing specific contexts with annotations.

According to the chunking principle neither the number of groups nor the total number of annotations should exceed the cognitive capacity. Therefore, the experimental application allows the user to select a certain context within the taxonomy and to exclusively emphasize 3D parts of the selected group. In order to emphasize 3D parts, the relevant ones were annotated, while the remaining parts were rendered semitransparently. Thus, if relevant parts are annotated exclusively, the textual information itself becomes an emphasis technique (see Figure 5.5).

Annotations focus viewers' attention

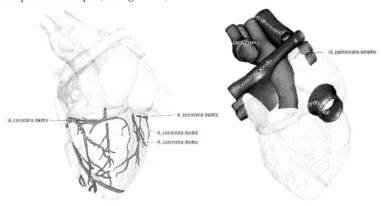

(a) Arteries (b) User selected contextual group

Figure 5.5: Different exclusively annotated contexts (supported by transparency).

5.3.3 Experimental Application

This section briefly introduces an experimental application which was developed as a proof of concept and implemented both the grouped annotation and exclusive annotation according to predefined contexts.

Domain experts were able to interactively structure the domain entities by creating groups of related 3D parts. The interactive system also integrated a drag&drop editor to inspect and define hierarchical structures (see Figure 5.6). The domain taxonomy was stored in an XML format, which offered a flexible interface to other applications and allowed to define multiple contexts of a model. For the exclusive annotation the user was able to choose one of the defined contexts by selecting a group defined in the taxonomy editor. Additionally, the experimental application allowed to view multiple contexts by annotation groups, which could be focused by clicking on the textual annotations of a group or their referred 3D parts (see Figure 5.7).

Taxonomy editor

Watch scene 3–2

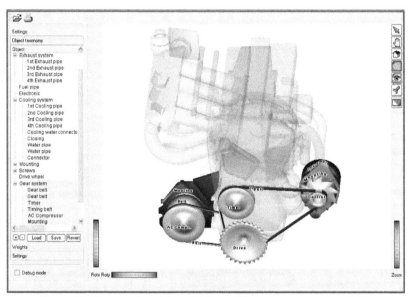

Figure 5.6: The experimental application with the taxonomy editor (left).

5.3.4 Discussion

Depending on the target application, the designations of the groups defined by the authors could be visualized in accordance to the annotation clusters. However, placing these annotations alongside the groups (see Figure 5.1) would require an extensive amount of the illustration background. Hence, it may be more efficient to place those group annotations above their groups, e.g., by using a different font style. Furthermore, the annotation boxes share their presentation space on the illustration background. Due to this fact, the number of concurrent groups which can be accommodated is limited. To cope with this problem, the user could be constrained in interacting with the model. *Group designations as headlines* *Limited space*

By reducing the number of annotations to those which are relevant to a defined context, the contextual annotation can support the understanding of complex spatial configurations. Therefore, online tutoring systems with contextualized illustrations may be more effective than pure adaptations of traditional textbooks with generalized illustrations. However, domain experts have to define these contextual groups manually, which requires manual pre–processing and limits the number of contexts available for each 3D model. For prospective approaches techniques could be integrated which allow the use of external application–independent ontologies like *WordNet* [Fel98] or their language–specific variants like *GermaNet* [KL02] could be integrated. *Manual context definition* *Link to external taxonomies*

In this approach, users are bound to those contexts defined by the taxonomy. If the application allows it, they can also use an taxonomy editor to organize the 3D parts'

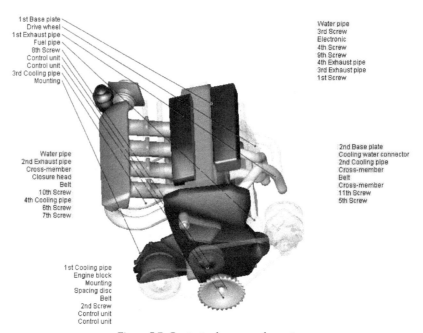

1st Base plate
Drive wheel
1st Exhaust pipe
Fuel pipe
8th Screw
Control unit
Control unit
3rd Cooling pipe
Mounting

Water pipe
3rd Screw
Electronic
4th Screw
9th Screw
4th Exhaust pipe
3rd Exhaust pipe
1st Screw

Water pipe
2nd Exhaust pipe
Cross-member
Closure head
Belt
10th Screw
4th Cooling pipe
6th Screw
7th Screw

2nd Base plate
Cooling water connector
2nd Cooling pipe
Cross-member
Belt
Cross-member
11th Screw
5th Screw

1st Cooling pipe
Engine block
Mounting
Spacing disc
Belt
2nd Screw
Control unit
Control unit

Figure 5.7: Contextual groups of a motor.

Intuitive definition of contexts by user — annotations to groups. However, such an editor is an additional structural interface. Since educational material uses illustrated objects in conjunction with descriptive text, it would be optimal if users could easily select segments of the continuous text they are interested in, and if this selection would be directly reflected in a modified presentation of the 3D model.

Semantic dependencies — Finally, this approach only considered absolute relevance values of 3D parts, i.e., the selected subset of elements in a group was relevant, whereas the remaining were irrelevant. However, it could be desirable to present different levels of relevance, i.e., semantic dependencies between annotated 3D parts. An exemplary application could be the approach of HARTMANN AND STROTHOTTE [HS02] by selecting the rendering style and its parameters according to computed relevance values.

5.4 User Study

Evaluation by chronological measure — For the evaluation of the contextual annotation and the grouped annotation a user study was performed. This user study is in accordance with the statement of SCHUMANN AND MÜLLER [SM00]: 'The quality of a visualization is defined by the degree to which the depiction achieves the communicative goal of the presentation. It can be considered

80

as the relation between the information which the user perceives in a period and the information which is to be mediated in the same period'. [1]

In order to measure the time required to find a certain set of objects in an illustration by their technical terms, a test platform presented 20 buttons which were arranged in two columns. Those buttons were (partially) externally annotated by terms which consisted of four random letters. An algorithm ensured that those search terms had a minimum difference, i.e., when a search term was created, the subsequent term always differed only in one letter (Levenshtein distance of 1 [Lev66]).

20 buttons as different objects

The first part of the user study investigated if and how much the time required to locate relevant annotated objects is affected by presenting additional but unimportant annotated objects. In successive turns 5, 10 and 20 of the buttons were externally annotated. Out of the set of presented search terms, five terms were randomly selected and presented in random order to the subjects who had to click the corresponding buttons. The second part tested if and how much the grouping of annotations is an appropriate technique which reduces the search time. In order to do this, each of the 20 buttons were annotated by the search terms. For each of both columns of the buttons two clusters of annotations were built by spatially grouping the annotation texts. Again five of the search terms were presented to the subjects who had to click the corresponding buttons. If one search term was found in one of the four clusters, all of the remaining search terms were arranged in the same cluster in random order. Since the grouping technique provokes intersecting reference lines, the impact of them was investigated. During the second part of the user study within the annotation groups the intersections of the reference lines were alternating present and resolved.

Test for exclusive annotation

Test for grouped annotation

Influence of intersections

5.4.1 Method

Subjects and design. The user study was performed with 31 participants (12 female, 19 male) aged between 18 and 61 years. The search time defined the time that a subject required to read a searched term and to locate the button which is annotated with this term. The test application registered the time between two clicks on searched buttons as well as the number of clicks on wrong buttons.

Search time

Materials and apparatus. The user study consisted of seven test modes and was performed by an interactive application on a computer with a standard computer mouse, in order to prevent distortions in the search time by the input device. The buttons were externally annotated, whereas the searched terms were presented on the upper right side of the application screen. The subjects had to find the correct five buttons and click on them. They were instructed only to click on the correct buttons as fast as possible. In order to prevent users to click on buttons by chance or systematically click all the buttons, the test application counted the number of wrong button clicks. If the subjects clicked each of the searched buttons, the next test was presented immediately.

Only locate the searched buttons

---

[1]Original text in German: 'Die Qualität einer Visualisierung definiert sich durch den Grad, in dem die bildliche Darstellung das kommunikative Ziel der Präsentation erreicht. Sie läßt sich als das Verhältnis von der vom Betrachter in einem Zeitraum wahrgenommenen Information zu der im gleichen Zeitraum zu vermittelnden Information beschreiben.'

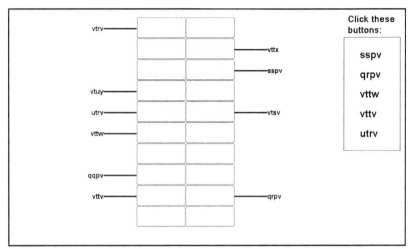

Figure 5.8: 10 out of 20 buttons are annotated, find those which are listed on the right.

In the first part of the study, three different test modes (t_1–t_3) were applied, which were alternatively presented for three repetitions. These tests determined the time required to locate the five searched buttons out of 20, whereas 5 (t_1), 10 (t_2), and 20 (t_3) buttons were annotated by random terms. A random subset of five terms was presented on the upper right side of the test application (see Figure 5.8) in random order. The subjects first had to read the searched terms, subsequently find the corresponding annotated buttons and finally click on them. The test application recorded the time required for the search task and the number of wrongly clicked buttons.

The second part of the user study consisted of two different test modes (t_4, t_5), which were repeated three times. Additionally, these six tests were repeated twice in two different modes (t_6, t_7) in order to test the influence of reference lines' intersections. Four clusters each with five annotations were built by spatially grouping the individual annotations of a group (see Figure 5.9). Again five buttons had to be found which annotations corresponded to the search terms presented. However, one of the four clusters contained all the search terms. In test mode t_4 all of the reference lines were presented in the normal way, which caused various line intersections. Thus, test mode t_5 focused on the reference lines of the searched buttons by presenting the remaining ones with a lower contrast. Whereas test mode t_4 and t_5 comprised reference line intersections within the clusters, the same tests were performed in test mode t_6 and t_7 except resolved intersections by sorting each clusters' annotations.

Procedure. First, the subjects had to carefully read the instructions explained by exemplary screenshots of the blind user study. In order to prepare users to the tests, they had to solve a test run of the user study which covered one of each test mode. Subsequently, the user study was performed.

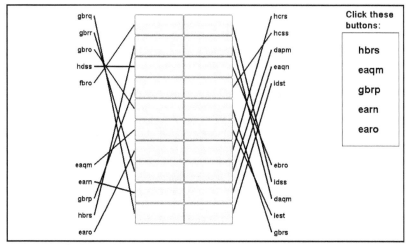

Figure 5.9: Grouped annotations without resolving reference line intersections.

5.4.2 Results

Scoring. The test application for the user study determined the time (in milliseconds) required for the correct location of all five searched buttons (see Figure 5.10). For the determination if two sets of timings significantly differed, the *One-Way ANOVA (Analysis of variance)* method was applied, which considers that there is no statistical significance with a result of $p \geq 0.05$.

Hypothesis 1: Annotation of unimportant objects negatively affects search time.

The test modes t_1–t_3 were designed to investigate if and how the annotation of unimportant objects influence the search time. For the timings of each test mode there was a significant difference (t_1 vs. t_2: $F = 127.88, p < 0.001$), (t_2 vs. t_3: $F = 58.74, p < 0.001$), and (t_1 vs. t_3: $F = 200.19, p < 0.001$). Additionally, the median of the test modes $t_1 : 6055ms$, $t_1 : 16364ms$, and $t_3 : 30513ms$ fulfilled the criterion ($t_1 < t_2 < t_3$). Thus, the more annotations were presented, the more time users required to locate the five searched buttons.

Search time for 5, 10 and 20 buttons

Hypothesis 2: The clustering technique reduces the search time.

The second part of the user study evaluated the grouping technique. Whereas test mode t_3 presented 20 annotations without grouping, test mode t_4 grouped them into clusters. The timings significantly differed for t_3 vs. t_4: $F = 13.68, p < 0.001$ and the median timing of the grouped test mode $t_4 : 24419ms$ was lower than for the test mode without the grouping technique $t_3 : 30513ms$. Hence, the grouping technique reduced the search time.

Normal vs. grouped

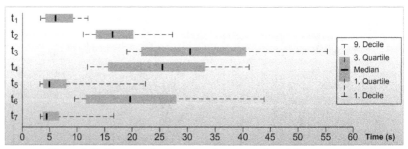

Figure 5.10: Time required to solve the test modes of the user study.

Hypothesis 3: Focus on context reduces search time.

Grouped vs. focused grouped

A negative effect of the grouping technique is that intersections of the annotation's reference lines cannot by avoided. Test mode t_5 investigated if focusing on the reference lines of searched annotations reduces the search time compared to test mode t_4. The ANOVA showed a significant difference ($F = 83.51, p < 0.001$) between both test modes, while the median search time for the focused test mode $t_5 : 4946ms$ was substantially lower than for the unfocused test one $t_4 : 24419ms$.

Hypothesis 4: Sorted clusters reduce search time.

Sorted vs. unsorted

As mentioned before, intersections of reference lines cannot be avoided when using the annotation grouping technique. However, it is possible to sort the annotations of the groups so that there are no intersections within the groups. The test modes t_6 and t_7 presented the same tests than test mode t_4 and t_5, except the intersections of the annotations within each group were resolved. Although the median timings of both sorted test modes $t_6 : 19478ms$ and $t_7 : 4367ms$ were lower than the test modes without sorting $t_4 : 24419ms$ and $t_5 : 4946ms$, no significant difference for t_6 vs. t_4: $F = 2.66, p = 0.105$ and t_7 vs. t_5: $F = 2.00, p = 0.159$ could be determined.

5.4.3 Discussion

Unnecessary annotations delay search time

The first part of the user study gave evidence that the number of annotated objects may influence the search time. For a given context the search time was minimized by exclusively annotating the mentioned terms. If multiple contexts have to be shown at a time, the technique of grouping the annotations for each context can reduce the search times. Additionally, using a focus on the annotation group on the context which is currently investigated, may significantly speed up the search time.

Line intersections slow down only slightly

The results of hypothesis 4 give the impression that sorting of annotations for resolving line intersections might be useful for still images or before user interaction in interactive applications. However, during user interactions the sorting of annotations should probably not be carried out in order to improve the frame coherence of the animations. To obtain evidence about these considerations, a further user study could determine which of those factors outweigh the others.

84

5.5 Conclusion

This section presented an interactive approach for the exploration of 3D models which considers the limitations of the human cognitive processes. An taxonomy editor was implemented in order to allow to define context specific groups. Moreover, technical solutions for both the contextualized illustration by exclusive annotation and the grouped organization of annotations were proposed and developed in an experimental application. Additionally, a user study assessed the central statements of this section according to a computer based solution.

Exclusive annotation may support learning, because it only emphasizes those parts of 3D models which are relevant to a defined context and considers cognitive limitations. However, several limitations of this approach arise:

- The context has to be defined manually by an author,

- the user is bound to a priori defined contexts and cannot freely define those of the explanatory texts,

- the contexts have to be manually generated and selected by an additional interface, the taxonomy editor,

- the relevancies presented by the 3D model should be continuous.

These limitations form a basis for looking more deeply at the linkage of expository texts and illustrations in educational material. In the following, the second part of this book addresses the linkage of continuous text with annotated 3D models and adapts the annotation techniques developed in the first part.

6

Correlating Illustrations and Text

Outline

The research in the first part of this book aimed at technically enabling automatically determined annotation layouts while the user is exploring a 3D model. In contrast, the following part utilizes annotations for the linkage of 3D models with expository texts. Therefore, this chapter first motivates the issue of mutual search tasks arising with educational textbooks, proposes a concept and reviews the related work. Finally, two central elements of the proposed concept are contemplated concerning their applicability towards a practical solution.

Achievements

This chapter presents the usage of annotations to support the complementary presentation of illustrations and expository text, by matching their representations through textual descriptors. Provided that technical terms in expository texts correspond to the annotations of 3D parts, their descriptors can be compared. Hence, by determining the similarities between text contexts (paragraphs) and view contexts (3D model views) both media can be mutually searched. Furthermore, this concept applies the achievements of this thesis' first part in order to provide an improvement to traditional educational textbooks, without intending to replace them. Finally, this forms a basis for an experimental application, which is developed in Chapter 7.

6.1 Introduction

The first part of this book (Chapter 3–5) addressed an immanent problem of educational books which present spatial objects merely as 2D illustrations. The aim of this part was to gain the ability to explore approximations of those spatial objects with an interactive 3D browser, whilst computing layouts for secondary elements that are similar to those in illustrations of educational books. Hence, by the illustrations' annotations the user can visually link parts of the primary object to their technical terms. *First part: Annotation layout*

The second part examines a different problem with educational books, which make complementary use of both expository texts and illustrations. In this part, the formal annotations of 3D models are not necessarily visualized, but used as a logical link between the illustrations and the expository text. These formal annotations can be used to match technical terms of text segments with corresponding views of annotated 3D parts. *Second part: Annotations as link*

Contexts
Chapter 5 presented techniques to visualize annotated 3D models with respect to a certain context. However, this approach used predefined contexts manually prepared by an author prior to the illustration task. The following section addresses the actual search tasks which arise when reading educational books and allows to select free contexts.

Chapter outline
The short introduction is followed by a section explaining the search tasks which can arise by reading educational material. Section 6.2 covers the problem statement, reviews the related work and proposes a concept to support readers in the search tasks. At the end of this section it becomes obvious that in order to develop this concept—two aspects have to be investigated in more detail. Thus, Section 6.3 addresses the challenging task of introducing a problem–oriented quality measure for the evaluation of views on 3D models. Afterwards, Section 6.4 examines different techniques for searching text documents and Section 6.5 finally concludes this chapter.

6.2 Search Tasks

In educational material the conjunctive use of text and illustrations is superior to merely using one medium. For human illustrators it is a complex and time–consuming task to adapt illustrations to the contexts described in the expository texts. Regardless the resulting books are a sophisticated instrument for learning, their use can still be improved by the use of modern computers.

In the following the issue of search tasks is introduced by examples. Based on this problem statement, the existing approaches are reviewed which (partially) address these search tasks. Finally, by the use of electronic documents (text and annotated 3D models) a novel technique is introduced in order to tackle these problems.

6.2.1 Problem Statement

Annotations may link text with illustrations
As briefly introduced in Chapter 2, an important reason for the use of both expository text and illustrations in educational material is that both media have specific abilities and advantages. While text is usually superior to describe the functioning of objects, illustrations can clarify their visual attributes and spatial relations. Since annotated illustrations often use the same technical terms as the expository text, the annotations can serve as a bidirectional link between text and illustrations.

Illustrations and Text are often a n:m relation
In many cases, the objects explained in educational material are illustrated by multiple different views to disambiguate their spatial configuration and shape. On the other hand, multiple text segments refer to the same parts of the illustrated objects, and describe them by different aspects. Thus, two search tasks arise: from text to illustration and from illustration to text.

Text ↦ Illustration

Text context
The users read a segment of the expository text describing a certain context (see Figure 6.1). A number of technical terms is described in the text context they are interested in.

Now, they have to search for the illustration which is addressing the context and find each of the annotations which are corresponding to the technical terms in the expository text. Through the annotations they can now determine which parts of the illustration were described in the text context. This search task can get even more complicated, such as when multiple illustrations address a text context.

Which illustrations' parts belong to this text segment?

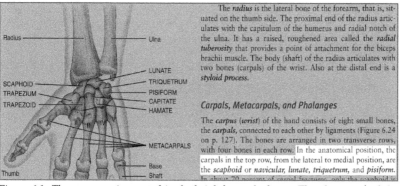

Figure 6.1: The users are interested in the brightly marked text. They have to find the illustrations' parts which accord with the technical terms. (Adapted from [Tor97, p.127])

Illustration ↦ Text

The users survey an illustration and are interested in a single or multiple parts of it, which constitute a view context (see Figure 6.2). They read the annotations belonging to these parts. Now, they encounter the search task to find the text segments in the expository text which are addressing those technical terms. In books normally illustrations are positioned near to those text segments. However, multiple interesting text segments on different pages and even different chapters may cover a view context.

View context

Which text segments belong to this illustration part?

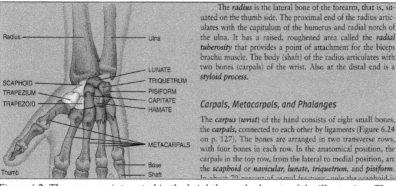

Figure 6.2: The users are interested in the brightly marked parts of the illustration. They have to find the text segments addressing these parts. (Adapted from [Tor97, p.127])

Electronic texts and annotated 3D models

Nowadays, numerous educational materials are also available in electronic versions which offer new possibilities to support learners. Besides electronic versions of books comprising text and illustrations, also annotated 3D models are available in multiple fields such as anatomy, natural science and the technical domain.

Electronic support for search tasks

In the following, a corpus of both annotated 3D models and electronic expository text of educational material forms the basis of the approach. A concept is introduced, which supports the previously identified search tasks by an automated approach, while adapting the advantages of the annotated exploration of 3D models elaborated in the first part of this thesis.

6.2.2 Related Work

This section reviews the related work in the field of retrieval between the media *text* and *images* or *3D models*.

Retrieval of Annotated Images and 3D Models

Feature based

Existing retrieval systems for images and 3D models comprise two basic techniques. Content–based retrieval techniques analyze images and 3D models in order to extract low–level image features like color histograms, shapes or textures (e.g., [FSN+95, JFS95]) or 3D features such as the 3D model's topology its curvature or symmetry (e.g., [Suz01, HSKK01]) which are stored in a database. These systems allow queries by example images in order to find images of similar low level features, but cannot handle textual queries.

Annotated multimedia objects

Annotation–based retrieval takes advantage of the fact that natural language documents can be retrieved with textual queries by very efficient techniques. In order to transfer these techniques to different media types, it is a common strategy to add formal annotations (i.e., keywords) to the media objects. Manually added by humans, these formal annotations contain information about the content and the context of the media object, which can be utilized for textual search queries for media such as images (e.g., [ATY+01, YDF04]) or 3D models (e.g., [ZC01, FMK+03]). In the case of 3D models, each individual geometric description of the 3D model's parts may be annotated with its unique term. Using the actual technical terms for each of the 3D parts' annotations, it can be determined which parts are included in the 3D model, even without utilizing a visualization tool for the geometric description. Hence, the sum of the textual annotations may represent a *contextual description* of the 3D model, which can be used for the linkage with text.

Linking Expository Text with Images and 3D Models

Illustration by text analysis

The *Agile* system by HARTMANN AND STROTHOTTE [HS02] based on a initial disambiguation on different term spellings in text documents and an analysis of the text structure. Additionally, a semantic network of terms was used with the text corpora. For the illustration of the texts, the approach deduced semantic associations between the text and 3D models, which were subsequently visualized by adapting these 3D models.

Recently, GÖTZE ET AL. [GNI05] presented a flexible text authoring tool which assists users to link texts with images. By selecting a text segment the user can define a query for common on–line search engines which retrieve images and 3D models. In this in- _Text authoring_ teractive system domain experts select those images which are appropriate in the current text context. In order to adjust the retrieved results to another context, often additional textual or visual elements have to be integrated into the final images. Therefore, GÖTZELMANN ET AL. [GGA⁺07] integrated the encapsulated annotation layout approach as presented in the first part of this book in order to enhance 2D images and 3D visualizations with secondary elements. Moreover, textual annotations were considered as an implicit description of the content of visual elements and might even reflect their intended usage.

Mutual Linkage of Expository Text with Images and 3D Models

Some approaches link text with images and vice versa. The *COMET* [FM93] and *WIP* [WAF⁺93] system pioneered this mutual linkage of text with several media (e.g., text, _Semi–automatic_ images, and animations). These prototypes adapted the content and presentation of doc- _illustration_ uments to user preferences or contextual requirements by the use of numerous planning mechanisms. However, the enormous amount of required formal descriptions impeded the application of this technique.

Another approach presented both text and 3D models in conjunction in order to support the browsing of long electronic texts. For that reason, the *Text Illustrator* by SCHLECHT- WEG AND STROTHOTTE [SS99] visualized annotated 3D models and expository texts in two widgets arranged side by side. An internal representation of the text ensured that _Interaction_ parts of the visualized 3D models and the terms can be linked with each other. Ad- _with text and_ ditionally, so called mediators allowed the adaptive linkage of 3D model and text. This _3D models_ system enabled interaction techniques on both the expository text and the 3D model. On the one side, by scrolling through the text, the 3D parts shown in the browser window were immediately highlighted in the 3D model. On the other side by clicking on a specific 3D part, the text browser immediately positioned the text onto the first occurrence of its denomination.

6.2.3 A Concept for Correlating Illustrations and Text through Annotations

This section introduces a novel concept how users, facing the identified search tasks, _Support of_ can be assisted by modern computers. Next, two computer–supported scenarios of the _search tasks_ search tasks are proposed, which are based on an interactive browser for textual documents (text) and a 3D browser for the annotated exploration of 3D models (illustrations).

Text↦Illustration. By marking some sentences of the expository text in the text browser, users should be able to select an arbitrary text context, that they are interested in. Imme- _1st scenario_ diately after the selection, the system searches for a correlating 3D model, calculates the view which optimally describes the text context and presents this view context enriched by textual annotations. Thus, users are able to link the information of the selected text with the 3D parts of the presented view context. Additionally, users can explore the 3D model in the 3D browser.

Illustration↦Text. By exploring 3D models in the annotated 3D browser users can select

2nd scenario

an arbitrary view context they are interested in. Immediately after the user request, the system searches for the paragraph which optimally describes the chosen view context and presents the corresponding document in the text browser. Thus, users are able to link the selected visual information with the presented text context. Additionally, users can browse the document to which the paragraph belongs.

In order to allow the realization of these scenarios, in the following the concept for mutually linking illustrations and text is introduced. After the presentation of the architecture of an prospective approach this section proposes techniques in order to make text contexts and view contexts comparable with each other, i.e., to describe them with the same representation.

Mutually Linking Illustrations and Expository Text

As described in the problem statement, in educational material there are multiple con-

Uniform
representation

texts for both expository text (text context) as well as illustrations (view context). The search tasks arise, if complementary contexts from one medium (e.g., text) have to be found in the other medium (e.g., image). The aim is to find almost congruent view contexts to given text contexts and vice versa. In order to be able to compare contexts of different media, their media representations can be described in the same manner.

As stated before, annotations may be used to textually describe the context and content

Textual
descriptors

of 3D models. Since the retrieval of text documents is a well–elaborated field of research and the search process can be performed in an efficient manner, in the following the context descriptions of media are of a textual nature. However, before these contexts are compared, both types of input media should be broken down into a finer level of granularity. Thus, the first step is to generate multiple textual descriptors of both media, which are similar to the level like contexts are described in traditional educational material.

Paragraph
descriptors

Authors of educational books often structure arguments for thematic contexts into individual paragraphs which set of words are considered as one text context in this thesis. In the following, a text parser is described which generates *paragraph descriptors* for each paragraph of the source text documents.

Illustrations in books may depict objects from different viewpoints in order to support

View
descriptors

the comprehension of specific parts' spatial configuration and shape. In this thesis, a set of 3D parts visible in a given view are considered as one view context. In the following, an approach is presented which samples each source 3D model from a certain number of different viewpoints. By analyzing the color–coded projections of the 3D model, the textual annotation of each visible 3D part is used to generate a (textual) *view descriptor* for each view rendered from the source 3D models.

Architecture

Preprocessing

In a preprocessing step, a set of descriptors is generated for each of the 3D models as well as for each of the textual documents (see Figure 6.3). Those media descriptors are stored in a database for the paragraph descriptors P and a database for the view descriptors V.

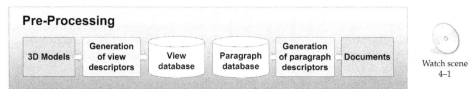

Figure 6.3: The preprocessing step for the creation of the textual descriptor databases.

At runtime the application provides both a text browser and an interactive 3D browser which allows to explore annotated 3D models. Using these interaction facilities, both search tasks can be supported by the application (see Figure 6.4) using the descriptor databases created in the preprocessing step. If users select an arbitrary part of text, the approach generates a new text descriptor and determines the most similar view descriptors stored in the database. As a result, the approach presents the 3D model's view, which possesses the best correlation with the chosen text. Subsequently, the user can explore the annotated 3D model in the 3D browser. The users can also request the application to determine correlating text segments. If they choose an arbitrary view of a 3D model, a new view descriptor is generated in order to determine the most similar paragraph descriptor stored in the database. The resulting paragraph is presented in the text browser, where users can browse the remaining text document.

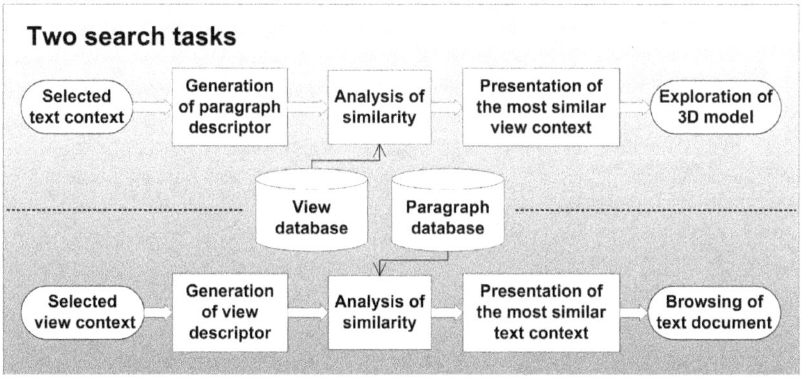

Figure 6.4: Both search tasks supported by the approach.

In the following the generation of descriptors for text documents and 3D models is described in more detail. For the sake of clarity, first *basic methods* are proposed. Subsequently, *optimized methods* are introduced which improve the descriptions by qualitative aspects.

Generation of Paragraph Descriptors

Usually, text retrieval engines store internal descriptions of complete document files in order to allow their retrieval. However, in order to generate individual text con-

93

texts from the expository text, approaches for question answering on text corpora (e.g., [HMP+00, PKW+02]) utilize a technique called paragraph–indexing which subdivides them into paragraphs. To ensure the minimality of the answers, they additionally test, if even a finer level of granularity—like sentences—is sufficient to answer a question. However, the smaller the text segments, the less likely they comprise multiple technical terms. Since thematic arguments in educational texts are usually structurally organized into paragraphs [Sch94], this seems to be a good compromise.

Paragraphs as text contexts

Basic method. This technique adapts the technique of paragraph–indexing and utilizes a simple text parser to subdivide each input text document $d \in D$ into individual paragraph descriptors p.

Optimized method. Authors may use several layout conventions to emphasize terms of increased relevance [Sch94]. In order to optimize the retrieval results, *importance values* for emphasized terms are introduced. An optimized text parser detects a set of emphasis techniques e (see Equation 6.1) for the terms t and transfers them into importance values i which are added for the specific term in the paragraph descriptor (see bold term Right Coronary Artery with the exemplary importance value $i_2 = 3.0$ in Figure 6.5).

Importance values

$$\text{importance}(t) = \begin{cases} i_1 : & e_t \equiv \text{normal;} \\ i_2 : & e_t \equiv \text{different font attribute (e.g., bold, italic);} \\ i_3 : & e_t \equiv \text{different font size;} \\ i_4 : & e_t \equiv \text{included structural element (e.g., heading).} \end{cases} \tag{6.1}$$

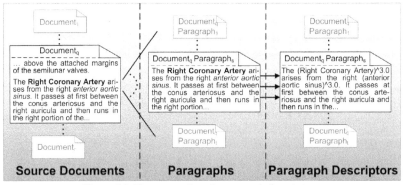

Figure 6.5: The generation of paragraph descriptors.

Generation of View Descriptors

In educational textbooks expository texts often describe spatial relations between complex–shaped objects respectively their parts. The perspective of such objects should be chosen in a context–sensitive way [RA90]. It is a challenging task for illustrators to select a single point of view, which depicts all relevant parts of such a context. Hence, the visibility of the individual components from a given point of view determines their potential to complement textual descriptions.

Sampled views as view contexts

Existing approaches for the determination of the *best view* of 3D models generate a finite set of orthogonal projections of those models and analyze them. This approach adapts this technique in order to generate a textual view descriptor for each of them. The camera positions are placed according to a sphere, which is circumscribing the 3D model (bounding sphere).

Sampling a set of views

In order to sample a number of projections, a method should be used which equally distributes n camera positions on this sphere. For the determination of equal camera point distributions algorithms for the approximation of the sphere by equilateral triangles [KSCT00] can be used or an energy–based algorithm which is placing the camera positions on a spiral [RSZ94].

Equal sample distribution

Theoretically, an infinite number of views could be sampled. However, it is dependent on the field of application and the individual 3D models, which resolution is purposive. In order to limit the preprocessing time and the storage size, a compromise has to be found. Granted that the total number of a 3D model's parts is known a priori. Thus, an adaptive algorithm can be used, which starts with a coarse number of camera positions and successively increases the number of camera positions until a distribution is found which sampled views cover all of the 3D model's color–IDs. In this case, the method of KUNSZT ET AL. [KSCT00] applying the hierarchical subdivision of the triangles is more advantageous, since the camera positions, which have already been analyzed, are valid until the minimal distribution is found (see Figure 6.6).

Purposive number of samples

Basic method. A set of equally distributed viewpoints is determined. According to the viewpoint coordinates, this technique renders multiple color–coded views v from each 3D model $m \in M$. Subsequently, each view is analyzed by using the color–ID of each 3D part to detect the visible parts. For each of the visible parts, their textual annotation is written into the view descriptor (see Figure 6.7).

Descriptors contain textual annotations of visible parts

Optimized method. Illustrators choose the view of illustrated objects very careful according to qualitative aspects (cf. Appendix C.8 and C.9). In contrast to the basic version, relevant parts should not only be visible, but also depicted in an advantageous manner. Hence, in order to determine the *importance values* of the visible parts in a view, qualitative measures have to be introduced. The more detailed topic of the non–trivial task to determine the quality of the depiction of visible parts in a view, is deferred to Section 6.3. Nevertheless, analog to the paragraph descriptors, the individual importance values are attached to the 3D parts' annotations in the descriptor (e.g., aorta with importance 2.5 in Figure 6.7). In order to improve the comparability of view descriptors with text descriptors the maximum importance value for visible parts of a view should be oriented at the maximum importance value for terms i_4.

Importance values

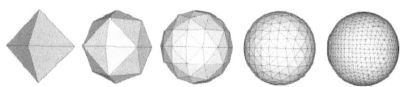

Figure 6.6: Recursive decomposition of the sphere (Levels 1 to 5). (Source: [SGF+05])

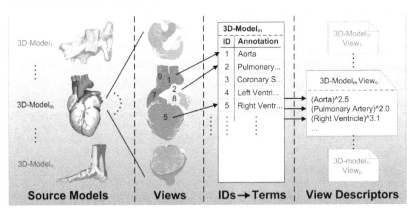

Figure 6.7: The generation of view descriptors.

Discussion

This section described how textual descriptions can be used for the retrieval of different media, i.e., text and 3D models. In educational textbooks, text and illustrations are used in conjunction, in order to explain contexts complementary. This approach assumes that a text context is covered in a paragraph, while multiple views of 3D models depict different view contexts. This section explained how to generate textual descriptors for each context defined in both text and 3D models. By equalizing the representations of their descriptions, contexts of both media can be compared. If one context is defined in one medium, a similar context in the other medium can be searched for.

Although this section introduced basic techniques to realize this concept, two questions arose, which have to be addressed more detailed in dedicated sections:

- How to determine the view quality of a set of relevant visible parts in a given view? This issue is addressed in Section 6.3.

- Which technique has to be used to determine correlating textual descriptors of both paragraphs and views? Section 6.4 explains foundations of this topic as well as problem–oriented specifications and solutions.

6.2.4 Conclusion

The aim of the second part of this book is to support users with the search tasks arising when reading educational books. In order to improve the spatial comprehension of users, they should be able to explore annotated 3D models, instead of static images. In the definition of the search contexts users should not be constrained, but supported by the system. As a basis there should be two databases containing natural language text and 3D models. The approach should be able to pre–process the input data (text documents and 3D models) in an automated way. However, none of the existing approaches satisfied the combination of those needs.

6.3 Qualitative Descriptions of Views

For the generation of textual descriptors from 3D models, Section 6.2.3 proposed a basic method to render a set of color–coded projections of the scene, whereas the viewpoints are placed on a sphere circumscribing the 3D model. Subsequently, these color–coded images are analyzed, whereas the textual annotations of the visible color–IDs of the 3D parts constitute the textual descriptor. *Analysis of color–coded images*

However, the textual descriptor generated from the optimized method should not only consider which 3D parts are visible, but also consider qualitative measures about their visibility in each view. These qualitative measures are used to define the importance value of each annotation of the visible parts mentioned in the view descriptors. *Qualitative measures for views*

In the following, specifications have to be defined which consider the necessity of the approach in order to assess existing approaches concerning their suitability. This forms the basis to develop a problem–oriented solution.

6.3.1 Specifications

There is a growing field of research which faces the challenge to compute the *best view* of arbitrary 3D models as a general goal. These approaches also sample and analyze the 3D model from a finite set of viewpoints and select the view, where their measure has the highest score. *Best view*

The proposed approach adapts these techniques to determine the scores of each sampled view, in order to mention it as a qualitative measure in the textual descriptor. First, for each visible 3D part of a view, a value is necessary which describes how good this specific part is visible in that view (cf. Appendix C.9). Second, in order to comprise information about the proximity of the important parts, a general measure should determine if the complete view of the 3D model is advantageous (cf. Appendix C.10). Third, this algorithm should be fast enough to allow user interaction, i.e., the view descriptor has to be determined in an acceptable amount of time (≤ 1 second). Hence, a suitable method should satisfy the following specifications: *How good are 3D parts visible in each view?*

- **Proximity.** The approach should be able to determine if the complete view is advantageous, i.e., how much contextual information an entire view possesses.

- **Specificity.** The approach should be able to describe the quality of the presentation of each individual visible 3D part in a given view.

- **Relevance.** It should be possible to assign individual relevance values to each 3D part. These values should be reflected in the approach's quality measure.

- **Interactivity.** In terms of time, the determination of the best view should be efficient enough for an interactive application.

6.3.2 Related Work

Two classes

Existing approaches can be subdivided into two different classes. Those approaches with *uninformed methods* determine the best views purely on topological properties of the geometric object or on evaluations of visible or occluded geometric features. Approaches using *informed methods* are able to determine object–specific quality measures for the components of a 3D scene and may consider object–specific relevance values defined by an external application.

Uninformed Methods

Projected area and visible faces

Many researchers propose measures that depend on the projected area of the models' 3D parts or on the number of visible faces (e.g., [PB96]). Some of these measures for the determination of the best view aim at minimizing the number of those faces that are displayed in a bad condition (e.g., [KK88]).

View entropy advantageous

Multiple applications

A very influential measure is based on the amount of information that can be captured from a certain view. The *viewpoint entropy* measure proposed by VÁZQUEZ ET AL. [VFSH01] yields a good balance between the number of visible faces and the area covered by them. When the projected area of a model's 3D parts is considered, it has the advantage that this measure is not influenced by different resolutions of the 3D models. This viewpoint entropy has also been successfully applied to the automatic selection of good views of molecular models [VFSL06], for volumetric models [BS05, TFTN05], or to compute paths through complex models [AVF04].

Informed Methods

Relevance with voxel parts

There are only few systems which consider the view quality of individual 3D parts. For the visualization of voxel models VIOLA ET AL. [VFSG06] used context–dependent relevance values to determine appropriate views on volumetric data sets.

Multiple measures

Canonical views not applicable

Recently, MÜHLER ET AL. [MNTP07] presented a system for surgeons, which employs an extensive amount of pre–processed information to determine several view–dependent quality measures and to weight their influence during run–time. Besides the view entropy, this system incorporates numerous parameters in a complex view metric. However, a user study did not point out significant results about their individual usefulness. A promising parameter that their system considers are *canonical views* that have been suggested by PALMER AND ROSCH [PRC81] in cognitive psychology. Canonical views ease the identification of visual parts. The substantial study of BLANZ ET AL. [BTB99] showed that these views were also preferred in interactive 3D visualizations. However, for unknown 3D models, canonical views cannot be computed, since they require at least the definition of its front view.

Discussion

The approaches, which belong to the class of the uninformed methods, are not able to evaluate the visibility of particular 3D parts. Thus, they are not sufficient in terms of the specificity. However, because of the allowed qualitative declarations about the entire view they can satisfy the proximity specification. The view entropy has been successfully applied in multiple approaches of different fields and is not biased of the geometric level of detail of (unknown) 3D models. Additionally, the necessary information could also be determined by hardware acceleration,[1] since this seems to be a sufficient measure for the overall view quality.

Uninformed methods partially sufficient

The approaches are sufficient in terms of specificity, since they consider the visibility of particular 3D parts. However, they have difficulties to meet all of the specifications. The approach of VIOLA ET AL. satisfies the relevance specification, because it is able to assign and evaluate relevance values to multiple 3D parts. But, in terms of interactivity, it fails to compute them in an acceptable time, which does not allow a free context selection. The system of MÜHLER ET AL. performs well in terms of interactivity, but it does not consider the impact of context–dependent relevance values of multiple 3D parts.

Informed methods partially sufficient

6.3.3 Approach

For the determination of the view quality with respect to a defined text context, a pragmatic solution has to be introduced. Although, in future, more factors could be tested regarding their influence on the assessment of a good view on 3D models, three measures which were discussed with human illustrators, are used for a foundational approach (cf. Appendix C.9 and C.10).

Pragmatic solution

Parts' Relative Size and Centricity. Important parts should be optimally visible. For a given view, the *relative size* of projected 3D parts can be computed in proportion to the set of views V. While A_p denotes the projected area of part p, their maximum area $A_m = max_{i \in V}(A_p(i))$ is pre–computed by the set of sampled views. Finally, the relative size is determined by $relsize_p = \frac{A_p}{A_m}$.

Bounding Box

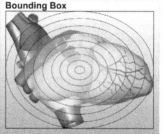

Informed methods

Figure 6.8: Centricity measure of 3D parts by concentric ellipses.

Moreover, the most important 3D parts are often presented in the center of an illustration. In order to determine the *centricity*, initially, the primary object's bounding box is determined. In this bounding box 10 concentric ellipses are inscribed which define a multiplicative factor for each pixel of the 3D parts (see Figure 6.8). Finally, the 3D parts' score is summed up in each elliptical region.

Views' Entropy. This measure reflects the available contextual information for a given view. The *viewpoint entropy* H for a specific view [VFSH01] is defined by Equation 6.2:

$$H = -\sum_{p=0}^{P} \frac{A_p}{A_t} \log \frac{A_p}{A_t},\qquad(6.2)$$

---

[1]The OpenGL Extension *Frame Buffer Objects* allows to obtain the number of rendered pixels of 3D parts.

Uninformed method

where A_t is the total area covered by the projected primary object $\sum_{j \in P} A_j$, and A_0 represents the projected area of the illustration background. Hence, if the whole viewport is covered by the primary object, consequently $A_0 = 0$. The maximum entropy is obtained when each 3D part is shown with the same relative projected area A_p/A_t.

6.3.4 Discussion

Independent measures

Some of the measures used by other approaches are inappropriate to the concept of correlating illustrations and text. Some methods are sensitive to the resolution of the approximated spatial objects or on their type of 3D model (cf. Chapter 2) and thus, conflict with the applicability specification , other methods require additional information in order to work reliable. However, the generation of view descriptors is intended to cope with unknown 3D models from arbitrary fields. Hence, the proposed methods work on the same image–based input data like the encapsulated annotation approach developed in the first part of this book (Chapter 3 to 5).

Combination of measures

While the proximity specification can be met by uninformed methods, i.e., the entropy measure, informed measures are required in order to satisfy the specificity measure. By additionally assigning relevance factors to individual 3D parts, contextually good views can be determined by the relative size and the centricity measure at interactive rates.

Weighted influence of measures

The informed methods for the relative size and centricity as well as the uninformed method for entropy were considered to be useful because of the consultancy of experts. In a specific application, their individual influence on the evaluation of good views could be controlled by a weighted sum. In order to determine appropriate weights, an application with a user study is postponed to Chapter 7. In future studies, additional measures (e.g., [MNTP07]) could be tested towards their usefulness.

6.4 Searching Text Documents

For the sake of simplicity, this section focuses on the discussion of the search task of text↦illustration (cf. Section 6.2): The users read a text segment in the educational book, and subsequently they are searching for the illustration that covers the context they read about. Hence, the text segments they read serve as search query, while the search space is the set of illustrations in the book.

In order to assess retrieval techniques, problem–oriented specifications have to be introduced first. Further on, the related discussion of approaches has to finalize with an introduction of the most appropriate retrieval technique. Finally, adaptations of this technique to the concept of correlating illustrations and text have to be presented.

6.4.1 Specifications

BAEZA–YATES AND RIBEIRO–NETO [BYRN99, p. 257] state: 'Information seeking is an imprecise process. When users approach an information access system they often have only a fuzzy understanding of how they can achieve their goals. Thus, the user interface should aid in the understanding and expression of information needs.' This section defines the specifications that a problem–oriented retrieval method should fulfill. These specifications are derived from the results of the approach on contextual annotation (see Chapter 5) and are adapted to the search tasks in educational books as described in Section 6.2.

Problem–oriented specifications

The search tasks address the challenge of finding corresponding view contexts to a given text context, and vice versa. Hence, an appropriate technique has to be used, which allows to compare the descriptors derived from both the text context and view context. Based on the requirements related to the concept of correlating illustrations and text as well as the presented statement, the following specifications can be defined:

Similarity of descriptors

- **Flexibility.** Expository text is written in natural language, which is 'not always well structured and could be semantically ambiguous' [BYRN99, p. 2]. The approach should be flexible, i.e., neither dependent on a limited set of supported types of text, nor force users to process the text manually. Furthermore, small differences in the spelling of the text should not impede the search success.

- **Intuitiveness.** The user interface should support users in expressing the query. The approach should provide an intuitive way to allow users to define the context they are interested in.

- **Integration.** Reinforcing the intuitiveness specification implies that, like in books, optimally only texts and illustrations should suffice. No supplemental manually added representations and structuring elements should be necessary for the definition of the contexts and the presentation of the search results.

- **Interaction.** Since information seeking is an imprecise process, the approach should provide intuitive techniques to support users to refine the query in order to find the desired information.

6.4.2 Retrieval Methods

A corpus of books electronically stored in a computer may be seen as a database. If users want to access the information stored in that database, they usually have an information need. The term *retrieval* addresses the challenge of gathering information from the database, concerning this information need.

Retrieval

Two fundamentally different types of retrieving information from a database can be distinguished [BYRN99]. The term *data retrieval* refers to a technique where users formulate a query in a specific notation (e.g., SQL) to articulate their information need. The search results are a set of exact matching data items. On the contrary, in *information retrieval*, the query can be a few terms or even complete sentences. However, in contrast to data retrieval, the query has to be interpreted by an information retrieval system. Instead of a set of accurately matching items, users obtain a list of documents which are relevant to the query in a certain degree. The documents in this list can be sorted by their degree

Data retrieval

Information retrieval

of relevance, while a threshold value of the minimum relevance may limit the number of documents.

Discussion In the following, both retrieval types are assessed with respect to their appropriateness to the concept specifications (see also Table 6.1). In terms of *flexibility* data retrieval is not optimal, since it expects the source documents to be manually preprocessed into a structured manner. Additionally, information retrieval may even determine documents which are slightly different to the query, data retrieval only determines data items which exactly match the query [BYRN99, Sch06]. Whereas data retrieval explicitly expects a specific notation of the query, information retrieval offers a more *intuitive* method by supporting natural language queries and copes with the information implicitly defined by the query [Sch06]. Due to this implicit interpretation by information retrieval, arbitrary textual contexts can be used as a query. Hence, on the contrary to data retrieval, this allows the *integrated* selection of an arbitrary text context or view context by interaction with the source medium.

If users are not satisfied with the retrieval results, they have the opportunity to modify the initial query by data retrieval, in order to obtain the desired results. However, if they did not define the query very well, they will not obtain any results. On the contrary, by information retrieval, users may get a list of documents which are similar to the query. This offers the opportunity to use the gathered information and to refine the query more intuitively. However, those adequate *interaction* techniques have to be adapted to the proposed approach.

	Data Retrieval	Information Retrieval
Flexibility	not sufficient	sufficient
Intuitiveness	not sufficient	sufficient
Integration	not sufficient	sufficient
Interaction	partially	partially

Table 6.1: Evaluation of the retrieval types according to the specifications.

Information retrieval Nearly each of the specifications are met by information retrieval, whereas data retrieval does not seem to be optimal for the support of the search tasks in educational material. Thus, the next section introduces different information retrieval models.

6.4.3 Information Retrieval Models

Formal description There are multiple different information retrieval models which can be formally described by a quadruple $[D, Q, F, R(q_i, d_j)]$ [BYRN99, p. 23]. D is the internal representation of the documents, i.e., the text descriptors and view descriptors. Q means the representation of the query.

Indexation First, in a preprocessing step called *indexation*, the information retrieval system transforms the documents to be indexed into an internal representation D, which only covers the relevant terms t of the documents (i.e., without *stopwords* like 'a', 'with', etc.). Additionally, in order to normalize morphological variants of words, a technique called *stemming* applies simple transformation rules on the remaining terms. Subsequently, these terms are used to construct the internal representation, called *dictionary*. In this dictionary, the documents are represented by their terms. A *term weight* can be used to define to which amount the document is described by a specific term.

In the proposed concept, the set of paragraph descriptors P as well as the set of view descriptors V are indexed to the dictionaries D_P respectively D_V. Additionally, the term importance values are reflected by term weights (see Section 6.4.6). The queries Q have to be transformed into the same internal representation than the documents D, in order to compare the similarity of the query q_i with each document d_j with a ranking function $R(q_i, d_j)$. This ranking function is depending on the framework F which is modeling D and Q, as well as their relationships.

Indexation of descriptors

Similarity by ranking function

The models can be applied for the retrieval of different media than text, i.e., audio, images, and video. However, since those *multimedia retrieval* techniques base on text retrieval, this section will focus on models to this media. In the following, four classic information retrieval models will be briefly explained, regarding their document representation, the query definition, their ranking function, and how they support term weights.

Multimedia retrieval

Boolean Model

The Boolean model is a rather simple retrieval model, based on set theory. It represents the documents as sets of terms, which means that for each term present in a document it is simply stored if it is present or not. The query is defined by terms combined with Boolean operators (e.g., 'and', 'or', 'not'). They are used for the ranking function in order to determine if there is an intersection among the documents and the query. The term weights are only represented by a Boolean value which only allows exact matches.

Binary term weights

Fuzzy Model

The Fuzzy model is an extension of the Boolean model, which copes with its disadvantage of having only binary term weights. In this model the documents are represented as fuzzy sets, whereas the query is defined the same way like it is done in the Boolean model. However, because of the fuzzy sets, different operators are used for the ranking function (e.g., minimum and maximum). By representing the documents as fuzzy sets, this allows continuous values for the term weights.

Fuzzy operators

Vector Space Model

The vector space model is a widespread retrieval model. In text retrieval each term defines its own dimension in a multidimensional vector space constructed of the dictionary. Hence, each document constructs a document vector. Additionally, in this model, the query also constructs an own vector based on the same dictionary as the documents. Thus, for the ranking function different measures can be applied for the determination of the similarity between the query vector and the document vectors. Usually, the quantity of occurrences of terms in documents— so called *term frequencies*—are used for the term weights. In order to implement the continuous term weights, a factor is used to adapt the vector in the term dimension.

Document vector

Term frequencies

Probabilistic Model

Relevance of documents
The probabilistic retrieval model [MK60] is based on a probability theory that (for a given user query) there is a set of relevant documents, whereas the remaining set of documents is irrelevant. Each of the documents is represented by a document vector and the query defines a subset of the dictionary. The ranking function consists of multiple parts. One part evaluates a score of each document by counting the number of matching terms according to the query. The original probabilistic model only uses binary term weights, however, extended models consider term frequencies of the source documents. Another part of the ranking function considers users to interact with the resulting documents of the initial search in order to mark relevant and irrelevant ones.

Probability estimation
It tries to estimate the probability (i.e., utilizing the Bayesian formula) that the user will find a certain document relevant in respect of the given query.

Discussion

Significant differences in applicability
Each of the presented information retrieval models meet the specification described in Section 6.4.1. Nevertheless, there are several significant differences in their applicability to the underlying problem. An important aspect is the ability to adapt their weights of single elements (i.e., terms) of the query. Unfortunately, the Boolean model only considers terms which are present or not present, and thus, does not suffice to represent the importance values of the source documents P and V. To cope with this problem, some researchers are proposing an extended boolean model (e.g., [Boo78, SFW82]) using continuous term weights between 0.0 and 1.0. Just as the Boolean model, the Fuzzy model also overcomes the binary term weight problems despite users do not tend to assemble complex queries [Kor97, p. 62], artificial expressions for the query formulation are required. Hence, it is not intuitive enough for an automated handling of the proposed approach.

Support of importance values

Intuitive query formulation
Since the vector space model transforms the query into the same vectorial representation than the document, it does not support Boolean operators. However, it offers an intuitive way for the query formulation and supports continuous values for the term weights. This outweighs the disadvantage of not being able to use Boolean operators, which can partially be compensated by modifying the term weights.

Relevance has to be known
The ranking function of the probabilistic model only works optimally, if user–defined relevance information about the documents is considered. Since this relevance information is not known a priori, the acquisition requires an iterative search process, in which users have to interact with the search results. These interaction techniques can also be applied to improve the results of the vector space retrieval method (see Section 6.4.5). Despite of interaction techniques, the vector space model is expected to outperform the probabilistic model [BYRN99, p. 34].

Same notation for q and d
Another advantage of the vector model is that it expects the same notation for queries than for documents, while considering term weights for both of them. This allows to determine the similarity of a view descriptor to the indexed paragraph descriptors and vice versa. Because of this, the following section introduces this retrieval model in more detail.

6.4.4 Vector Space Model

The vector space retrieval model [SWY75] is widely used. It is not only used for the indexation of textual documents, but also for low–level features extracted from multimedia content (e.g., histograms of images or frequency distributions of audio files).

Numerous applications

The indexation of textual documents is performed in several steps. After removing the stop words and the stemming process, the *dictionary* T is built from the remaining set of terms of D. It spans a multidimensional vector space, whereas each term of the dictionary constructs its own dimension. Subsequently, for each document $d \in D$ their own document vectors $\vec{d}$ are constructed and stored in the index I. The *term frequencies* tf_t^d of each term of d are determined and used as a factor of the term dimension in the according descriptor. Queries are processed in the same manner than the documents. Thus, they represent a vector $\vec{q}$ in the same vector space as D.

Document vector

Term frequency

The document vector specifies *term weights* w_t^d for all terms t in the dictionary for a given document d. In order to obtain descriptive weight vectors, SALTON proposes the standard measure [SABS94] that considers both the frequency tf_t^d of the term t in the current document d as well as its frequency in the respective database D:

Term weight

$$w_t^d = tf_t^d \cdot \log(\frac{N}{n_t}), \tag{6.3}$$

where N denotes the size of the document collection D and n_t refers to the number of documents in D that contain term t.

For illustration purposes, Figure 6.9 shows a simplified example. The exemplary dictionary comprises three different terms, which span a vector space T. Additionally, there are four document vectors constructed from the documents $D = d_1, d_2, d_3$, and the query q using the terms of the dictionary.

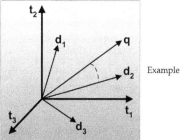

Example

Figure 6.9: According to the cosine measure the document d_2 is most similar to query q.

Based on the document vectors it is now possible to search for documents that are similar to a given query q or similar to another document d', in which case $\vec{q} := \vec{d'}$. By comparing the query vector with each document in the collection $d \in D$ all the documents can be ranked according to their similarity with the query q. The most common similarity measure is the *cosine similarity* [SABS94], which is computed by the inner product of both normalized document vectors $\vec{d}$ and $\vec{q}$ (see Equation 6.4) and represents the angle between both vectors (see Figure 6.9).

Cosine similarity measure

$$\text{sim}(\vec{d}, \vec{q}) = \frac{\vec{d} \cdot \vec{q}}{|\vec{d}| \cdot |\vec{q}|} \tag{6.4}$$

Threshold value

Search engines commonly return a list of search results, which are itemized in an abbreviated manner. This list is decreasingly ordered by the similarity of the documents d_i to the query q. To prevent the list getting huge and including even entries with nearly no similarity, a *threshold value* can be used to define a minimum degree of similarity as condition for documents to be listed in the results.

6.4.5 Interaction

Interaction for query refinement

By the vector space model, users get a list of documents which are similar to the query. However, this list is probably very extensive, thus, it is unlikely that users will investigate each of the search results until they have found an appropriate one. The user interface of the search system should support the user in finding appropriate documents.

Iterative process

Searching for appropriate documents is an iterative process based on the search results of the previous iteration. There are two common techniques for supporting this iteration, which are addressing the issue from different viewpoints. In the following, they are briefly introduced, followed by a short discussion.

Direct adaptation

Query Modification. The users inspect at least one of the search results and realize in which way they differ from their information need. Subsequently, they directly modify the search query by defining which of the terms are more respectively less important, or by appending respectively removing terms.

Indirect adaptation

Relevance Feedback. The users inspect at least a couple of search results and judge about whether they are relevant or irrelevant concerning their information need. This additional information can be used by the system, in order to modify the query (e.g., [Roc71, Sal71, Ide71]).

Discussion

Both techniques have advantages

Table 6.2 shows characteristics of the introduced techniques. An advantage of query modification is that users do not have to *inspect* multiple search results in order to refine the query. However, through this technique, the *query adjustment* is predominantly user–centered. Hence, they have to alter the query manually, which is tied with a more complex task than by relevance feedback, because it usually requires a deep understanding of the system [Sch06, p. 36].[2] In terms of immediacy of the *query adaptation*, the query modification is more direct. Using this technique the query can be adjusted more precisely than it is possible by relevance feedback, because this only offers an implicit technique to change the query. This can be of advantage, if some query terms are to be added or removed, or if users know well about the syntax of querying the system. Additionally, it is unlikely that users are willing to judge about relevant and irrelevant results through many iterations [Kor97, p. 221].

---

[2]Original statement in German: 'Der Anwender wird beim Relevance Feedback vom aufwändigen Modizieren der Anfrage, was in der Regel tiefe Systemkenntnis erfordert, befreit.'

Since the user is forced to know about the formulation of the query, in terms of intuitiveness, the query modification technique does not seem to be optimal. However, since the user cannot exactly define which parts of the query have to be changed by relevance feedback, this technique lacks of flexibility. Hence, they could be used in combination in order to complement their advantages and offer the optimal support to the user according to the specifications.

Combination of both techniques

	Query Modification	Relevance Feedback
Number of results to inspect	≥ 1	> 1
Query adjustment task	user centered	computer centered
Immediacy of query adaptation	direct	indirect

Table 6.2: Characteristics of search interaction techniques.

6.4.6 Necessary Adaptations

This section discussed different retrieval approaches and proposed the vector space model for the application of the concept introduced in Section 6.2.3. Finally, this section introduces necessary adaptations in order to apply the concept of correlating illustrations and text to the vector space model and to the interaction techniques.

Adaptation of the Vector Space Model

In order to apply the vector space retrieval model to the approach proposed in Section 6.2.3, some adaptations have to be made. As described, the approach uses two separate document databases, i.e., the set of paragraph descriptors D_P and the set of view descriptors D_V. Both of those descriptors define importance values in order to emphasize or de–emphasize the terms describing the paragraphs or views.

Importance values of descriptors' terms

For the indexation, the indexes I_P and I_V as well as their dictionaries T_P and T_V of these descriptors have to be built. In contrast to the standard model, the approach additionally integrates a *boost function*, which allows to implement the importance values of the descriptor files by modifying the document weight for a term t, where

Modification of document weights

$$\begin{array}{ll} \text{boost}(t) < 1.0: & \text{de–emphasized term } t; \\ \text{boost}(t) = 1.0: & \text{normal}; \\ \text{boost}(t) > 1.0: & \text{emphasized term } t. \end{array} \qquad (6.5)$$

Thus, the computation of the weights as defined in Equation 6.3 is changed to:

$$w_t^d = \text{boost}(t) \cdot \textit{tf}_t^d \cdot \log(N/n_t). \qquad (6.6)$$

This modification allows to consider qualitative aspects, i.e visual dominance of terms in paragraphs and visual quality of 3D parts in a view. Hence, correlations of text contexts and view contexts can be determined.

Adaptation of Interaction Techniques

A main disadvantage of query modification is that users have to modify the query manually. Thus, normally they must have a fundamental knowledge about the formal definition of queries. In order to individually adjust queries to the users requirements, interactive techniques should be provided that help users to refine their initial query. Those techniques should be designed in a *consistent* and *intuitive* manner for both illustrations and text. Additionally, they should be simply pluggable on top of the concept in a *transparent* way.

User interface should support query refinement

When the user chooses an view context or a text context in order to query the system, a view descriptor or a paragraph descriptor are generated. Visually dominant terms in the text context, respectively visually dominant 3D parts in the view context are considered with a higher importance value. The size (i.e., paragraph descriptor: font size, view descriptor: 3D part size) is used for the determination of the importance value of both the text context and the view context. Hence, this variable can be used for a *consistent* tool in order to modify the importance values in a *transparent* fashion, i.e., without change of the concept. By realizing a tool for the size adjustment of terms and 3D parts, an *intuitive* facility for users could be created in order to adjust their queries.

Size parameter of fonts and 3D parts

Size modifies importance

Additionally, relevance feedback could be implemented for both illustrations and text by adding options to the search results whether the retrieved paragraphs or views are relevant. Although this technique could improve the search results significantly, it is not ideal to express user interests in specific parts of the illustrations or text.

Relevance feedback

6.5 Conclusion

Starting from a practical description of the immanent problem of search tasks between illustrations and expository text in educational material, this chapter discussed a concept for the support of learners. By the use of annotated 3D models, multiple textual descriptions of different views can be generated and compared to the textual descriptions generated from the paragraphs of expository text. This equalization of both media allows to mutually search both representations.

Concept

In order to describe this concept, elaborately two aspects had to be addressed more extensively. In order to generate qualitative textual descriptions of a 3D model's views, algorithms had to be assessed which are normally used to determine their best view. These algorithms had to be adapted and extended to the underlying problem specifications. In order to determine correlations between qualitative descriptions of text contexts and view contexts, an appropriate technique had to be found and adapted to an intended solution specifications.

Two excursuses

Based on the concept of correlating illustrations and text, the following Chapter 7 introduces an experimental application as proof–of–concept, and evaluates its use.

7

Application Scenario
and Evaluation

Outline

This chapter picks up the concept of correlating illustrations and text introduced in Chapter 6. An experimental application is developed, which uses an
electronic version of a popular anatomic text book and a database of anatomic
3D models. The retrieval task is performed by a widespread open–source
approach. For both media representations, i.e., expository text and 3D models, new objects can be easily added to the database and immediately used.
Furthermore, this application shows how the encapsulated approach for the
annotation layout and the concept of correlating illustrations and text work
together, and that the studies undertaken in first part of this book are a requirement for the concept of the second part.

Achievements

The experimental application developed in this chapter serves as proof of
concept for both parts introduced in this book. It clarifies, why the first part
had to be addressed prior to the second one. The concept of correlating
illustrations and text is evaluated by a user study, that does not only validate
the central statements of the concept and its applicability, but also grants
additional insights in the practical use of applications.

7.1 Introduction

This chapter addresses the theoretic concept introduced in the previous chapter and
applies it to a practical context. While Chapter 6 developed the concept of correlating illustrations and text in general, this section applies it exemplary to the domain of
anatomy.

*Application of
theoretic concept*

This section highlights the necessary of adaptive and coordinated multi–modal presen-
tations in this application domain. As in many scientific or technical areas, students
of human anatomy have to learn a large amount of human organs' technical terms,
their appearance, and their functioning. Moreover, anatomic textbooks focus on descriptions of geometric properties: chapters on *osteology*, for example, contain descriptions
of characteristic features of complex–shaped bones, chapters on *myology* employ the
features of these bones as landmarks in order to describe the run of muscles, and the
syndesmology explains the direction of movements in joints.

*Medical
application
domain*

Need of text and illustrations
These examples demonstrate the suitability of annotated illustrations for learning purposes of a domain–specific terminology, the relevance of basic learning tasks in anatomy for almost all scientific or technical domains, and the need to complement expository text with expressive illustrations. The integration of a real–time annotation layout system and the automatic selection of appropriate 3D models and views from a database in this system aim at supporting all these learning tasks. The experimental application implemented in this chapter serves as proof of concept and discusses its realization. Finally, the concept is evaluated by a user study which verifies the central statements of the concept and the applicability of its experimental implementation.

Proof of concept and evaluation

Chapter overview
Followed by this introduction, Section 7.2 briefly explains the application of the concept of correlating illustrations and text to the medical domain and presents an experimental application. Section 7.3 evaluates both the central statements of the concept and its application. Subsequently, Section 7.4 discusses the achievements, and Section 7.5 concludes this chapter.

7.2 Experimental Application

In order to describe the application of the concept of correlating illustrations and text to the medical domain, its framework and components are defined in the following. Based on this framework, this section presents the graphical user interface and also discusses how the user interaction is handled. Besides initiating queries and interacting with the search results, appropriate methods are proposed in order to support users in refining their queries.

7.2.1 Framework

Implementation
An interactive application was implemented, where users can interact with elements of both media (expository text and 3D models). When browsing of the expository text respectively exploration of the 3D model, users can initiate both search tasks by simply selecting a context they are interested in, i.e., a text segment or a view of a 3D model. Automatically, the application generates queries which serve as input for the application's search engine. Finally, users merely have to choose one of the search results.

Preprocessing
In order to enable the use of a search engine to process the users search requests at runtime, an automated preprocessing step has to be performed for each document of the collection of descriptive texts and 3D models. When users add a document to the search engines database, first of all multiple context descriptors are generated (see Section 6.2.3) in order to append their document vectors to the paragraph index I_P respectively the view index I_V.

Search engine
In order to handle the user interaction and the text interaction, the *Qt library* [Tro] was applied, whereas the open–source library *Coin3D* [Sys] provided as a basis for the 3D browser. The open–source search engine *Lucene* [Dou] was used in order to determine similarities between text contexts and view contexts. Hence, appropriate views for the content of user–selected text segments and vice versa can be determined during runtime. As an

110

exemplary application domain, the human anatomy was chosen because of several rea- Underlying
sons. On the one hand, comprehensive corpora of tutoring material are available[1]. On corpora
the other hand, the comprehension of a domain–specific terminology as well as complicated spatial configurations are important learning tasks.

7.2.2 Interactive Browser and Mutual Queries

The interactive browser allows to explore both expository text and 3D models, whereas Input formats
their widgets are placed side by side. The text browser allows to load documents from
the text corpus stored in the *Hypertext Markup Language* format (HTML). The 3D model
browser allows to load documents of the 3D model corpus stored in the *Open Inventor*
format (IV).

In order to add documents to the search engines databases users can influence the num- Adjustable
ber of sampled contexts which can be found by the system. For text documents, it can be indexing
chosen if they should be broken up into sentences, paragraphs or sections. Since other
approaches use paragraphs (e.g., [HMP+00]) for an appropriate level of granularity, this
serves as default value. For 3D models users can choose the number of views to be sampled, which is depending on the geometric complexity of the model. The text browser
can be used by scrolling through text documents which are enriched by illustrations Exploration of
from the book and following the integrated hyperlinks. The 3D models can be explored text and
by scaling, translating, and rotating. Furthermore, they are annotated by the encapsu- 3D models
lated annotation approach introduced in the first part of this book. In the following, it is
described how users can initiate text $\mapsto$ view queries as well as view $\mapsto$ text queries and
in which way the results are presented.

Text $\mapsto$ view queries

In order to induce a text $\mapsto$ view query, users can select arbitrary text segments in the
expository text displayed in the text browser (see Figure 7.1). This interaction initiates
the retrieval of 3D views of the indexed 3D models which correspond to the terms used
in the text segment.

Watch scene
4–2

As described in Section 6.2.3, this action transforms the content of user–selected text
segment into a text descriptor, considering emphasized terms with an increased level of Transformation
importance, i.e., higher weights for the corresponding query terms. This text descriptor and query
is subsequently used as a query vector for the search engine. Using the view index I_V
allows to retrieve views on 3D models that correlate with the terms used in the query.

The best fitting 3D model in the best view is loaded and presented immediately; the Presentation
remaining good views of other 3D models are presented in small overview windows on of results
the side of the 3D screen; they are loaded when they are selected by the user. In order
to support the interactive exploration of the 3D model, a colored sphere in the upper
left corner is presented. The colors of the sphere represent the similarities determined
by the search engine, i.e., yellowish parts are relevant to the chosen text context and Exploration

---

[1]The underlying corpus comprises an electronic version of *Gray's popular textbook on human
anatomy* [Gra18] and all anatomic models contained in the *Viewpoint library* of polygonal 3D models [Dig].

111

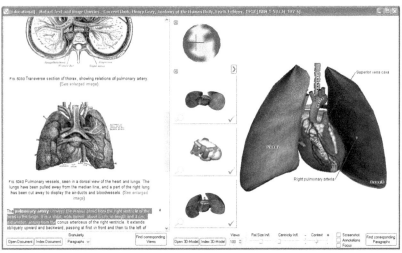

Figure 7.1: A text $\mapsto$ view query (left) with its results (right).

bluish parts are not relevant. If the user rotates the 3D model, the sphere is rotated as well. Hence, users can see the level of relevance of the view according to the text context chosen before.

Annotation   In order to enable the user to understand which 3D parts are addressed in the expository text, it is a necessary precondition to annotate the 3D model which was retrieved by the system. Thus, the encapsulated annotation approach developed in the first part of this Contextual   book is integrated into the 3D browser. Moreover, the annotation layout within these annotation   computer–generated illustrations should reflect this new context (see Chapter 5). Hence, users can cause the system to annotate the 3D model exclusively according to the chosen text context. This means that only the annotations which correspond to the terms used in the selected text context are displayed and the remaining 3D parts are de–emphasized by transparency.

View $\mapsto$ paragraph queries

Watch scene 4–3

In order to support the search task view $\mapsto$ text, users can induce a visual query. They simply have to choose the arbitrary 3D model's view they are interested in (see Figure 7.2) in order to initiate the retrieval of text segments (e.g., paragraphs) of indexed text documents which correspond to the 3D parts visible in the selected view.

Transformation   Followed by the selection of a view, its color–coded rendition is analyzed (see Section 6.2.3) in order to transform this view into a view descriptor. The visible size of and query   the 3D parts and their centricity are considered with a pertinent level of importance, i.e., higher weights for the corresponding query terms. Subsequently, this descriptor serves as a query vector for the search engine, which uses the paragraph index I_P to retrieve

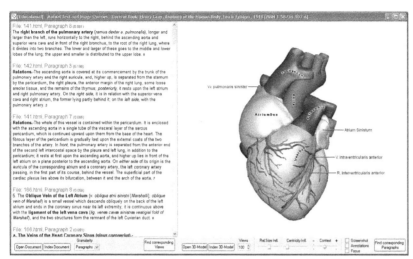

Figure 7.2: A view ↦ text query (right) and its results (left).

text segments of text documents in the text corpus that correlate with the annotations of the visible 3D parts of the query.

The list of retrieved text segments is presented in a list sorted by their relevance. In order to give an overview of the search results, they are displayed in an abbreviated manner with a small numerical note about their degree of relevance. By clicking on one of the text segments, its original text document is immediately loaded and the text browser is positioned to the chosen text segment. Additionally, a functionality is integrated to get back to the list of search results.

Presentation of results

Exploration

Combined query

As an additional feature users can induce a combination of the previously described queries. Hence, the system offers the alternative to type in an arbitrary text query by a plain text dialog, in order to search both text segments and views that correlate to the query. To retrieve correlating illustrations and texts, the users' text query is processed by the search engine using both the paragraph index I_P and the view index I_V. The search results are displayed in both the text browser and the 3D model browser as described above. Likewise, the exploration of both representations takes part.

Initiating combined search

Results for both illustrations and text

7.2.3 Interactive Query Refinement

This section presents the facility for the interactive refinement of the initial query for both text ↦ view queries as well as view ↦ text queries. As Section 6.4.6 explained this

Refine initial search

113

technique should be consistent for both search tasks, performable in an intuitive manner, and transparently plugged onto the existing application.

Size for modification of illustrations and text
The dimension *size* has influence on the importance values of both text queries and view queries, i.e., altering the font size of the text and the size of the visible parts in the rendered view may be used for expressing a refined information need. In the following, intuitive techniques are discussed to influence the importance values for specific terms respectively their rendered 3D parts.

Refining text ↦ view queries

Modification of font size
Since the layout is tightly coupled with the relevance of terms (see Section 6.2.3), users are allowed to emphasize or de-emphasize text segments interactively. Text selections in combination with control keys directly increase or decrease the font size of the selection text.

Mapping font size to term weights
Modifying the font size can be used intuitively for expressing the importance of text parts. As described in Section 7.2.2, when users induce a text ↦ view query, the system generates a text descriptor which considers emphasized words with higher importance values. Hence, this influences the weights of the corresponding query terms which may help users to improve the retrieval results, i.e., 3D models and their views.

Watch scene 4–4

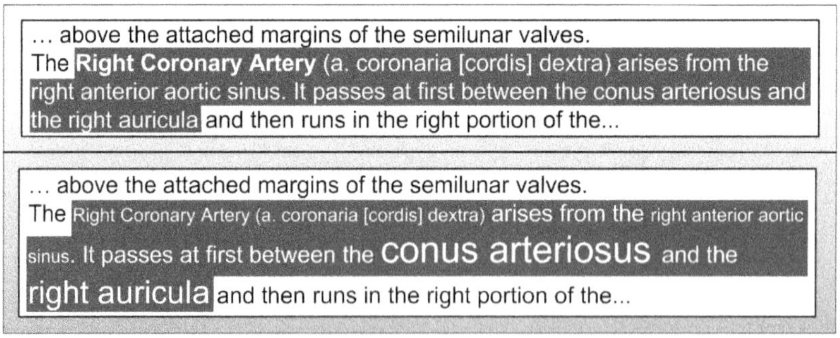

Figure 7.3: Refinement of a text query.

Figure 7.3 presents an example of a refinement to a text query (blue mark). The top part of Figure 7.3 shows the original paragraph as printed in the textbook, a user modified the font size to signal a major interest in some terms (i.e., conus arteriosus) and minor interest in another term (i.e., right coronary artery). Moreover, additional terms can be added to the query.

Refining view ↦ text queries

Modification of 3D parts' size
Analog to the modification of the font sizes for the refinement of text ↦ view queries, the influence of 3D parts in a view ↦ text query can be controlled by the visible size of the rendered 3D parts. Hence, an appropriate technique has to be implemented, which allows to increase respectively decrease the size of the visible 3D parts.

114

Likewise for font sizes of text, magnifying and shrinking 3D parts can be used as an intuitive technique to express the importance of specific 3D parts. When users induce a view
↦ text query, the system analyzes the views' color–coded rendition in order to generate
a view descriptor which is considering the visible 3D part sizes with appropriate importance values (see Section 7.2.2). This directly influences the weights of the query terms
corresponding to the visible 3D parts, and may help to improve the retrieval results, i.e.,
text segments.

Mapping
3D part size
to term weights

In order to magnify respectively shrink rendered 3D parts, an appropriate technique has
to be used. Even though many approaches have been proposed for this task, the majority
can only be applied on predefined focus objects like circles etc. (e.g., [CM01, YCB05]).
However, the technique leveraged should allow to merely modify the size of one 3D part
at a time without influencing the size of neighboring 3D parts. Until now, algorithms
which satisfy this condition for arbitrarily shaped objects (rendered 3D parts) are quite
rare. For general distortions there are powerful approaches, e.g., proposed by KEAHEY
AND ROBERTSON [KR97], however real–time algorithms are not available yet.

Discussion about
technique

Recently, two novel approaches have been developed which allow the magnification of
arbitrarily shaped objects in real time. SPINDLER ET AL. [SBGS06] proposes an approach
in real time using textures. While this technique performs well for simpler geometries,
it cannot be adapted to complex and fine structures (e.g., arteries, tendons or veins).
Another approach proposed by GERMER ET AL. [GGSS06] may use the ID–buffer in
order to control magnifications of arbitrarily shaped objects in real time. The *SpringLens*
algorithm treats images as flexible surfaces which are covered with a grid of particles
connected with springs. By changing the rest lengths of the springs and applying a
physical simulation, the grid is distorted. The particles self–organize, such that the focus
regions are magnified.

Appropriate
approach:
SpringLens

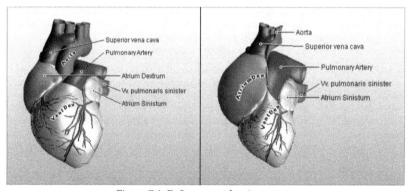

Watch scene
4–5

Figure 7.4: Refinement of a view query.

Figure 7.4 presents an exemplary refinement of a view query (blue mark). The left illustration shows the 3D model from a selected view with its original size. On the right side
the user enlarged some 3D parts (i.e., atrium dextrum) while others were shrunk (i.e.,
aorta). The search results (paragraphs) are affected by these refinements.

115

7.3 User Study

In order to evaluate the concept of correlating illustrations and text, a user study was designed which consisted of two parts. The first part, the low level study, aimed at determining the influence of metrics for the relative size and centricity. The second part, the high level study, tested whether the algorithms used for the determination of good views for given text segments as well as the determination of text segments for given specific views are appropriate. To address the first study, the problem was simplified to a set of eight spheres that were spatially arranged in a cubical manner. Some of the spheres were important (green colored), whereas the remaining spheres were not important (gray colored). By rotating this 3D arrangement, it was possible to derive several configurations, covering visibility and centricity problems. The second study used a well–known spatial object (car) and applied the proposed algorithms in order to either derive a set of good views for a specified textual description or good textual descriptions for a specified view.

Combination of low and high level study

7.3.1 Method

Subjects and design. The test was designed in three different languages (Catalan, English, and German); the user study was carried out with 115 subjects. The subjects (47 female, 68 male) were subdivided into one test group g_1 (76 participants) without prior knowledge of 3D software (e.g., 3D games, 3D modeling software), and one test group g_2 (39 participants) with knowledge in that field. Both test groups had to solve the same blind tests.

Materials and apparatus. The user study consisted of 12 single tests, where the subjects had to choose one out of three alternatives. The test was presented in a printable document, but could also be performed on a computer monitor. The users were also asked if they had problems in understanding the test or recognizing the illustrations. Thus, those results were excluded from the study to remove distortion by uncertainty.

The first part p_1 of the study consisted of six single tests (t_1–t_6). In order to avoid distortions, the tests were extremely simplified and presented eight cubically arranged spheres. It evaluated, which criteria (relative size or centricity) humans consider as su-

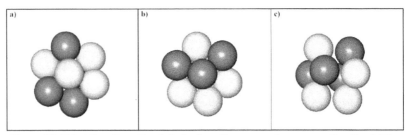

Figure 7.5: Select the alternative (a,b,c) where the green spheres are optimally visible.

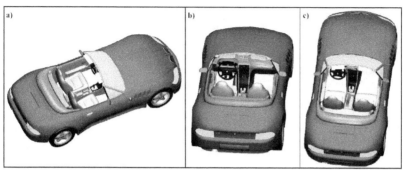

Figure 7.6: Which view (a,b,c) shows the optimal visibility of the *steering wheel*, the *gearshift lever*, and the *center console*?

perior for a 'good view' and to which level. To determine the three alternatives, the measures of visible relative size and centricity were used as described in Section 6. The users had to select the view they preferred in terms of visibility (see Figure 7.5).

The second part p_2 consisted of another six tests (t_7–t_{12}) for the investigation of text↔illustration correlations with a well–known spatial object. Since the approach was designed for tutoring purposes in general (i.e., in the fields of medical, natural science, engineering etc.) a model of a BMW Z3 car was chosen, since most subjects know its interior parts by its denomination. The tests (t_7–t_9) assessed, whether the approach algorithmically determines the same views users would select for a given text (see Figure 7.6). In the tests (t_{10}–t_{12}) users were presented a specific view of the car and they had to select one of three alternative textual descriptions in order to find out if the proposed algorithm correlates with the users selections (see Figure 7.7).

Procedure. A short preliminary user test with two subjects (excluded from the user study), followed by a short interview about their decisions, revealed minor problems in understanding the tests. Their choices of views were distorted by a preference of several

| a) Rear lights, Center console, Mirrors |
| b) Rear lights, Door, Leather seats |
| c) Rear lights, Mirrors, Wind shield |

Figure 7.7: Which text (a,b,c) describes the visible parts of the illustration most appropriate?

spatial arrangements (i.e., canonical views [PRC81]), which negatively influenced the visibility. Thus, a note was included in the user study, remarking that the focus of the test is on the visibility of the important parts.

7.3.2   Results and Discussion

Scoring. In the tests t_1–t_6, the value of both measures (visible relative size and centricity) was calculated. Since users chose one favored alternative, is was possible to determine whether the results of both measures corresponded to the preferences of users.

In the tests t_7–t_9 100 views of the car model were indexed. Then, the system was queried by two respectively three technical terms of well–known car components (e.g., steering wheel, leather seats). The top scored results, together with two lower scored results, were presented to the user in a random order. In the tests t_{10}–t_{12}, three different descriptions (each with two or three technical terms of well–known car components) were indexed and queried the system with a specific view of the car, in order to find out which description optimally fits to the illustration. The top scored and the lower scored descriptions were presented to the user in a random order.

Hypothesis 1: Subjects with knowledge of 3D software select different illustrations than those without.
Since the approach is based on 3D models, first it was determined if participants with knowledge of 3D software (3D modeling, 3D games etc.) have different preferences in the selection of 3D views than those without. The majority of the subjects of both groups g_1 and g_2 chose the same alternatives. The *One-Way ANOVA (Analysis of variance)* method was applied in order to obtain evidence if at least the percentages for each selection differ significantly. Statistical significance cannot be considered with a result of $p \geq 0.05$. The ANOVA neither determined a significant difference for p_1 (F=0.062, p=0.808) nor for p_2 (F=0.278, p=0.610). In the following, the groups g_1 and g_2 were merged to group G.

Hypothesis 2: Relative visible size is more important than centricity.
The tests t_1–t_6 aimed at determining the influence of both measures *relative visible size m_1* and *centricity m_2* (see Figure 7.8). The χ^2–test was used, since 115 subjects contributed to the user study and each of the tests had three alternatives—there was an expected

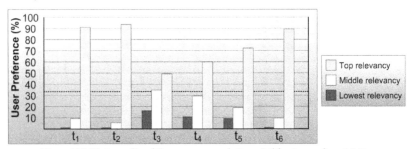

Figure 7.8: Test results of the measures relative visible size and centricity.

frequency of 38.333 of choosing an alternative. For statistical significance χ^2 has to be ≥ 5.99 ($\alpha = 0.05$).

In order to test m_1, t_1 and t_2 equalized m_2 of the important parts, while m_1 differed. There was a strong significance for m_1 ($t_1 : \chi^2 = 169.793$ and $t_2 : \chi^2 = 184.976$). In t_1 90.43% chose the alternative with highest value for m_1, while 93.04% did for t_2.

For testing m_2, the tests t_3 and t_4 equalized m_1 of the important parts, while m_2 differed. There was a significance for m_2 ($t_3 : \chi^2 = 17.965$ and $t_4 : \chi^2 = 40.192$). In t_3 only 48.7% chose the alternative with highest value for m_2, while 59.13% did for t_4. Thus, m_2 is significant, but seems to be much less important than m_1. Finally, t_5 and t_6 tested m_1 and m_2 against each other. m_1 had a higher support (t_5: 73.04% and t_6: 88.70%) than m_2 (t_5: 19.13% and t_6: 9.57%), while the remaining subjects chose the alternative where neither m_1 nor m_2 was maximized (t_5: 7.83% and t_6: 1.74%). As assumed, relative visible size was clearly more important than centricity. Thus, the following tests were carried out with an unequal weight on both measures m_1 and m_2 (5:1).

Hypothesis 3: The approach presents desired views for a given paragraph.
In the tests t_7–t_9 a set of common technical terms of the car was presented and showed three alternative views of the car. Users had to select the one where the named parts were optimally visible. The higher the computed relevance of the algorithm, the more users preferred the view (see Figure 7.9–left). Most of the subjects chose the highest ranked alternative (t_7: 86.09%, t_8: 84.35%, t_9: 89.57%). At a relevance of less than 0.8 only a few subjects preferred the view, but with a relevance larger than 0.8 the preference increased exponentially. Thus, this seems to be a rough measure for a cutoff of retrieval results.

Hypothesis 4: The approach presents desired paragraphs for a given view.
In the tests t_{10}–t_{12} an illustration of a car was presented and showed three alternatives with multiple common technical terms of the car. The subjects had to choose the alternative that optimally describes the illustration. Like in the previous test, the higher the computed relevance of the algorithm, the more users preferred the view (see Figure 7.9–right). Most subjects chose the highest ranked alternative (t_{10}: 100.00%, t_{11}: 95.65%, t_{12}: 95.65%). Again, a cutoff of 0.8 for the relevance of retrieval results seems to be a rough measure.

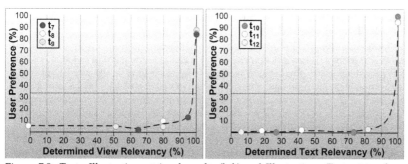

Figure 7.9: Text$\mapsto$Illustration retrieval results (left) and Illustration$\mapsto$Text retrieval results (right).

Discussion.
First, the study gave evidence that there was no difference in the preference of 3D views for subjects with or without prior 3D knowledge. Both, the tests for the relative visible size and the centricity were significant, while the relative visible size is much more preferred than the centricity. In the tests for text $\mapsto$ illustration queries as well as illustration $\mapsto$ text queries, the relevance determined by the algorithm correlated with users' preferences. In each of the tests more than 80% of the subjects chose the top ranked view. Since with a relevance value less than 0.8—only few subjects chose the view, this value seems to be a good measure for a cutoff of the retrieval results.

7.4 Discussion

Other levels of granularity The very efficient indexing mechanism of vector–based search engines permits the access to an almost unlimited number of documents. In this approach, content descriptions are constructed for all paragraphs within voluminous tutoring documents and for a user–selected number of views onto a library of 3D models. User evaluations have to analyze whether a finer level of granularity (e.g., sentences) in the representation of the textual content or more view descriptors could be advantageous.

Multiple annotations The text retrieval system determines similarities of the query with the documents stored in the search index by constructing document vectors of their terms. Despite the indexed terms are simplified (stemming) as well as fuzzy searches can be performed, the terms of the query and the documents have to correspond to a certain degree. Applied to this system, this means that annotations used for the 3D parts have to correspond to those terms used in the expository texts. For some applications this does not constitute a problem, e.g., in the medical domain a standardized terminology of Greek and Latin terms exists for the denomination of organs, and in the technical domain, 3D parts are usually annotated with unique part identifiers. However, in some cases objects may have multiple different denominations. In this case, the 3D parts should be annotated with multiple denominations (e.g., in different languages). This strategy would allow to integrate interactive 3D visualizations into a multi–lingual tutoring environment based on translated documents or completely different documents for all languages. Alternatively, specialized thesauri could be employed to expand the query by similar terms in order to improve the search results (see e.g., [QF93]).

Multi–word terms Furthermore, multi–word terms are another challenging problem for information retrieval approaches. When a document vector is created of a query or a document, the text is segmented into single–word terms. Hence, instead of multi–word terms only their components are represented in the document vectors, which may cause suboptimal search results. To cope with this problem, two solutions could be considered for this approach in future work. On the one hand, automated text mining techniques could be used for the detection of the multi–word term boundaries (e.g., [FAM00, KN04]). On the other hand, the corpus of the 3D models' annotations constitutes a rich dictionary of (single– and multi–word) technical terms. Each technical term of the whole corpus of annotated 3D models could be collected and used with the corpus of text documents, in order to extract the complete technical terms used in there.

Other researchers proposed additional measures for the evaluation of the quality of a view (e.g., [MNTP07]). Since neither formal comparisons have been performed, nor significant evaluation results of their impact on specific tasks in learning environments have been been achieved yet, it remains unclear whether these measures improve the quality of the retrieval results. Therefore, additional user studies should be designed in order to determine the impact of different view descriptors for both search tasks by relating the content presented within multi–modal tutoring systems. Moreover, the field of view selection for 3D models is a relatively new and rapidly developing field of research—new measures could be integrated and compared to the results of this user study.

Additional measures for good views

The user study evaluated the statements of the concept of correlating illustrations in general using well–known 3D models. In order to determine domain–specific requirements, professional subjects (e.g., medical students) could be introduced to the system and asked for further ideas to improve the application for the specialized domain. Furthermore, using domain experts would enable to test a future implementation of relevance feedback techniques (as proposed in Section 6.4.6) and to assess the expected improvement of search results.

Evaluating with domain experts

7.5 Conclusion

The second part of this book proposed a novel approach for the support of learners in the interactive exploration of comprehensive multi–modal tutoring material. As a proof of concept, this chapter applied the approach to the domain of medical education. However, as the concept is developed for being applied in general, it could also be applied to other specific domains.

Chapter survey

Furthermore, the experimental application pointed out that the annotation approach developed in the first part of this book as well as the constitutive contextual annotation technique are pre–requirements to the concept of correlating illustrations and text. Thus, the annotated exploration of 3D models correlating with the expository text can be used in addition to the static illustrations used in books.

Annotation as requirement

Finally, an extensive user study with 115 participants has been performed. The first part of the study significantly demonstrated the appropriateness the measures used for this approach and raised additional information about the adjustment of the algorithms. The second part gave evidence that the overall approach can be used to support users with the search tasks between illustrations and text. The majority of users chose the same views on 3D models to a given text segment, and they chose the same text segments to a given view of a 3D model.

User study

The following Chapter 8 finally concludes this thesis, addresses some points of criticism, and offers suggestions for future developments.

8 Concluding Considerations

This chapter summarizes the achievements of this work through a number of central statements, reflects them by critical remarks, addresses open questions and provides ideas about future directions of research.

8.1 Theses

Annotations as Bidirectional Link

Educational books usually complement expository texts with illustrations in order to support the learner's comprehension of complex spatial objects. For that reason, book authors often collaborate with illustrators who carefully adapt their depictions to the semantic focus of the text segments. In order to improve the link between expository texts and the illustrations, annotations can be used. Typically, annotations like figure captions refer to the whole illustration while internal and external annotations establish the bidirectional link between individual parts of the illustration and their technical terms.

1st Thesis. Annotations play an important role in visually associating technical terms used in expository texts with their corresponding parts in the illustrations.

Illustration Layers

The design of illustrations is an iterative process. According to SOUSA [Sou03], there are multiple stages in which illustrators communicate with the book author. In the last stage illustrators determine an appropriate layout for the annotations belonging to the individual parts of the illustration. To do so, they utilize different information about the illustration, such as the depiction of the spatial object itself, its segmentation and the remaining space on its background. These components can be described by a layered model in order to allow the automatic adaptation of the annotation layout process.

2nd Thesis. A layered model can be facilitated to describe the individual components used by illustrators for the determination of annotation layouts.

Annotation Types

The first part of this book starts with an extensive analysis of annotations in illustrations. Based on the most common annotation types determined in the corpus, it describes their prevalent representatives. In order to allow the development of an automated annotation approach, their layout specific parameters are determined. Finally, this enables to group the annotation types into three different layout containers which share their layout requirements.

3rd Thesis. The annotation types in illustrations can be classified into different types, whose layout necessities can be handled by three different containers.

Annotation Styles

The analysis of the annotations used in illustrations revealed that instead of a single dominant layout style, human illustrators use a wide variety of different styles for each different annotation type. These styles are influenced by functional and esthetic requirements as well as subjective preferences. In order to develop a framework which allows to define multiple annotation styles, a set of frequently used layout parameters was identified for each layout container.

4th Thesis. Human illustrators use multiple annotation styles, which should be supported by an annotation approach.

Specifications

In literature there are no definite rules for the annotation of spatial objects' illustrations. In fact, there is a multitude of different considerations which may conflict with each other and influence the illustrator's complex task to determine an appropriate annotation layout. The informal guidelines of human illustrators had to be carefully straightened to specifications in order to allow an automated annotation approach which approximates the most common annotation styles of human illustrators.

5th Thesis. Illustrators use different partially conflicting considerations in order to determine an appropriate annotation layout.

Annotation Metrics

Based on the specifications constituted from the illustrators' guidelines, metrics can be deduced in order to evaluate the quality of computed annotation layouts. By weighting the metrics' influence, task– and user–specific preferences can be realized.

6th Thesis. By weighting the influence of metrics for the evaluation of computed annotation layouts, individual preferences can be defined.

Applicability

In order to make the annotation approach applicable to different types of 3D models as well as different target applications, a narrow interface can be facilitated between the applications for the visualization of 3D models and the annotation approach itself. The application's supply of both the primary object layer (frame–buffer) and the segmentation layer (ID–buffer) is sufficient to allow the computation of defined annotation layouts for visible 3D model parts.

7th Thesis. By providing the primary object layer and the segmentation layer, defined annotation layouts can be computed for different types of 3D models and target applications.

Real–time Layout

Since multiple metrics are based on distance functions, an initial distance transformation on the ID–buffer builds the foundation for the container layout algorithms. In order to enable a real–time layout, several heuristics have to be applied. First of all, the search space has to be reduced to a set of possible layout candidates. Using the weighted metrics, the placement of the individual layout containers can be evaluated.

8th Thesis.   A real–time annotation layout can be determined by reducing the search space and the application of heuristic methods based on a pre–computed distance field.

Frame Coherence of Layout Elements

During the exploration of the 3D models, the user interaction may cause severe changes in the annotation layout. However, in order not to divert viewers, these changes should be minimal and the layout elements should neither be hidden nor pop in and out at completely different positions. Hence, techniques have to be facilitated which ensure smooth (frame coherent) transitions of the annotations, while considering the influence of other metrics.

9th Thesis.   The interaction of users with 3D models may cause changes in the annotation layout which have to be minimized by appropriate strategies.

Interactive versus Static Layout

Frame coherence of layout elements may be beneficial for the interactive exploration of 3D models. However, the quality of annotation layouts suffers from coherence techniques, such as annotation agents, since they minimize the flow of secondary elements by merely considering local improvements of their placement. Hence, annotation layouts intended to serve for static illustrations should be computed by neglecting coherence techniques.

10th Thesis.   Frame coherence of layout elements is beneficial for interactive applications but should be refrained from the annotation of static illustrations.

Adaptivity

Internal annotations are accommodated on a different layout space than external annotations and annotation boxes. Due to the user interaction, one of the two disjoint layout spaces may become very limited or even vanish. However, in return, this expands the available area of the other layout space. Hence, the annotation approach should allow multiple types of annotations in order to take advantage of this fact and to optimally use possibilities to accommodate annotations.

11th Thesis.   In order to cope with the varying layout space of internal and external annotations by user interactions, the annotation approach should adapt their annotation type.

125

Search Time

Due to the publishing costs, illustrators are often forced to design illustrations which cover multiple text segments describing different contexts of an object. Amongst others, this constraint involves a high number of annotations. Unfortunately, larger quantities of annotations may increase the time that users need to locate a specific part of an illustration which is referred by its annotation.

12th Thesis. Larger quantities of annotations may increase the time that users need to locate their referred parts of illustrations.

Grouped and Exclusive Annotation

Since interactive annotation approaches can determine individual annotation layouts by user requests, the limitations of publishing costs faced by book illustrators, are not given. Based on taxonomies built by domain experts, parts of 3D models which are relevant in a certain context can be organized into contextual groups. In order to visualize these contexts, two different concepts can be applied, i.e., for multiple contexts, an annotation grouping technique supports the user, whereas an exclusive annotation technique focuses on a single context. Both techniques can reduce the time that users need in order to locate the referred parts of an illustration for given contexts.

13th Thesis. Corresponding to given contexts, both grouped and exclusive annotation can reduce the time users need to locate referred parts of illustrations.

Annotation as Emphasis Technique

Besides the use of graphical abstraction techniques, annotations themselves can be used to focus the viewer's attention to specific 3D parts. Through the exclusive annotation of those 3D parts, which are relevant in a given context, the viewer's attention may be focused on these parts, without the necessity of additional graphical abstraction techniques.

14th Thesis. Exclusive annotation may be used as an emphasis technique.

Complementary Use of Illustrations and Text

The complementary use of expository text and illustrations in educational textbooks entails the problem of search tasks between both representations. One search task arises when users are reading a text segment and have to find the corresponding illustration and its parts which correspond to the terms described in the text. Another search task occurs when the users are interested in certain parts of an illustration and have to find corresponding text segments which describe these parts.

15th Thesis. Learners are faced with search tasks when reading educational textbooks with complementary use of illustrations and text.

Correlation of Views and Text Segments

Book authors and illustrators carefully coordinate the usage of expository texts and illustrations of educational textbooks. For both of the search tasks, contexts may be defined, i.e., a certain set of terms (expository text) or a set of visible parts (illustration). In order to automatically match the contexts of both media, they must be comparable. The crucial step is to sample multiple text segments and 3D model views in order to describe them by the same representation. Using these descriptors, the similarity of the contexts between both media can be determined in order to support the search tasks.

16th Thesis. By describing text and illustrations through the same representations, their similarity can be determined.

Textual Description of 3D Views

While textual descriptors of text segments can be generated by a text parser, textual descriptors of 3D models' views can be generated by their formal annotations. Hence, an analysis of the 3D models' segmented rendition reveals which 3D parts are visible in the view, which enables annotations to be used in order to generate a textual descriptor.

17th Thesis. Formal annotations of 3D models may be used to automatically generate textual descriptions of the visible parts of rendered 3D models.

Information Retrieval to Support Search Tasks

Information retrieval methods such as the vector space model constitute a good platform to perform mutual search tasks. This method transforms the textual descriptors of both media into an internal representation which allows for efficiently determining their similarities. If the users select a context of interest of the one media (i.e., a text segment respectively a 3D model's view), another textual descriptor is generated. This query descriptor may be used to determine the most similar descriptors of the other media stored in the internal representation.

18th Thesis. The search tasks can be supported by the use of information retrieval techniques.

Interactive Search Refinement

The user's information needs cannot always be optimally described by a chosen text segment or a chosen view. However, by emphasizing and deemphasizing particular terms in the text or visible parts of the 3D model, users may adjust their information need.

19th Thesis. Users may be supported with both search tasks by interactive techniques for the refinement of their search request.

Association between Illustrations and Expository Text

Educational textbooks which complement expository texts with illustrations may use annotations in order to allow the user to associate terms addressed in the expository text with the visible parts of illustrations. Likewise, in order to support the search tasks, the concept of correlating illustrations and text requires an annotation approach which allows the interactive visualization of 3D models.

20th Thesis. The encapsulated annotation approach is an important requirement for applications using the concept of correlating illustrations and text.

127

8.2 Critical remarks

The encapsulated annotation approach is intended to annotate 3D models which are interactively visualized by the world–in–hand metaphor (cf. Chapter 2). Due to its narrow interfaces (see Section 4.3), this approach might also be applied towards the annotation of different applications. However, other fields of annotation (e.g., charts, tables, maps, information visualization) may have different specifications and annotation layouts. Regardless it is possible to apply this approach to these applications with several constraints; it might not generate optimal results unless problem–specific adaptations are made.

Focus on illustrations

The annotation layouts generated by this approach may not reproduce each subjective esthetic consideration of human illustrators. However, it was not the objective of this book to replace human illustrators in the task of annotating, but to technically allow to generate similar annotation layouts at interactive rates in order to support the exploration of 3D models. Because of this no comparison or user study was performed about the effectiveness of the interactively annotated 3D models in terms of esthetic and communicative goals. Likewise, the concept of correlating illustrations and text was intended to support the learning process of students. This means that this approach should be used in combination with traditional textbooks, instead of replacing these sophisticated learning tools.

Joint use with educational books

8.3 Future Directions

Besides the technical improvements discussed for the encapsulated annotation approach (Section 4.5) and the concept of correlating illustrations and text (Section 7.4), this section addresses future directions of research.

Improvements

The bottleneck of the encapsulated annotation approach is the computation of the distance field based on the ID–buffer. In order to meet real–time constraints, some compromises regarding its resolution have to be made. In future work, novel techniques could be employed in order to achieve a faster computation of the distance field (e.g., by the support of standard graphics hardware). Through comparing the different resolutions of the distance field by annotation metrics it would be possible to evaluate potential improvements of the annotation layout.

Bottleneck distance buffer

Recently, a rather promising approach for the annotation of 2D images has been proposed by VOLLICK ET AL. [VVAH07]. This approach describes annotation layouts as energy functions to be minimized. In order to obtain suitable parameters for different annotation metrics, a learning algorithm tunes them according to annotation layouts manually defined by example. However, the approach does not meet several specifications for the interactive exploration of 3D models and only considers external annotations. By combining this approach with the annotation approach developed in the first part of this book both works could benefit from each other. Especially the technique

Learning of layout parameters

to learn different layout parameters could be used in order to intuitively define layout styles and the specifications' weights for the interactive exploration of 3D models.

In order to visualize contexts of 3D models it could be desirable to annotate even hidden parts of the primary object, e.g., in order to indicate their location in the 3D model. This is unusual for static illustrations in books, but could be used to guide the navigation of the user to specific parts of the 3D model. The developed annotation approach does not consider the annotation of hidden 3D parts, but in future work the suitability of annotations for supporting the contextual exploration of 3D models could be evaluated.

Annotation of hidden parts

The concept of correlating illustrations and text proposes a contextual annotation layout in order to highlight the relevance of 3D parts. Moreover, the rendering engine of the experimental application employs semi–transparency in order to focus the attention of the user to the most salient visual parts in result of a text↦illustration query. In future works, more elaborate illustration techniques could be integrated, such as cut–aways, ghosting, adjusted lighting, or NPR rendering styles which were proposed for interactive 3D visualizations of surface (e.g., [HIR+03, KD05]) and voxel models (e.g., [DWE02, VFSG06]).

Extended context visualization

Especially an approach of LI ET AL. [LRA+07] seems to be promising since it aims at applying dynamic cutaway views in order to support the comprehension of complex 3D models and to ensure the visibility of their 3D parts. Hence, these contextualized cutaway views could be combined with the techniques for determining good views on relevant parts of the 3D models. However, this approach could not only be useful for the contextualized presentation of 3D models, but also for the concept of correlating illustrations and text. Their approach additionally proposes an interactive authoring tool for intuitively defining cutaway views. Hence, this could also be used to refine view↦text queries (see Section 7.2.3). By interactively cutting unimportant parts, the queries for corresponding text segments could be focused on relevant parts. Finally, a user study could reveal whether the cutaway technique outperforms the query refinement by magnification, or if a combination of both techniques is promising.

Improved presentation

Improved query refinement

Even 3D animations consisting of cyclic sequences of slightly different 3D models can be explored by interactive applications. By adapting the encapsulated annotation approach to additional specifications, those 3D animations can be annotated (see Appendix A). Additionally, those animated 3D models can also be integrated into the concept of correlating illustrations and text. In future work, the learning benefit of the enhancement by 3D animations (e.g., a beating heart or a working cycle of a combustion motor) could be evaluated by a user study.

Animated 3D models

Applications

Since the concept of correlating illustrations and text is expandable, users or domain experts can easily add new text documents or 3D models. Besides a batch processing index creation, the support of more file formats, drag&drop mechanisms, or a plug–in to import data from a web browser could improve the user interface. Medical tutoring systems might benefit from expressive renditions of volumetric datasets in addition to or in combination with renditions of polygonal models. Especially the visible human

Integration of voxel models

dataset [Nat] has been exhaustively annotated. Hence, this dataset is very attractive for a tutoring application. Several approaches deal with the visualization of volumetric data in real time (e.g., [VKG04, BG05]). Since the algorithms proposed for both the application of the concept of correlating illustrations and text as well as the encapsulated annotation approach consequently work in image space, those visualization approaches for volumetric data could be integrated nearly seamlessly.

Application to augmented reality
The encapsulated annotation approach is independent of the type of 3D models used and the individual interactive application. For the specified layout of the annotations, merely the rendered rendition (frame–buffer) as well as segmentation information (ID–buffer) is required. Combined with tracking techniques this approach could be used for augmented reality purposes, i.e., real existing objects could be explored whereas the annotation layout would be computed in order to augment the user's view. This approach could be applied in the education of students in the fields of medicine or engineering. The annotations could support the identification of parts while segmenting or assembling a real existing object like a torso of the human body, an engine, or technical device.

Abstraction

Systematization of metrics
Finally, there is no general approach for the annotation of arbitrary images. Applications in different fields have differing specifications that have to be attentively determined in order to develop problem–oriented solutions. Hence, as a perspective, the annotation types and styles of other fields (e.g., Maps, Geographic Visualization, Information Visualization, Information Graphics) could be investigated and their specifications as well as their metrics could be derived. Finally, consistencies and individualities of the specifications of multiple fields could be determined in order to find more general annotation metrics. Hence, a framework of metrics could help to systematize the evaluation of annotation layouts. A hierarchical structure of metrics could build the basis for the construction of a general approach and possibly help to improve the performance of individual annotation tasks by synergy effects.

A	# Annotation of Animated 3D Models

A.1 Introduction

This appendix presents an optional extension based on the encapsulated annotation approach developed in the first part of this thesis. In order not to disrupt the argumentative flow, it has been postponed to this appendix. It addresses the usefulness of the interactive exploration of animated 3D models in combination with the advantage of annotated illustrations. Additionally, this appendix suggests a possibility to integrate animated 3D models into the concept of correlating illustrations and text introduced in the second part of this thesis.

Extension to both parts of the thesis

The following sections introduce the underlying issue (Section A.2), define specifications for the annotation of animated 3D models and identify necessary adaptations to existing approaches (Section A.3). An experimental application exemplifies the practicability of the developed techniques, followed by the discussion of the achievements. Subsequently, the central statements are evaluated by a user study (Section A.4), whereas Section A.5 concludes this appendix.

Chapter overview

A.2 Problem Analysis

Educational books may not only comprise descriptions and explanations of static objects, but also of dynamic processes. Usually, such dynamic processes are described by instructive texts [Bal97]. However, illustrations may support the textual explanations. In order to indicate dynamic processes, these illustrations may facilitate additional secondary elements, i.e., arrows can be used to clarify the movements of the primary objects' parts (see Figure A.1).

According to PALMITER AND ELKERTON [PE93] animations may support the understanding of learners. They compared the learning benefit of instructions presented by text to those presented by animated demonstrations. During the training process, compared to the text–only group users of the animation group were faster and more accurate in recalling the procedures. However, some researchers criticize that animations do not necessarily support learners. Hence, a small set of static illustrations may not be sufficient for the narration of animations. TVERSKY ET AL. [BT02] challenged the benefit of illustrated animations in printed material and mentioned: 'The information that might be more effectively portrayed in an

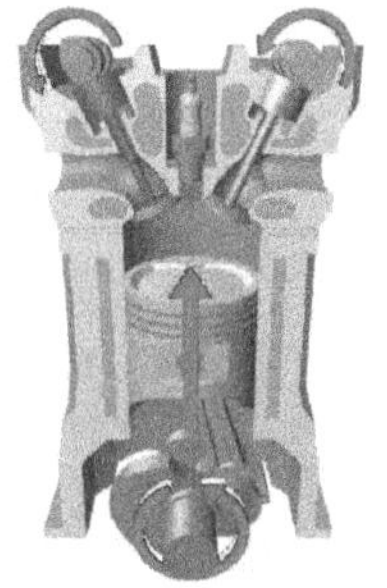

Figure A.1: Working combustion engine. (Source: [Pie])

Arrows may indicate movements

Animations may improve understanding

Exact movements should be indicated

Annotation is important

animated graphic might include the qualitative aspects of motion or the microsteps, the exact sequence and timing of complex operations.' However, MAYER ET AL. [MHMC05] compared annotated illustrations with narrated animation for multimedia instruction and found out that in 50% of the tests annotated illustrations outperformed computer–based animations. Hence, it would be desirable to combine the animations of objects with the possibility of an annotated exploration.

Animation as a cyclic sequence

Many processes can be explained by a cyclic sequence of slightly different 3D models (e.g., pumping of a heart or a work cycle of a combustion engine), which can be modeled by standard software. Likewise, interactive 3D browsers allow to explore the animated 3D models. However, existing 3D annotation approaches (cf. Chapter 3) are not capable of those animations, because they only consider changes in the presentation of 3D models induced by user interactions and are therefore not able to stabilize annotations throughout continual animations. Hence, they either conflict with the *unambiguity* specification induced by a static placement of the secondary elements or they conflict with the *legibility* and *frame coherence* specification through their perpetual restlessness. Additionally, those approaches neither analyze the trajectories of the 3D parts throughout the animation sequence nor they provide techniques and secondary elements to indicate them.

Conventional approaches are not capable

Video–based techniques

For the purpose of annotating video streams, the flow of visual elements is often analyzed by image processing techniques. These algorithms either determine trajectories of moving elements or evaluate the potential of regions to accommodate annotations. YAN ET AL. [YKCK06] developed several tracking algorithms to detect a moving ball in tennis matches in order to display trajectories on selected (key) frames. GOLDMAN ET AL. [GCSS06] analyzed trajectories of moving objects to generate storyboards from video streams automatically. THANEDAR AND HÖLLERER [TH04] employed a uniform grid to determine so–called *calm* and *dormant* regions. ROSTEN ET AL. [RRD05] used a feature density operator based on pixel intensity values to determine positions and regions of low visual interest in an augmented reality scenario.

Differing challenges

The major challenge of these video–based approaches is the segmentation of the video streams' frames into foreground and background and the evaluation of regions in order to find good placements for annotations. Whereas there is the possibility for 3D models to compute ID–buffers that offer the segmentation without substantial computational effort. Furthermore, as the video analysis techniques cannot exploit semantic information, they do not have any constraints on the layout of the annotations. Moreover, none of those approaches considers coherence aspects. Hence, the demands of video–based annotation considerably differ from those for the annotation of 3D models.

A.3 Approach

Cyclic sequence of 3D models

In order to comply with the specifications for a functional and esthetic annotation layout, this approach bases on the encapsulated annotation approach (cf. Chapter 4). Instead of a single 3D model, a finite set of slightly different 3D models which approximate movements of their 3D parts serves as input. This *3D animation* is presented frame by frame in a cyclic sequence while the user may explore these 3D models. According to the world–in–hand metaphor (cf. Chapter 2), user interactions define camera parameters and view transformations, which are not only applied for the 3D model of the current frame, but for all 3D models of the cyclic sequence.

In the original annotation approach the segmentation of the 3D parts' projections is based on an ID–buffer (cf. Chapter 4). In contrast to this, for this issue an ID–buffer for each frame of the animation sequence is rendered in the background. These ID–buffers can be used to determine *calm regions*, i.e., positions on the view–plane which do not change during the whole animation. These calm regions can be used by the original annotation approach. If a 3D part that has to be annotated does not offer calm regions for the accommodation of the annotation, trajectories (*animation paths*) of the 3D part's movements are determined that can be annotated.

Calm regions

Animation paths

In the following, the additional requirements for the annotation of animated 3D models are illustrated by examples. Subsequently, both the strategy for the determination of calm regions in animated 3D scenes is described and the novel approach for the visualization of animation paths of moving 3D parts in animation is presented.

A.3.1 Necessary Adaptations to the Layout Approach

Conventional coherence strategies for the annotation of interactive 3D visualizations are not sufficient for the annotation of 3D animations. In order to motivate new functional requirements and heuristics to implement them, the initial observations are briefly summarized:

Initial observations

Moving Text. As introduced in Chapter 3, internal annotations should be placed on salient regions of the referred part and should not overlap the remaining parts, whereas external annotation texts should be placed as near as possible to their referred parts (*unambiguity*). For considering this specification the annotation texts could continuously move with the 3D parts (see Figure A.2). However, this strategy would massively decrease their *legibility* and *frame coherence*.

(a) Moving internal text.   (b) Fixed external text, moving reference line.

Figure A.2: Problems induced by moving secondary elements.

Moving Reference Line. In learning material the majority of annotated illustrations employs external annotations. As an alternative strategy the annotation texts of external annotations could be fixed to a certain location. However, since the 3D parts are moving, this fixation could violate the claim not to overlap the primary object. Additionally, the reference lines have to connect the annotations text with salient regions of the part of the illustration they refer to. Hence, they would be affected by the continuous movement of the 3D parts that would violate the claim not to intersect themselves (*legibility*) and their unsteady appearance possibly could divert the viewer (*frame coherence*).

In contrast to unpredictable effects of user interactions to the spatial arrangement of foreground elements on the projection, these considerations should be taken into account for the annotation of pre–defined animations. The methods introduced in the following aim at achieving a layout of secondary elements according to the annotation specifications for *all* frames of an animation. The first layout method proposed makes use of spatial coherence within animations, i.e., it is based on the assumption that 3D parts move only slightly on the view–plane. Therefore, there are areas that belong to a single 3D part during the entire animation. These *calm regions*, which are not affected by the animation are determined and used with the strategies of the original encapsulated annotation approach developed in Chapter 4.

A.3.2 Determination of Calm Regions

Multiple ID–buffers

Unlike in the original annotation approach, this method does not only determine the ID–buffer of the current 3D model projected on the viewplane, but of each 3D model of the sequence according to the given camera position. Those regions where the color–ID values do not change throughout all frames of the animation can be considered as

Calm means IDs do not change

calm and used for annotation (see Figure A.3). By applying a simple AND operation on the captured ID–buffers, another G–buffer is created. In contrast, zero values in that G–buffer indicate *fluctuating regions* where annotations should not be placed.

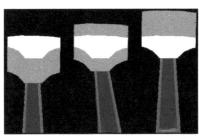 

(a) The uniform gray region denotes the ID of the piston, white areas designate calm regions.

(b) A 3D part without calm regions.

Figure A.3: Detection of calm areas.

Discussion

By neglecting these fluctuating regions the encapsulated annotation approach determines a layout for the secondary elements. However, for 3D parts that move extensively, calm regions can be very small or even they may not exist at all. In these cases, another strategy for the annotation of those parts has to be found. In the next step the movement of the 3D parts is determined and visualized.

A.3.3 Analysis of the 3D Parts' Movements

The analysis of the 3D parts' movements in animations is simplified by abstracting the parts' locations by points. These points should be placed unambiguously, i.e., viewers should easily determine the referred part of annotations. Therefore, the mid–point is determined on salient regions of the referred part. Two methods were compared in order to determine the midst position for complex–shaped 3D parts (3D shape approximations via bounding boxes and distance transformations of the projected 3D parts, see Table A.1) with respect to their *exactness*,[1] *performance*, and the *coherence* of their results within subsequent frames of an animation.

3D part locations

Method	Exact	Outliers	Performance	Coherence
Distance transformation	yes	no	slow	jumps
Bounding box	no	possible	fast	coherent

Table A.1: Comparison of two alternative methods for the determination of the midpoint of complex–shaped 3D parts.

Distance transformations. For interactive applications it is too time–consuming to compute distance transformations for all ID–buffers associated with the frames of an animation. Down–sampled ID–buffers ease this problem, but possible incoherences between the results in subsequent frames disqualify that technique for its application.

Shape approximations by bounding boxes. For complex–shaped 3D parts, the bounding box center may not lie within the projected area of the referred part and thus can produce invalid animation paths. An additional check of the ID–buffer whether the center point of the bounding box is an outlier easily manages this problem. If the determined point is an outlier, the bounding box can be hierarchically subdivided until one segment is not an outlier any more.

Method	# resulting points	Curvature control
Point averaging routines	fixed	bad
Mathematical curve fitting routines	variable	good
Tolerancing routines	some are fixed	bad

Table A.2: Comparison of line smoothing methods.

In a second step the midpoints of moving 3D parts within the frames of an animation are connected. These trajectories are smoothed in order to achieve an esthetic appearance such as those arrows in hand–made illustrations. Several line smoothing algorithms were evaluated with respect to the requirements of this application. Table A.2 shows the number of *resulting points* and the influence about the *curvature* according to the classification of MCMASTER AND SHEA [MS92].

Line smoothing

Large changes in the position of a 3D part in subsequent frames of an animation frame would produce long line segments and a rough appearance of the animation path, thus point averaging routines (e.g., median) are not sufficient in this application. Tolerancing routines cannot be used since they smooth lines by eliminating points within a given

---

[1]*Outliers* denote proposed mid–points that are actually not contained in the 3D parts' projections.

135

radius, and thus would even decrease the number of line segments. Finally, due to the good control over the resulting curvature of the line stroke, curve fitting routines are applied (in this case B–splines).

(a) Internally annotated animation path. (b) Externally annotated animation path.

Figure A.4: Annotation of animation paths.

Visualizing animation path
The results are visualized with additional arrows at the ends of the determined line. If there is enough space for the annotation stroke, the letters of the annotation are directly projected onto the animation path (*internal path annotation*). If the space is not sufficient, the annotation's text is placed on a calm region of the illustration background (*external path annotation*) whereas a reference line connects the text with the animation path of the referred part (see Figure A.4).

A.3.4 Comparison

Both methods have advantages
Both of the previously described methods have advantages. The annotation placement in calm regions minimizes the overlaid space on the 3D part whereas arrows presenting the trajectories of moving 3D parts can also be found in hand–made illustrations. Thus, it is application dependent, which method should be preferred. In interactive applications, however, the animation itself may communicate the part's movement. Therefore, the annotation placement in calm regions should be preferred whereas trajectories should only be used for parts without calm regions. For still images and screenshots trajectories can convey the movement of parts.

A.3.5 Experimental Application

In order to test the practicability of both strategies an experimental application was developed that integrated annotations for animated 3D models into an interactive 3D visualization according to the proposed techniques. Therefore, several 3D models of the *Viewpoint 3D* library [Dig] were enhanced with common 3D modeling programs in order to generate sequences of moving 3D parts. The annotation process performed with all models at interactive frame rates. The computational performance of the annotation process is almost independent from the geometric complexity of the 3D models. However, for very complex 3D animations the *Coin3D* library [Sys] as used in this system might not be the best choice in terms of performance.

The determination of calm regions required color–coded renditions of a complete animation sequence. The performance depended on the number of animation frames and the rendering speed of the graphics hardware. With three different animated 3D models (animations of 16 frames) the determination of calm regions required less than a second on the reference systems. Therefore, the layout process started whenever the user stopped the interaction with the 3D model. Figure A.5 shows the calm and fluctuating regions of a V8 Motor with a rotating ventilator and accordingly moving pistons.

3D model animation

Figure A.6 shows the same motor which external annotation texts and their anchors are exclusively placed on calm regions. Figure A.7 presents an illustration where the pistons are enriched by arrows showing the trajectories of their movement in the animation. These trajectories could be integrated into static illustrations of instructive texts. In order to provide spatial indications (i.e., depth information), this approach can modify the appearance of arrows.

Watch scene 5

Figure A.5: Calm (white) and fluctuating (grey) regions of a motor (animated ventilator and pistons).

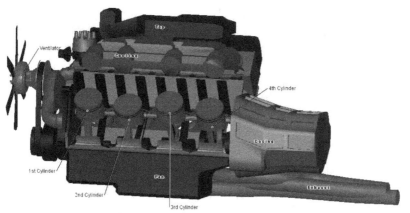

Figure A.6: Annotated calm regions.

A.3.6 Discussion

This section discussed the benefits and issues of an annotation layout for the exploration of animated 3D models. The initial observations revealed that the coherence strategies of existing annotation layout algorithms did not achieve sufficient results in a new application field: the integration of secondary elements in 3D animations, which can be inspected from user–selected viewpoints. Therefore, two novel techniques were proposed in order to overcome those problems in interactive environments. Moreover, the view-dependent determination of animation paths is useful in order to generate visual summaries for animations (i.e., for printed material) which depict the animation sequences.

Visual summaries

137

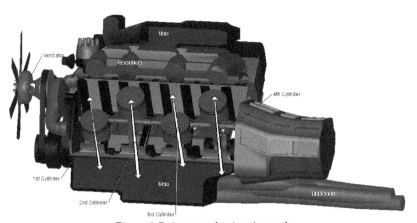

Figure A.7: Annotated animation paths.

Different operators For performance reasons a simple strategy was used to detect calm regions in subsequent frames (blending of ID–buffers with an AND operations). More sophisticated methods for the evaluation of the calmness of regions could help to find even better placements of annotations. The AND function, however, guarantees that calm areas are disjoint—their associated annotations cannot overlap. More intuitive combinations of ID–values throughout an animation (scoring with an OR function) would require to solve annotation–annotation overlaps or a selection of non–overlapping annotations. Task–dependent dynamic relevance values could be considered for the annotation selection and the selection of annotation styles.

Applicability Furthermore, if the determination of the animation paths could be completely realized by image–based techniques (i.e., distance–transformation), regarding the applicability, this approach could be used with different types of 3D models. However, as mentioned before, the computational effort might be too demanding for interactive approaches.

Linkage of images and text Annotated 3D animations combine the features of annotated illustrations and the spatial exploration of 3D animations. However, MAYER ET AL. [MA92b] stated that based on the continuity principle learning with animations and textual explanations presented concurrently performs much better than presenting animation and text separately. Hence, the exploration of annotated 3D models should be linked with expository text.

A.4 User Study

Evaluation of methods In order to evaluate if the proposed methods are appropriate for the annotation of animated 3D models and in order to improve the comprehension of animated 3D models several tests were developed and performed. The test application showed five different shapes that were annotated in different fashions. These shapes moved along defined paths; the annotations followed these movements or remained on fixed positions. The

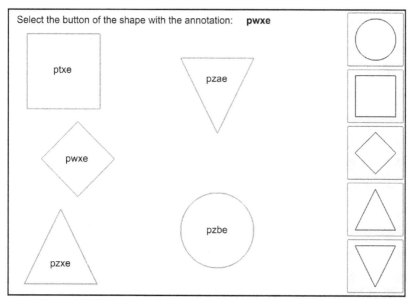

Figure A.8: Test scene of the user study: Select the corresponding button.

participants were asked to read the texts presented as annotations and to associate them to their corresponding shape.

A.4.1 Method

Subjects and design. The tests were conducted with 30 subjects (computer graphics students; 8 female, 22 male) who were subdivided into two test groups of 14 and 16 participants. Both test groups completed the same blind tests with different types of hardware.

Materials and apparatus. The first group completed the test on a 19 inch TFT monitor (Belinea 101920) at 75 Hz refresh rate. The second test group was tested on a 21 inch CRT monitor (Fujitsu–Siemens MCM213V) at 80 Hz refresh rate. The visible diagonal size of both was almost equal (TFT: 48.3cm, CRT: 50.0cm). The test application initially presented five different shapes (circle, square, square 90° rotated, triangle, triangle 180° rotated) on five different starting positions (see Figure A.8). These assignments were chosen randomly in each test. On the right side of the display there were 5 large corresponding buttons for the user interaction.

In order to measure the impact of different annotation strategies, these five shapes were annotated with slightly differing annotation texts without any semantic relation to their associated shape. Once again, those assignments were chosen randomly. In order to generate textual annotations with terms consisting of four letters, each letter of the initial string was chosen randomly. Out of this string, four other strings were generated by minimally alternating one of the four letters (LEVENSHTEIN distance of 1 [Lev66]). An instruction *'Select the button of the shape with the annotation:'* was presented on the upper side of the display, followed by one of the 4–digit strings that were randomly chosen.

Procedure. The test subjects were randomly assigned to the groups TFT or CRT. Initially, the test was presented to the participants. They were instructed to read the 4–digit string on the top of the display, to find the corresponding annotation on the left side of the display and to assign the correct shape by pushing the appropriate shapes on the right side of the display. Additionally, they were instructed to prioritize accuracy over urgency. After this introduction users started the tests. Each test had a preparation screen that showed the identical consecutive test, except for the string 'Preparation:'. After clicking on a button the actual test was performed.

A.4.2   Results

Scoring. For each test the application logged if the subjects selected the *correct* shape and the selection *time* in milliseconds. The preparation time was not considered. For a better comparison the timings of each subject were subsequently normalized by dividing them by the results median. The *One–Way ANOVA (Analysis of variance)* method was applied in order to determine whether or not the results of two tests mean a significant difference. Statistical significance cannot be considered with a result $p \geq 0.05$.

Hypothesis 1: Moving text is better readable on CRT than on TFT monitors.

CRT vs. TFT First, the influence of display types was evaluated. The ANOVA attested that no significant difference could be determined both with respect to the correct shape selection ($F = 0.274, p = 0.604$) and the selection time ($F < 0.001, p = 0.984$). Thus, both test groups for the display types were merged in the following tests.

Hypothesis 2: Fixed texts are better readable than moving texts.

Fixed vs. moving text The tests t_1 and t_2 were designed to evaluate the placement of internal annotation in calm regions (see Section A.3.2). The shapes oscillated between the end points of an invisible vertical or horizontal line. In the first test t_1 the annotation texts followed their parts' movements. In the second test t_2 textual annotations resided on calm areas of moving parts. The test revealed that a movement of textual annotations worsens the subjects' performance with respect to the accuracy of the assignment ($t_1 : 93\%, t_2 : 100\%$) and with respect to the response time. For the latter criterion there was also a significant difference ($F = 12.692, p < 0.001$) between t_1 and t_2 (see Figure A.9).

Hypothesis 3: Annotation of animation paths is better than moving text.

Moving text vs. animation path The tests t_3 and t_4 were designed to evaluate the annotation within trajectories of parts' movements (see Section A.3.3). For both tests complex–curved paths of oscillating shapes were defined. In test t_3 these trajectories were hidden whereas the annotation texts

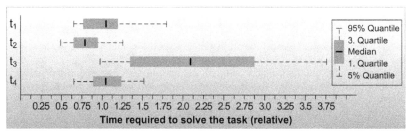

Figure A.9: Relative time required for the tasks (normalized by median).

were centered on the moving shapes. However, in test t_4 these trajectories were presented whereas the annotations were attached to the corresponding trajectories. Once again, the performance of test subjects using this method (test t_4) was better than with moving annotation texts (test t_3) both with respect to the accuracy of the assignment ($t_3 : 87\%, t_4 : 100\%$) and with respect to the response time. For the latter criterion there was also a significant difference ($F = 19.881, p < 0.001$) between t_3 and t_4 (see Figure A.9).

A.4.3 Discussion

By means of test t_1 and t_2 it has been collected evidence that users performed worse in solving the tasks with moving text than with fixed text. Both the correct shape assignments and the selection time required for solving the task were better with fixed text. The additional cognitive load necessary for reading moving texts seems to cause these effects. Thus, fixed positions of the texts should be preferred.

Fixed text performed better

For the recognition of the annotations moving with the shapes along the predefined path (t_3), users significantly required more time than they required for the recognition with less complex movements (t_1). The results of t_3 and t_4 showed that animation paths significantly decrease both the failure rate and the time required for the recognition of the annotations (see Figure A.9).

Annotated path performed better

A.5 Conclusion

Since animations may improve understanding of the dynamic processes, this extension adapted the encapsulated annotation approach in order to annotate animated 3D models. Due to its results, animated 3D models such as a running motor or a beating heart can be explored by the user, while preserving a frame coherent annotation of them. However, MAYER ET AL. [MA92b, May01] state that concurrently presenting illustrations respectively animations with expository text significantly outperforms the learning benefit of the separate presentation of those media. Hence, it would be desirable to link expository text with annotated illustrations and animations.

In order to link expository text with these 3D animations, the annotation techniques developed in this appendix could be used in the concept of correlating illustrations and text (cf. Chapter 6 and 7). Whilst the presentation and exploration of the 3D animations can be integrated without additional effort, the procedure of adding new 3D animations to the corpus of 3D models has to be adapted. As explained in Chapter 6, when adding new 3D models, multiple view descriptors are generated which allow a context–driven retrieval of the 3D models in the corpus. However, unlike for static 3D models, for each 3D model of the animation sequence the visible relative size, centricity, and entropy of the 3D parts may be different. Hence, view descriptors had to be generated that consolidate all 3D models of the animation sequence.

This could be achieved by generating preliminary view descriptors for each 3D model of the animation sequence. In a subsequent consolidating step, a strategy had to be applied which combines those preliminary view descriptors to one descriptor which describes the complete sequence. For example, this could be done by either computing the average of the importance values for each 3D part, or by selecting the maximum values of the preliminary view descriptors. However, future user studies would be necessary in order to evaluate which of those consolidation methods would be appropriate.

B Investigated Corpus of Illustrations

This appendix presents statistics about the books that were investigated in order to be able to describe different phenomena of annotations (cf. Chapter 3).

Selection of Book Corpus

In order to obtain a substantial corpus of heterogeneous illustrations, 28 books of different fields, comprising a minimum of 50 illustrations, were examined. For the sake of uniformity, the analysis merely incorporated content pages of the books, but no indices, appendices, and bibliographies.

Selection of Specimen

There was a large variance in the number of content pages (59–2167 pages) of the books as well as in the comprised quantity of illustrations. In order to obtain an equally distributed set of illustrations over the whole range of the book content pages, an algorithm was developed, which ensured a deterministic selection.

The selection algorithm was developed for the selection of N illustrations. It started with the selection from the first content page, skipped a certain number of pages (*pageStep*) and selected the next illustration. This process was continued until either 50 specimen were analyzed or no content pages remained. To cope with the big variance in the amount of the book pages, the value of *pageStep* represented $\frac{1}{50}$th of the content pages.

```
x:=y
for (...
  :c /
```
See Appendix D.5

If there were multiple illustrations on a selected book page, the algorithm chose those which were the topmost (first priority) and the leftmost (second priority). However, only illustrations that fit to the following definition were selected: the illustration presents the spatial shape of a real existing object and has at least one textual annotation. If this condition was not fulfilled, it was proceeded with the nearest following illustration. In the case that no illustration fulfilled the condition within the interval of *pageStep* pages, the analysis of this particular specimen was skipped and the algorithm continued with the next one. Hence, it was possible that the algorithm selected less than 50 specimen.

Statistics

Table B.1 shows the results of the analysis. The table is divided into two segments. The first part consists of *Visual Dictionaries*, whereas the remaining part lists *Text Books*. The left column shows the references of the books examined and their bibliography can be found at the end of this appendix. The asterisk sign marks those books, which were also used for the informal study of the first analysis pass.

The field *Page Step* documents which pages were considered as content pages and thus, which illustrations were investigated. Besides the topic of the annotated illustrations

Book	Investigated Pages (Page Step)	Field				Annotation Type					
		Human Anatomy	Natural Science	Technical	Other	Figure Captions	External Annotations	Internal Annotations	Object Descriptions	Figure Descriptions	Legends
						Text Books					
[AA05]	1-755 (15)	0	50	0	0	50	30	2	0	0	1
[BB90]	1-889 (17)	0	50	0	0	50	50	11	0	0	2
[BH96]	3-475 (9)	0	49	0	0	49	49	8	0	0	3
[Daw92]	1-236 (4)	0	0	46	0	46	34	10	1	1	0
[Dul96]	10-211 (4)	0	33	0	0	33	22	16	0	2	5
[Gra18]*	1-1615 (32)	50	0	0	0	50	47	18	0	0	0
[Gud01]	10-341 (6)	0	49	0	0	49	48	15	0	0	1
[Har89]	1-288 (5)	0	0	41	0	41	41	9	0	0	1
[HN04]	1-755 (15)	0	50	0	0	50	50	21	0	2	4
[JM00]	3-826 (16)	0	0	50	0	50	47	11	0	0	0
[KM98]	3-955 (19)	0	0	48	0	48	40	9	0	0	1
[Lip00]*	1-754 (15)	50	0	0	0	50	50	5	0	0	49
[Maj95]	1-276 (5)	0	1	49	0	50	44	10	0	0	0
[Rog92]*	1-720 (14)	50	0	0	0	50	50	1	0	1	0
[Smi02]	1-295 (5)	0	0	49	0	49	46	3	1	0	2
[SPP01]*	1-384 (7)	50	0	0	0	50	49	6	0	9	3
[SPP97]*	1-384 (7)	50	0	0	0	50	50	1	0	7	7
[Ste02]*	44-805 (15)	0	50	0	0	50	33	9	14	0	8
[Sum95]	1-873 (17)	0	0	47	0	47	47	12	0	1	0
[SW97]	1-745 (14)	0	50	0	0	50	50	4	0	0	0
[Tor97]*	1-574 (11)	50	0	0	0	50	50	5	0	6	3
		300	**382**	**330**	**0**	**1012**	**927**	**186**	**16**	**29**	**90**
						Visual Dictionaries					
[Doc02]*	10-616 (12)	4	22	24	0	50	49	1	0	1	0
[FM99]*	2-441 (8)	0	0	41	0	42	33	7	0	0	0
[Par98]	1-2167 (43)	5	24	21	0	50	39	7	0	0	0
[PS79]	16-677 (13)	0	10	21	19	0	50	40	0	0	50
[Rau05]*	1-415 (8)	1	13	19	17	0	50	43	0	0	50
[Tho86]	10-589 (11)	1	0	49	0	49	46	8	0	0	0
[Tri92]	1-59 (1)	0	0	50	0	50	50	0	0	0	0
		11	**69**	**225**	**36**	**241**	**317**	**106**	**0**	**1**	**100**
		311	**451**	**555**	**36**	**1253**	**1244**	**292**	**16**	**30**	**190**

Table B.1: Results of the analysis of the investigated corpus of books.

(*Human Anatomy*, *Natural Science*, *Technical*, and those from *Other* fields), frequencies of appearances of the different annotations types were counted.

Initial Observations

Since the transitions between the types of annotations are fluent, it is extremely difficult to classify them into a small set of choices. Thus, the analysis results can only be considered as a rough measure. However, it is obvious that nearly each illustration utilizes figure captions. Exceptions are visual dictionaries [FM99, Rau05] which deploy figure legends instead of figure captions. Figure descriptions, object descriptions, and legends are commonly placed beside the primary object, while figure captions are placed below or above it. Some authors favor using figure legends, whilst colors, numbers or letters as internal and external annotation establish the assignment to the primary object's parts. However, each of those annotation types can contain nearly arbitrary content or even combinations of text, images, and tables. It can only be classified by regarding its most prominent trait.

External annotations are applied with a significantly higher frequency than internal ones. While external annotations are used with an average frequency of 95%, internal annotations are only used with an average of 20%, and some illustrators did not use them at all. A possible reason may be that preserving the contrast and legibility of internal annotations is harder than for external ones. Moreover, internal annotations overlay their referred parts to a higher extent than external annotations. In most cases, internal annotations are used in combination with external annotations. A conspicuous fact is that internal annotations are often used, if there is not much space to accommodate external ones. An exception is the popular work of Henry Gray [Gra18] which aesthetically integrates internal annotations in the majority of illustrations.

Bibliography of Corpus

[AA05]   Sandra Alters and Brian Alters. *Biology*. John Wiley & Sons, Hoboken, NJ, 2005.

[BB90]   Richard C. Brusca and Gary J. Brusca. *Invertebrates*. Sinauer, Sunderland, Massachusetts, 1990.

[BH96]   Ann B. Butler and William Hodos. *Comparative Vertebrate Neuroanatomy*. Wiley Liss, New York, 1996.

[Daw92] Christopher Dawes. *Laser Welding*. Abington Publishing, Cambridge, 1992.

[Doc02] Paul Docherty, editor. *DK Ultimate Visual Dictionary*. Dorling Kindersley Publishing, New York, revised edition, 2002.

[Dul96] Michael Dultz, editor. *Lebensraum Erde*. ADAC Verlag, München, 1996.

[FM99]   Heinz K. Flack and Georg Möllerke. *Illustrated Engineering Dictionary*. Springer, London, 2nd edition, 1999.

[Gra18]   Henry Gray. *Anatomy of the Human Body*. Lea & Febiger, Philadelphia, 20th edition, 1918.

[Gud01]   Wolf–Eckhard Gudemann, editor. *Enzyklopädie der Natur*. Orbis Verlag, München, 2001.

[Har89]   Nigel S. Harris. *Modern Vacuum Practice*. McGraw–Hill, New York, 1989.

[HN04]   Gerhard Heldmaier and Gerhard Neuweiler. *Vergleichende Tierphysiologie*. Springer, Berlin, 2004.

[JM00]   Robert C. Juvinall and Kurt M. Marshek. *Fundamentals of Machine Component Design*. John Wiley & Sons, New York, 3rd edition, 2000.

[KM98]   Igor J. Karassik and J. Terry McGuire. *Centrifugal Pumps*. Chapman & Hall, New York, 2nd edition, 1998.

[Lip00]   Herbert Lippert. *Lehrbuch Anatomie*. Urban & Fischer, München, 2000.

[Maj95]   Shri R. Majumdar. *Pneumatic Systems: Principles and Maintenance*. McGraw–Hill, New York, 1995.

[Par98]   Sybil P. Parker, editor. *McGraw–Hill Concise Encyclopedia of Science & Technology*. McGraw–Hill, New York, 4th edition, 1998.

[PS79]   John Pheby and Werner Scholze, editors. *The Oxford–Duden Pictorial English Dictionary*. Bibliographisches Institut, Mannheim, 1979.

[Rau05]   Karin Rautmann, editor. Duden: *Das Bildwörterbuch*. Bibliographisches Institut & F.A. Brockhaus AG, Mannheim, 6th edition, 2005.

[Rog92]   Andrew W. Rogers. *Textbook of Anatomy*. Churchill Livingstone, Edinburgh, 1992.

[Smi02]   Graham T. Smith. *Industrial Metrology*. Springer, London, 2002.

[SPP97]   Johannes Sobotta, Reinhard Putz, and Reinhard Pabst, editors. *Sobotta: Atlas of Human Anatomy. Volume 2: Thorax, Abdomen, Pelvis, Lower Limb*. Lippincott Williams & Wilkins, Baltimure, 12th English edition, 1997.

[SPP01]   Johannes Sobotta, Reinhard Putz, and Reinhard Pabst, editors. *Sobotta: Atlas of Human Anatomy*. Lippincott Williams & Wilkins, Baltimore, 13th edition, 2001.

[Ste02]   Michael C. Sternheimer, editor. *Die große Larousse Natur–Enzyklopädie*. Gondrom Verlag, Bindlach, 2002.

[Sum95]   David A. Summers. *Waterjetting Technology*. Spon Press, London, 1995.

[SW97]   Volker Storch and Ulrich Welsch. *Systematische Zoologie*. Gustav Fischer Verlag, Stuttgart, 5th edition, 1997.

[Tho86]   Klaus Thome. *Die Technik im Leben von heute*. Meyers Lexikonverlag, Mannheim, 3rd edition, 1986.

[Tor97]   Gerhard J. Tortora. *Introduction to the Human Body: The Essentials of Anatomy and Physiology*. Benjamin Cummings, Redwood City, CA, 1997.

[Tri92]   Roger Tritton, editor. *The Visual Dictionary of Ships and Sailing*. DK Publishing, London, 1992.

C Expert survey

In the context of this book several questions arose that could not be answered by the review of literature. In order to obtain evidence, multiple experts of the domain of illustration were consulted. The experts interviewed were academic professors in the fields of illustration and design (see Table C.1). This section presents the questions addressed by a guided interview that was held in German.

Expert	Affiliation	Area of Expertise
Prof. Silvia Beck	FH Niederrhein (University of Applied Sciences)	Depiction in Drawing
Prof. Ingo Garschke	HS für Grafik und Buchkunst Leipzig (Academy of Visual Arts)	Artistic Anatomy and Depiction
Prof. Uwe Göbel	FH Bielefeld (University of Applied Sciences)	Book Design, Creative Usage of Text and Image
Prof. Jochen Stücke	FH Krefeld (University of Applied Sciences)	Illustration and Depiction in Drawing

Table C.1: List of the experts consulted.

Because of the complexity of the questions, performing the survey by a questionnaire seemed to be inadequate. Thus, the survey had to be performed orally, and the questions were motivated by examples in order to clarify their context. Subsequently, the experts were asked the questions listed below.

Often considerations about design and esthetic cannot be expressed by absolute answers for agreement respectively disagreement. Hence, the experts were asked to describe whether they predominantly agree or not as well as additional comments were recorded.

The following segment consists of the questions in English, the German questions (in brackets), the experts' answers and the combined additional comments of the experts:

Question 1

Is it safe to say, that annotated depictions of real existing objects are always illustrations? (Kann man sagen, dass Abbildungen von realen Objekten mit Annotationen immer Illustrationen sind?)

Answer. Agreement (4 out of 4 experts)

Comment. The type of depiction does not play a role. Even augmenting parts of a photo with text may be the act of illustration.

Question 2

Which term could be used for annotated illustrations?
(Wie lassen sich die annotierten Illustrationen am besten bezeichnen?)

Answer.   Illustrations in educational books (2 out of 4 experts)/Scientific illustrations (4 out of 4 experts)

Comment.   Dependent from the area; even in other books than educational ones may be annotated illustrations.

Question 3

It seems that there is no dedicated literature for the annotation of illustrations.
(Es scheint keine spezielle Literatur zur Annotation von Illustrationen zu geben?)

Answer.   Agreement (4 out of 4 experts)

Comment.   –

Question 4

Are internal annotations predominantly used if there is not much space for external ones or if there are many annotations to accommodate?
(Werden interne Beschriftungen hauptsächlich genutzt, wenn Platz zur Verfügung steht oder viele Beschriftungen unterzubringen sind?)

Answer.   Agreement (3 out of 4 experts)

Comment.   Possibly not the only reason, there are further advantages which illustrators could consider, i.e., internal annotations are more direct. However, legibility has to be considered.

Question 5

Roughly speaking can be said that there is a semantic gap between illustrations and text?
(Kann man zwischen einer Illustration und Text von einer semantischen Lücke sprechen?)

Answer.   Agreement (3 out of 4 experts)

Comment.   Both media have different strengths, however maybe the word gap could be understood somehow misleading. Additionally, the level of abstractness between illustrations and text is different.

Question 6

Are illustrations in educational books often summarized, i.e., do multiple contexts of the text (e.g., paragraphs) relate to the same illustration?
(Werden Illustrationen in Lehrbüchern häufig zusammengefasst, d.h. mehrere Kontexte beziehen sich auf eine Illustration?)

Answer.   Agreement (4 out of 4 experts)

Comment.   –

Question 7

Would it be desirable to be able to design one illustration for each context?
(Wäre es wünschenswert, zu jedem Sachverhalt (Kontext) eine Illustration erstellen zu können?)

Answer. Agreement (4 out of 4 experts)
Comment. It would be more effective, but designing the illustrations and printing the book would be very expensive in terms of time and money. Maybe the flow of text would be disrupted by that big number of illustrations.

Question 8

Should a view on the illustrated object should be chosen in a way that each important part is visible?
(Sollte eine Sicht auf das illustrierte Objekt so gewählt werden dass alle wichtigen Teile gut zu erkennen sind?)

Answer. Agreement (4 out of 4 experts)
Comment. Additionally, techniques like cutting and transparency can be used.

Question 9

Provided that several parts of the illustrated object are important in a given context, which criteria would influence the selection of the view?
(Angenommen, einige Teile eines illustrierten Objektes sind wichtig in einem gegebenen Zusammenhang, welche Kriterien haben Einfluss auf die Wahl der Sicht?)

Answer. Visible size (3 out of 4 experts)/Mediality (4 out of 4 experts)
Comment. Another criterion could be canonical views of known objects. The size of the object should be indicated or comparable.

Question 10

For a given context, it is desirable to indicate the neighboring regions or the whole object?
(Ist es wünschenswert, auch angrenzende Regionen anzudeuten, d.h. einen Gesamtkontext?)

Answer. Agreement (4 out of 4 experts)
Comment. It is important for the orientation, and it improves the ability to remind. Only if the orientation is clear to the viewer it can be left out. Thus, it is dependent of the experience of the target viewers.

Question 11

Are annotations in illustrations sequentially accommodated?
(Werden die Positionen der Annotationen werden der Reihe nach ermittelt?)

Answer. Agreement (4 out of 4 experts)
Comment. –

Question 12

If the process of accommodating annotations is sequential, which is the rule to select the sequence?

(Wenn Annotationen der Reihe nach platziert werden, nach welcher Regel wird dann die Reihenfolge ausgewählt?)

Answer.	Hard cases first (3 out of 4 experts)/important cases first (3 out of 4 experts)
Comment.	Both rules can be applied, however there is no universal rule; it is depending on the object and the task. Another rule could be accommodating the annotations in a clockwise sequence.

Question 13

Is a human heart relatively complex natured? Hence, are multiple views needed to depict it?

(Kann man sagen, dass ein menschliches Herz relativ komplex geartet ist, sodass man gewöhnlich mehrere Ansichten braucht um es darzustellen?)

Answer.	Agreement (4 out of 4 experts)
Comment.	There are multiple human organs which are quite complex, such as the heart. Furthermore, the human brain could also be used since it is very complex as well.

D

Pseudocode Segments

The algorithms described in this book are designated to be implementable by an experienced programmer. The following only presents a small set of algorithms. Most algorithms described in the book can be sufficiently explained by verbal descriptions. However, the use of pseudocode seemed to be adequate to clarify the description of some algorithms. In order not to distract the continuity of the text, the pseudocode segments have been postponed to this chapter.

Input.	Disjoint *layoutSpace[]* of each *colorID*, belonging to the illustration background and the part of the primary object; distance buffer.
Output.	Result lists of disjoint salient areas of size d_{min}.

```
 1. for each colorID i do
 2.     layoutSpace[i] ← unallocated
 3.     allocationsLeft ← true
 4.     while (allocationsLeft) do
 5.         d=determineMaximumOnRemainingArea(layoutSpace[i])
 6.         if (d ≥ d_min) then
 7.             if not (checkOverlapWithAllocated(d.pos, 2d_min)) then
 8.                 addSalientAreaToResults(i, d.pos, 2d_min)
 9.                 allocateSalientArea(d.pos, 2d_min)
10.             else markAsInappropriate(d.pos)
11.             end if
12.         else allocationsLeft ← false
13.         end if
14.     end while
15. end for
```

The algorithm iterates for each disjoint layout space which can be masked by the color-ID on the ID-buffer, i.e., the illustration background and each part of the primary object. Initially, this layout space is unallocated. The function *determineMaximumOnRemainingArea* is used to determine the maximum value d of the unallocated distance buffer. Subsequently, if d value is greater than the defined minimum size d_{min}, function *checkOverlapWithAllocated* ensures that the square of the edge length $2d_{min}$ at the determined maximum's position $d.pos$ does not overlap already allocated areas; otherwise $d.pos$ is marked as inappropriate. Next, function *addSalientAreaToResults* stores its position in a result list. Additionally, function *allocateSalientArea* allocates a square of the edge length $2d_{min}$ at $d.pos$. This process is continued until no more maximum greater than d_{min} can be found in the distance field of the remaining unallocated space. Finally, the result list contains disjoint salient points.

Algorithm D.1: Determination of annotation boxes' and internal annotations' candidates.

Input. Metrics M; candidates C; determined values $V[m][c]$; weights $W[m]$.
Output. Candidate with best score s_{top}.

1. # Normalizing the determined values
2. **for each** *metric i* **do**
3.   **for each** *candidate j* **do**
4. $v_{ij} \leftarrow \dfrac{v_{ij}}{\max(v_i)}$
5.   **end for**
6. **end for**

7. # Choosing the best one (minimum score s) of the n candidates
8. **for each** *candidate j* **do**
9. $s_j \leftarrow 0$
10.   **for each** *metric i* **do**
11. $s_j \leftarrow s_j + w_i * v_{ij}$
12.   **end for**
13. **end for**
14. $s_{top} \leftarrow \min(s_1, ..., s_n)$

This algorithm consists of two parts. In order to allow comparability between the different metrics' values, the first part normalizes the determined values of each metric, i.e., these values are scaled to a range between 0.0 and 1.0. The second part determines the score s of each candidate by computing the weighted sum (according to the users preferences) of their metrics' values. Since the metrics are designed to express better scores by lower values, the algorithm selects the candidate with the minimum score.

Algorithm D.2: Determination of the best candidate.

Input. Best score for internal s_{ci} and external s_{ce} placement; cutoff parameter for internal cf_{ci} and external cf_{ce} annotations; hysteresis parameter cf_{hyst}.
Output. Value *answer* denoting whether an adaptation is allowed or denied.

1. **if** $s_{ce} > cf_{ce}$
2.   **if** $s_{ci} < \frac{cf_{ci}}{cf_{hyst}}$
3.   *answer* $\leftarrow$ *adaptation permitted*
4.   **end if**
5. **end if**
6. **else** *answer* $\leftarrow$ *adaptation denied*

Adaptation of external to internal annotation: If the score of the best external placement is worse (higher) than the container's cutoff value, it is verified if the best internal placement candidate's score is significantly better than its containers cutoff value. The higher the hysteresis value, the less agile performs the adaptation. For the adaptation of internal to external annotations, s_{ci} and cf_{ci} are interchanged with s_{ce} and cf_{ce}.

Algorithm D.3: Annotation type hysteresis algorithm.

Input. Positions of anchor points $\vec{A} \in \mathbb{N}^2$ of visible parts; *groups* G consisting individually of M visible parts; n positions of annotation box candidates $\vec{C} \in \mathbb{N}^2$.
Output. Annotation layout for each *group* g.

1. **for each** *group* i **do**
2. $centroid_i \leftarrow \frac{1}{m_i} \sum_{j \in g_i} \vec{a}_j$
3. $c_{selected} \leftarrow \min(\text{dist}(centroid_i, \vec{c}_k), 1 \leq k \leq n)$
4.   accommodateExternalAnnotations($c_{selected}$, g_i)
5.   resolveLineOverlaps(g_i)
6. **end for**

For each group the algorithm determines the *centroid* of the anchor points of the group parts. To this centroid, the nearest annotation box candidate is located in order to accommodate the group's external annotations inside it (*accommodateExternalAnnotations*). Finally, line overlaps within the group are resolved by function *resolveLineOverlaps*.

Algorithm D.4: Group annotation layout algorithm.

Input. Educational book with annotated illustrations (see Appendix B).
Output. Equally distributed set of n specimen for the book analysis (see Table B.1).

1. *numberOfSpecimenAnalyzed* $\leftarrow 0$
2. *pageStep* $\leftarrow \frac{nrOfContentPages}{n}$
3. *currentPage* $\leftarrow$ *beginningOfContentPages*
4. **while** (*numberOfSpecimenAnalyzed* $\leq n$ **and** *currentPage* $<$ *endOfContentPages*) **do**
5.   *specimenTested* $\leftarrow$ *false*
6.   **while** (*specimenAnalyzed* = *false*) **do**
7.   **if** (*pageContainsAnnotatedIllustration* = *true*) **then**
8.   analyzeFirstSuitableAnnotatedIllustration(priorities: 1st top, 2nd left)
9.   *specimenAnalyzed* $\leftarrow$ *true*
10.   *numberOfSpecimenAnalyzed* $\leftarrow$ *numberOfSpecimenAnalyzed* + 1
11.   *currentPage* $\leftarrow$ *currentPage* + *pageStep*
12.   **else** nextPage()
13.   **end if**
14.   **end while**
15. **end while**

In order to analyze n illustrations *pageStep* is used to skip a certain number of pages. As long as less than n illustration are analyzed and the end of the book is not reached, the algorithm performs as follows. Continuing from the *currentPage*, the first annotated illustration (1st priority: topmost, 2nd priority: leftmost) is selected and analyzed by the surveyor (*analyzeFirstSuitableAnnotatedIllustration*). If there is no suitable illustration on the *currentPage*, it is progressed with the *nextPage*.

Algorithm D.5: Algorithm for the selection of the books' specimen.

Data Structures

This appendix briefly introduces exemplary XML documents including their *Document Type Definition (DTD)* for both annotation files and context files.

```
<?xml version="1.0" encoding="UTF-8" standalone="yes"?>
<!DOCTYPE Model [
  <!ELEMENT Model (Part+) >
  <!ELEMENT Part (Annotation, Description) >
  <!ELEMENT Annotation EMPTY >
  <!ATTLIST Annotation caption CDATA #IMPLIED >
  <!ATTLIST Annotation external CDATA #IMPLIED >
  <!ATTLIST Annotation id NMTOKEN #REQUIRED >
  <!ATTLIST Annotation internal CDATA #IMPLIED >
  <!ELEMENT Description (#PCDATA) >
]>
<Model>
  <Part>
    <Annotation id="0" caption="The human heart and its parts."/>
    <Description>
      The heart is a muscular organ responsible for pumping blood through the blood vessels
      by repeated, rhythmic contractions... <br>
      <center><img src="/images/HeartLocationHumanBody.gif" width=300></center>
    </Description>
  </Part>
  ...
  <Part>
    <Annotation id="23" external="Left Atrium" internal="L. Atrium"/>
    <Description>
      <p>The <i>left atrium</i> is one of the four chambers in the human heart. It
      receives oxygenated blood from the <i>pulmonary veins</i>, and pumps it into the
      <i>left ventricle</i>.</p>
    </Description>
  </Part>
</Model>
```

The annotation files are defined in the *Extensible Markup Language (XML)* which assigns the color–ID (*id*) of each 3D part (*Part*) of the 3D model (*Model*) to its annotations. Hence, for each color–ID there is a field for the text of internal annotations (*internal*), the external annotations (*external*) and annotation boxes (*description*). In order to format texts, to define tables or to embed images, the *Hypertext Markup Language (HTML)* may be used. The color–ID 0 represents the illustration background, whereas its field *caption* holds a short version of the *description* which may consist of more extensive information about the 3D model.

Data Structure E.1: Exemplary annotation file.

```
<?xml version="1.0" encoding="UTF-8" standalone="yes"?>
<!DOCTYPE Taxonomy [
  <!ELEMENT Taxonomy (Context+) >
  <!ELEMENT Context (Group, Childs) >
  <!ELEMENT Childs (Part+, Context*) >
  <!ELEMENT Group EMPTY >
  <!ATTLIST Group name CDATA #REQUIRED >
  <!ELEMENT Part EMPTY >
  <!ATTLIST Part id NMTOKEN #REQUIRED >
]>
<Taxonomy>
  <Context>
    <Group name="Mounting"/>
    <Childs>
      <Part id="1"/>
      <Part id="15"/>
      <Part id="23"/>
      <Part id="24"/>
      <Part id="25"/>
    </Childs>
  </Context>
  <Context>
    <Group name="Gear System"/>
    <Childs>
      <Part id="31"/>
      <Part id="32"/>
      <Part id="33"/>
      <Context>
        <Group name="Gear belts"/>
        <Childs>
          <Part id="36"/>
          <Part id="37"/>
        </Childs>
      </Context>
      <Context>
        <Group name="Screws"/>
        <Childs>
          <Part id="27"/>
          <Part id="28"/>
          <Part id="29"/>
          <Part id="30"/>
        </Childs>
      </Context>
    </Childs>
  </Context>
  ...
</Taxonomy>
```

Taxonomy files are defined in the *Extensible Markup Language (XML)* and contain a set of contexts (*Context*) which consist of a group name (*name*) and a set of child elements (Childs). These child elements may include the color–IDs (*id*) of the 3D parts that the group includes as well as other contexts.

Data Structure E.2: Exemplary taxonomy file.

Reference Systems

In order to test the applicability and real–time constraints of the experimental applications developed for this thesis, different reference systems served as platform.

First reference system

- CPU Type: AMD Athlon XP 2200+ (1.8 GHz)
- Mainboard: ECS L7S7A2
- RAM: 512 MB (PC2100 DDR SDRAM)
- Graphics Controller: ASUS N6200
- Monitor: Yakumo TFT19AL
- Operating System: Windows XP Professional

Second reference system

- CPU Type: Intel Pentium 4 640 (3.20 GHz)
- Mainboard: Fujitsu Siemens D1961
- RAM: 1024 MB (PC3200 DDR SDRAM)
- Graphics Controller: Leadtek WinFast A6600 GT
- Monitor: Maxdata Belinea 101980
- Operating System: Windows 2000

Third reference system

- CPU Type: Intel Pentium M 725 (1.6 GHz)
- Mainboard: Acer Travelmate 4000
- RAM: 512 MB (PC2700 DDR SDRAM)
- Graphics Controller: ATI Mobility Radeon 9700
- Monitor: (built in)
- Operating System: Windows XP Home Edition

Video Scenes

This appendix provides the URLs of the video scenes linked to several parts of this thesis. The videos can be accessed by the web page:

> http://wwwisg.cs.uni-magdeburg.de/~timo/book/index.html

or by the links listed below:

- Scene 1-2: Adaptation (subtitled) [0:32]
  http://wwwisg.cs.uni-magdeburg.de/~timo/book/Scene1-2.avi

- Scene 2-1: Candidates (with audio) [1:29]
  http://wwwisg.cs.uni-magdeburg.de/~timo/book/Scene2-1.avi

- Scene 2-2: Weighted Evaluation (with audio) [1:51]
  http://wwwisg.cs.uni-magdeburg.de/~timo/book/Scene2-2.avi

- Scene 2-3: Annotation Agents (with audio) [1:21]
  http://wwwisg.cs.uni-magdeburg.de/~timo/book/Scene2-3.avi

- Scene 3-1: Grouped Annotation [0:27]
  http://wwwisg.cs.uni-magdeburg.de/~timo/book/Scene3-1.avi

- Scene 3-2: Contextual Annotation [0:54]
  http://wwwisg.cs.uni-magdeburg.de/~timo/book/Scene3-2.avi

- Scene 4-1: Introduction Correlating Illustrations and Text (with audio) [1:20]
  http://wwwisg.cs.uni-magdeburg.de/~timo/book/Scene4-1.avi

- Scene 4-2: Text to Illustration Query (with audio) [1:36]
  http://wwwisg.cs.uni-magdeburg.de/~timo/book/Scene4-2.avi

- Scene 4-3: Illustration to Text Query (with audio) [0:58]
  http://wwwisg.cs.uni-magdeburg.de/~timo/book/Scene4-3.avi

- Scene 4-4: Refinement Text to Illustration Query (with audio) [0:42]
  http://wwwisg.cs.uni-magdeburg.de/~timo/book/Scene4-4.avi

- Scene 4-5: Refinement Illustration to Text Query (with audio) [0:51]
  http://wwwisg.cs.uni-magdeburg.de/~timo/book/Scene4-5.avi

- Scene 5: Annotation of Animated 3D Models (with audio) [1:55]
  http://wwwisg.cs.uni-magdeburg.de/~timo/book/Scene5.avi

Bibliography

[Ade99]   Frank Adegeest. Method and System for Improving Legibility of Text and Graphic Objects Laid Over Continuous–tone Graphics. United States Patent 5872573, February 16, 1999.

[AHS05]   Kamran Ali, Knut Hartmann, and Thomas Strothotte. Label Layout for Interactive 3D Illustrations. *Journal of the WSCG*, 13(1):1–8, 2005.

[ATY+01]   Y. Alp Aslandogan, Chuck Thier, Clement T. Yu, Jon Zou, and Naphtali Rishe. Using Semantic Contents and WordNet in Image Retrieval. *SIGIR Forum*, 31(SI):286–295, 2001.

[AVF04]   Carlos Andújar, Pere-Pau Vázquez, and Marta Fairén. Way–Finder: Guided Tours Through Complex Walkthrough Models. *Computer Graphics Forum*, 23(3):499–508, 2004.

[Bal97]   Steffen-Peter Ballstaedt. *Wissensvermittlung: die Gestaltung von Lernmaterial.* Psychologie Verlags Union, Weinheim, 1997.

[BB98]   Mireille Bétrancourt and Andre Bisseret. Integrating Textual and Pictoral Information via Pop–up Windows: an Experimental Study. *Behavior and Information Technology*, 17(5):263–273, 1998.

[BF00]   Blaine A. Bell and Steven K. Feiner. Dynamic Space Management for User Interfaces. In *Symposium on User Interface Software and Technology*, pages 238–248, 2000.

[BG05]   Stefan Bruckner and Eduard Gröller. VolumeShop: An Interactive System for Direct Volume Illustrations. In *IEEE Visualization*, pages 671–678, 2005.

[Blu67]   Harry Blum. A Transformation for Extracting New Descriptors of Shape. In *Models for the Perception of Speech and Visual Form*, pages 362–380. MIT Press, Cambridge, 1967.

[Bol01]   Max Bollwage. *Typografie Kompakt.* Springer, Berlin, 2001.

[Boo78]   Abraham Bookstein. On the Perils of Merging Boolean and Weighted Retrieval Systems. *Journal of the ASIS*, 29(3):156–158, 1978.

[Bri90]   Mary H. Briscoe. *A Researcher's Guide to Scientific and Medical Illustrations.* Springer Verlag, Berlin, 1990.

[Bri96]   Mary H. Briscoe. *Preparing Scientific Illustrations*. Springer, New York, 2nd edition, 1996.

[BS05]   Udeepta Bordoloi and Han-Wei Shen. View Selection for Volume Rendering. In *IEEE Visualization*, page 62, 2005.

[BT02]   Mireille Betrancourt Barbara Tversky, Julie Morrison. Animation: Can It Facilitate? *International Journal of Human Computer Studies*, 57:247–262, 2002.

[BTB99]   Volker Blanz, Michael J. Tarr, and Heinrich H. Bülthoff. What Object Attributes Determine Canonical Views? *Perception*, 28(5):575–600, 1999.

[BY90]   Christina Burbeck and Yen L. Yap. Spatiotemporal Limitations in Bisection and Separation Discrimination. *Vision Research*, 30(11):1573–1586, 1990.

[BYRN99]   Ricardo Baeza-Yates and Berthier Ribeiro-Neto. *Modern Information Retrieval*. Addison Wesley, New York, 1999.

[CJ90]   Anthony C. Cook and Christopher B. Jones. A Prolog Rule–based System for Cartographic Name Placement. *Computer Graphics Forum*, 9(2):109–126, 1990.

[CM99]   Olivier Cuisenaire and Benoit M. Macq. Fast Euclidean Distance Transformations by Propagation Using Multiple Neighbourhoods. *Computer Vision and Image Understanding*, 76(2):163–172, 1999.

[CM01]   M. Sheelagh T. Carpendale and Catherine Montagnese. A Framework for Unifying Presentation Space. In *14th Annual ACM Symposium on User Interface Software and Technology (UIST '01)*, pages 61–70, 2001.

[CMS95]   Jon Christensen, Joe Marks, and Stuart Shieber. An Empirical Study of Algorithms for Point–Feature Label Placement. *ACM Transactions on Graphics*, 14(3):203–232, 1995.

[CMS99]   Stuart K. Card, Jock D. Mackinlay, and Ben Shneiderman, editors. *Readings in Information Visualization: Using Vision to Think*. Morgan Kaufmann Publishers Inc., San Francisco, 1999.

[CS02]   Wallace Chigona and Thomas Strothotte. Contextualized Text Explanation for Visualizations. In *2nd International Symposium on Smart Graphics*, pages 27–34, 2002.

[CSRS03]   Wallace Chigona, Henry Sonnet, Felix Ritter, and Thomas Strothotte. Shadows with a Message. In *3rd International Symposium on Smart Graphics*, pages 91–101, 2003.

[Dal97]   Gerard M. Dalgish. *Random House Webster's Dictionary of American English*. Random House Value Publishing, New York, 1997.

[DeM82]   Tom DeMarco. *Controlling Software Projects: Management, Measurement and Estimation*. Yourdan Press, New Jersey, 1982.

[Dig]   Digimation Inc. Viewpoint 3D Library. http://www.digimation.com/home-/modelhome.html, Accessed July 1, 2007.

[Dou]   Doug Cutting. Lucene Text Retrieval Engine. http://lucene.apache.org/, Accessed July 1, 2007.

[DWE02]   Joachim Diepstraten, Daniel Weiskopf, and Thomas Ertl. Transparency in Interactive Technical Illustrations. *Computer Graphics Forum*, 21(3):317–325, 2002.

[DWE03]   Joachim Diepstraten, Daniel Weiskopf, and Thomas Ertl. Interactive Cutaway Illustrations. *Computer Graphics Forum*, 22(3):523–532, 2003.

[EF00]   Albert Endres and Dieter W. Fellner. *Digitale Bibliotheken — Informatik–Lösungen für globale Wissensmärkte*. dpunkt Verlag, Heidelberg, 2000.

[FAM00]   Katerina Frantzi, Sophia Ananiadou, and Hideki Mima. Automatic Recognition of Multi–word Terms: the C–value/NC–value Method. *International Journal on Digital Libraries*, V3(2):115–130, 2000.

[Fel98]   Christiane Fellbaum, editor. *WordNet: An Electronic Lexical Database*. MIT Press, Cambridge, MA, 1998.

[FM93]   Steven K. Feiner and Kathleen R. McKeown. Automating the Generation of Coordinated Multimedia Explanations. In Mark T. Maybury, editor, *Intelligent Multimedia Interfaces*, pages 117–138. AAAI Press, Menlo Park, 1993.

[FMK+03] Thomas Funkhouser, Patrick Min, Michael Kazhdan, Joyce Chen, Alex Halderman, David Dobkin, and David Jacobs. A Search Engine for 3D Models. *ACM Transactions on Graphics*, 22(1):83–105, 2003.

[FMN+91] Elliot Fishman, Donna Magid, Derek Ney, Edward Chaney, Stephen Pizer, Julian Rosenman, David Levin, Michael Vannier, Janet Kuhlman, and Douglas Robertson. Three–Dimensional Imaging. *Radiology*, 181(2):321–337, 1991.

[FP99]   Jean-Daniel Fekete and Catherine Plaisant. Excentric Labeling: Dynamic Neighborhood Labeling for Data Visualization. In *SIGCHI Conference on Human Factors in Computing Systems*, pages 512–519, 1999.

[FS92]   Steven K. Feiner and Dorée D. Seligmann. Cutaways and Ghosting — Satisfying Visibility Constraints in Dynamic 3D Illustrations. *The Visual Computer*, 8(5&6):292–302, 1992.

[FSN+95] Myron Flickner, Harpreet Sawhney, Wayne Niblack, Jonathan Ashley, Qian Huang, Byron Dom, Monika Gorkani, Jim Hafner, Denis Lee, Dragutin Petkovic, David Steele, and Peter Yanker. Query by Image and Video Content: the QBIC System. *Computer*, 28(9):23–32, 1995.

[FvDFH90] James D. Foley, Andries van Dam, Steven K. Feiner, and John F. Hughes. *Computer Graphics: Principles and Practice*. Addison–Wesley, Boston, 2nd edition, 1990.

[GAHS05]   Timo Götzelmann, Kamran Ali, Knut Hartmann, and Thomas Strothotte. Form Follows Function: Aesthetic Interactive Labels. In *Eurographics Workshop on Computational Aesthetics in Graphics, Visualization and Imaging*, pages 193–200, 2005.

[GCSS06]   Dan B. Goldman, Brain Curless, David Salesin, and Steven M. Seitz. Schematic Storyboards for Video Editing and Visualization. *ACM Transactions on Graphics*, 25(3):862–871, 2006.

[GGA+07]   Timo Götzelmann, Marcel Götze, Kamran Ali, Knut Hartmann, and Thomas Strothotte. Annotating Images through Adaptation: An Integrated Text Authoring and Illustration Framework. *Journal of the WSCG*, 15(1):115–122, 2007.

[GGSS06]   Tobias Germer, Timo Götzelmann, Martin Spindler, and Thomas Strothotte. SpringLens: Distributed Nonlinear Magnifications. In *Eurographics '06 Short Papers*, pages 123–126, 2006.

[GNI05]   Marcel Götze, Petra Neumann, and Tobias Isenberg. User–Supported Interactive Illustration of Text. In *Simulation und Visualisierung*, pages 195–206, 2005.

[Göt04]   Timo Götzelmann. Interaktive Visualisierung Interner Beschriftungen in 3D–Oberflächenmodellen. Diplomarbeit, Fachhochschule Fulda, FB Angewandte Informatik und Mathematik, 2004.

[Gra18]   Henry F. R. S. Gray. *Anatomy of the Human Body*. Lea & Febiger, Philadelphia, 20th edition, 1918.

[HAS04]   Knut Hartmann, Kamran Ali, and Thomas Strothotte. Floating Labels: Applying Dynamic Potential Fields for Label Layout. In *4th International Symposium on Smart Graphics*, pages 101–113, 2004.

[HBMB05]   Graeme S. Halford, Rosemary Baker, Julie E. McCredden, and John D. Bain. How Many Variables Can Humans Process? *Psychological Science*, 15(1):70–76, 2005.

[Hir94]   Gerhard Hirtlreiter, editor. *Knaurs Weltatlas*. Lexigraphisches Institut, München, Deutsche Ausgabe edition, 1994.

[HIR+03]   Nick Halper, Tobias Isenberg, Felix Ritter, Bert Freudenberg, Oscar Meruvia, Stefan Schlechtweg, and Thomas Strothotte. OpenNPAR: A System for Developing, Programming, and Designing Non–Photorealistic Animation and Rendering. In *Pacific Graphics*, pages 424–428, 2003.

[HMP+00]   Sanda Harabagiu, Dan Moldovan, Marius Pasaca, Rada Mihalcea, Mihai Surdeanu, Razvan Bunescu, Roxana Girju, Vasile Rus, and Paul Morarescu. FALCON: Boosting Knowledge for Answer Engines. In *9th TREC Conference (TREC–9)*, pages 479–488, 2000.

[HO97]   David Haussler and Manfred Opper. Mutual Information, Metric Entropy, and Risk in Estimation of Probability Distributions. *Annals of Statistics*, 26(6):2451–2492, 1997.

[Hod03]   Elaine R. S. Hodges. *The Guild Handbook of Scientific Illustration*. John Wiley & Sons, Hoboken, 2nd edition, 2003.

[HP98]   Ralf Helbing and Bernhard Preim. Interaction Facilities and Highlevel Support for Animation Design. In Thomas Strothotte, editor, *Computational Visualization: Graphics, Abstraction, and Interactivity*, pages 259–276. Springer–Verlag, New York, 1998.

[HS02]   Knut Hartmann and Thomas Strothotte. A Spreading Activation Approach to Text Illustration. In *2nd International Symposium on Smart Graphics*, pages 39–46, 2002.

[HSKK01]   Masaki Hilaga, Yoshihisa Shinagawa, Taku Kohmura, and Tosiyasu L. Kunii. Topology Matching for Fully Automatic Similarity Estimation of 3D Shapes. In *28th Annual Conference on Computer Graphics and Interactive Techniques (SIGGRAPH '01)*, pages 203–212, 2001.

[HV96]   Beverly L. Harrison and Kim J. Vicente. An Experimental Evaluation of Transparent Menu Usage. In *SIGCHI Conference on Human Factors in Computing Systems (CHI '96)*, pages 391–398, 1996.

[Ide71]   Eleanor Ide. New Experiments in Relevance Feedback. In Gerard Salton, editor, *The SMART Retrieval System — Experiments in Automatic Document Processing*, chapter 16, pages 337–354. Prentice Hall, Englewood Cliffs, 1971.

[Imh75]   Eduard Imhof. Positioning Names on Maps. *The American Cartographer*, 2(2):128–144, 1975.

[JFS95]   Charles E. Jacobs, Adam Finkelstein, and David H. Salesin. Fast Multiresolution Image Querying. *Computer Graphics*, 29:277–286, 1995.

[JRS02]   Roland Jesse, Felix Ritter, and Thomas Strothotte. Bewegung als Präemptive Präsentationsvariable in einem Interaktiven System. In *Simulation und Visualisierung*, pages 275–288, 2002.

[KD05]   Florian Kirsch and Jürgen Döllner. OpenCSG: A Library for Image-Based CSG Rendering. In *USENIX 2005 Annual Technical Conference, FREENIX Track*, pages 129–140, 2005.

[KK88]   Tomihisa Kamada and Satoru Kawai. A Simple Method for Computing General Position in Displaying Three–Dimensional Objects. *Computer Vision, Graphics, and Image Processing*, 41(1):43–56, 1988.

[KL02]   Claudia Kunze and Lothar Lemnitzer. GermaNet — Representation, Visualization, Application. In *3rd International Conference on Language Ressources and Evaluation*, pages 1485–1491, 2002.

[KN04]   Michael Krauthammer and Goran Nenadic. Term Identification in the Bio-
           medical Literature. *Biomedical Informatics*, 37(6):512–526, 2004.

[Kön04]   Anne R. König. *Lesbarkeit als Leitprinzip der Buchtypographie*. Universität
           Erlangen–Nürnberg Buchwissenschaft, Erlangen, 2004.

[Kor97]   Robert R. Korfhage. *Information Storage and Retrieval*. John Wiley & Sons,
           New York, 1997.

[KPT⁺04]   Atanas Kiryakov, Borislav Popov, Ivan Terziev, Dimitar Manov, and Damyan
           Ognyanoff. Semantic Annotation, Indexing, and Retrieval. *Web Semantics:
           Science, Services and Agents on the World Wide Web*, 2(1):49–79, 2004.

[KR95]   Antonio Krüger and Thomas Rist. Since Less is Often More: Methods for
           Stylistic Abstractions in 3D–Graphics [Electronic version]. In *ACM Workshop
           on Effective Abstractions in Multimedia: Layout, Presentation, and Interaction*,
           1995.

[KR97]   T. Alan Keahey and Edward L. Robertson. Nonlinear Magnification Fields.
           In *IEEE Symposium on Information Visualization (InfoVis '97)*, page 51, 1997.

[Krü98]   Arno Krüger. Automatic Graphical Abstraction in Intent–Based 3D–Illustra-
           tions. In *Working Conference on Advanced Visual Interfaces (AVI '98)*, pages
           47–56, 1998.

[KSCT00]   Peter Z. Kunszt, Alex S. Szalay, Istvan Csabai, and Aniruddha R. Thakar.
           The Indexing of the SDSS Science Archive. In Nadine Manset, Christian
           Veillet, and Dennis Crabtree, editors, *ASP Conference Series*, volume 216, 141.
           Astronomical Society of the Pacific, 2000.

[KW03]   Ralf Kalmar and Volker Wulf. Das Virtuelle Software–Engineering–Kompe-
           tenzzentrum (ViSEK). In *6th International Conference Wirtschaftsinformatik*,
           pages 987–1006, 2003.

[LBWR94]   Gerald L. Lohse, Kevin Biolsi, Neff Walker, and Henry H. Rueter. A Classifi-
           cation of Visual Representations. *Communications of the ACM*, 37(12):36–49,
           1994.

[Lev66]   Vladimir I. Levenshtein. Binary Codes Capable of Correcting Deletions,
           Insertions, and Reversals. *Soviet Physics Doklady*, 10(8):707–710, 1966.

[Lip00]   Herbert Lippert. *Lehrbuch Anatomie*. Urban & Fischer, München, 2000.

[LL82]   W. Howard Levie and Richard Lentz. Effects of Text Illustrations: A Review
           of Research. *Educational Communication and Technology Journal*, 30(4):195–
           232, 1982.

[LRA⁺07]   Wilmot Li, Lincoln Ritter, Maneesh Agrawala, Brian Curless, and David
           Salesin. Interactive Cutaway Illustrations of Complex 3D Models. In *34th
           Annual Conference and Exhibition on Computer Graphics and Interactive Tech-
           niques (SIGGRAPH '07)*, (in print) 2007.

[LT04]   Alex Leykin and Mihran Tuceryan. Determining Text Readability over Tex-
            tured Backgrounds in Augmented Reality Systems. In *ACM SIGGRAPH
            International Conference on Virtual Reality Continuum and its Applications in
            Industry (VRCAI '04)*, pages 436–439, 2004.

[LVK+06]   Jan-Maarten Luursema, Willem B. Verwey, Piet A. M. Kommers, Robert H.
            Geelkerken, and Hans J. Vos. Optimizing Conditions for Computer–assisted
            Anatomical Learning. *Interacting with Computers*, 18(5):1123–1138, 2006.

[MA92a]   Richard E. Mayer and Richard B. Anderson. The Instructive Animation:
            Helping Students Build Connections Between Words and Pictures in Multi-
            media Learning. *Journal of Education Psychology*, 84(4):444–452, 1992.

[MA92b]   Richard E. Mayer and Richard B. Anderson. The Instructive Animation:
            Helping Students Build Connections between Words and Pictures in Multi-
            media Learning. *Educational Psychology*, 84(4):444–452, 1992.

[Mar89]   Judy Martin. *Technical Illustration : Materials, Methods and Techniques*. Child
            & Associates, Sydney, 1989.

[Mar95]   Gary Marchionini. *Information Seeking in Electronic Environments*. Cambridge
            University Press, 1995.

[Mar98]   Catherine C. Marshall. Making Metadata: A Study of Metadata Creation
            for a Mixed Physical–digital Collection. In *3rd ACM Conference on Digital
            Libraries (DL '98)*, pages 162–171, 1998.

[May89]   Richard E. Mayer. Systematic Thinking Fostered by Illustrations in Scientific
            Text. *Journal of Education Psychology*, 81(2):240–246, 1989.

[May01]   Richard E. Mayer. *Multimedia Learning*. Cambridge University Press, Cam-
            bridge, 2001.

[MD06a]   Stefan Maaß and Jürgen Döllner. Dynamic Annotation of Interactive En-
            vironments using Object–Integrated Billboards. In *14th International Confer-
            ence in Central Europe on Computer Graphics, Visualization and Computer Vision
            (WSCG)*, pages 327–334, 2006.

[MD06b]   Stefan Maaß and Jürgen Döllner. Efficient View Management for Dynamic
            Annotation Placement in Virtual Landscapes. In *6th International Symposium
            on Smart Graphics*, pages 1–12, 2006.

[MHMC05]   Richard E. Mayer, Mary Hegarty, Sarah Mayer, and Julie Campbell. When
            Static Media Promote Active Learning: Annotated Illustrations Versus Nar-
            rated Animations in Multimedia Instruction. *Journal of Experimental Psychol-
            ogy: Applied*, 11(4):256–265, 2005.

[Mil56]   George A. Miller. The Magical Number Seven, Plus or Minus Two: Some
            Limits on Our Capacity for Processing Information. *Psychological Review*,
            63(2):81–97, 1956.

[MK60]   Melvin E. Maron and John L. Kuhns. On Relevance, Probabilistic Indexing and Information Retrieval. *Journal of ACM*, 7(3):216–244, 1960.

[MM99]   Roxana Moreno and Richard E. Mayer. Cognitive Principles of Multimedia Learning. *Journal of Education Psychology*, 91(2):358–368, 1999.

[MMW01]   Frederick C. Mish and Merriam-Webster, editors. *Merriam–Webster's Collegiate Dictionary*. Merriam–Webster, Springfield, 10th edition, 2001.

[MNTP07]   Konrad Mühler, Mathias Neugebauer, Christian Tietjen, and Bernhard Preim. Viewpoint Selection for Intervention Planning. In *EG/IEEE–VGTC Symp. on Visualization*, pages 267–274, 2007.

[Moo02]   Antoni Moore. The Case for Approximate Distance Transforms. In *14th Annual Colloquium of the Spatial Information Research Centre (SIRC 2002)*, pages 137–148, 2002.

[MS92]   Robert B. McMaster and K. Stuart Shea. *Generalization in Digital Cartography*. The Association of American Geographers, Washington, 1992.

[Nat]   National Library of Medicine. Visible Human Project. http://www.nlm.nih.gov/research/visible/visible$_{human.html, Accessed July}$1, 2007.

[Nat04]   National Information Standards Organization. *Understanding Metadata*. NISO Press, Bethesda, 2004.

[NCFD06]   Daren T. Nicholson, Colin Chalk, W. Robert J. Funnell, and Sam J. Daniel. Can Virtual Reality Improve Anatomy Education? A Randomised Controlled Study of a Computer–generated Three–dimensional Anatomical Ear Model. *Medical Education*, 40(11):1081–1087, 2006.

[Olb06]   Martin Olbrich. Beschriftung von 3D–Modellen. Diplomarbeit, Technische Universität Dresden, 2006.

[Pai71]   Allan Paivio. *Imagery and Verbal Processes*. Holt, Rinehart and Winston, New York, 1971.

[PB96]   Dimitri Plemenos and Madjid Benayada. Intelligent Display in Scene Modeling. New Techniques to Automatically Compute Good Views. In *International Conference on Computer Graphics & Vision*, 1996.

[PE93]   Susan Palmiter and Jay Elkerton. Animated Demonstrations for Learning Procedural Computer–Based Tasks. *Human–Computer Interaction*, 8(3):193–216, 1993.

[Pea99]   Judy Pearsall, editor. *Oxford Concise English Dictionary*. Oxford University Press, Oxford, 10th edition, 1999.

[PGP03]   Ingo Petzold, Gerhard Gröger, and Lutz Plümer. Fast Screen Map Labeling — Data Structures and Algorithms. In *21st International Cartographic Conference*, pages 288–298, 2003.

[Pic00]   Joseph P. Pickett, editor. *The American Heritage Dictionary of the English Language*. Houghton Mifflin, Boston, 4th edition, 2000.

[Pie]   Eric Pierce. Four Stroke Cycle (Illustration). http://en.wikipedia.org/wiki/ Image:Four_stroke_cycle_compression.jpg, Accessed July 1, 2007.

[PKW+02]   Sameer Pradhan, Valerie Krugler, Wayne Ward, Daniel Jurafsky, James H. Martin, Kathy McKeown, and Vasilis Hatzivassiloglou. Using Semantic Representations in Question Answering. In *International Conference on Natural Language Processing (ICON '02)*, pages 195–203, 2002.

[PPP+05]   Nathalie Pavy, Charles Paule, Lee Parsons, John A. Crow, Marie-Josee Morency, Janice Cooke, James E. Johnson, Etienne Noumen, Carine Guillet-Claude, Yaron Butterfield, Sarah Barber, George Yang, Jerry Liu, Jeff Stott, Robert Kirkpatrick, Asim Siddiqui, Robert Holt, Marco Marra, Armand Seguin, Ernest Retzel, Jean Bousquet, and John MacKay. Generation, Annotation, Analysis and Database Integration of 16,500 White Spruce EST Clusters. *BMC Genomics*, 6(1):144, 2005.

[PR02]   Bernhard Preim and Felix Ritter. Techniken zur Hervorhebung von Objekten in medizinischen 3D–Visualisierungen. In *Simulation und Visualisierung*, pages 187–200, 2002.

[PRC81]   Stephen E. Palmer, Eleanor Rosch, and Paul Chase. Canonical Perspective and the Perception of Objects. In John Long and Alan Baddeley, editors, *Attention and Performance*, volume 9, pages 135–151. Erlbaum, Hillsdale, 1981.

[Pre98]   Bernhard Preim. *Interaktive Illustration und Animation zur Erklärung Komplexer Räumlicher Zusammenhänge*. PhD thesis, Otto–von–Guericke–Universität Magdeburg, 1998.

[PRS97]   Bernhard Preim, Andreas Raab, and Thomas Strothotte. Coherent Zooming of Illustrations with 3D–Graphics and Text. In *Graphics Interface*, pages 105–113, 1997.

[PSS91]   Kenneth N. Purnell, Robert T. Solman, and John Sweller. The Effects of Technical Illustrations on Cognitive Load. *Instructional Science*, 20(5–6):443–462, 1991.

[QF93]   Yonggang Qiu and Hans-Peter Frei. Concept Based Query Expansion. In *16th Annual International ACM SIGIR Conference on Research and Development in Information Retrieval (SIGIR '93)*, pages 160–169, 1993.

[RA90]   Thomas Rist and Elisabeth André. Wissensbasierte Perspektivenwahl für die Automatische Erzeugung von 3D–Objektdarstellungen. In *Graphik und KI*, pages 48–57, 1990.

[Ran89]   Robert O. Rankin. The Development of an Illustration Design Model. *Educational Technology Research and Development*, 37(2):25–46, 1989.

[Rey87]   Craig W. Reynolds. Flocks, Herds, and Schools: A Distributed Behavioral Model. *Computer Graphics*, 21(4):25–34, 1987.

[Roc71]   Joseph J. Rocchio. Relevance Feedback in Information Retrieval. In Gerard Salton, editor, *The SMART retrieval system — experiments in automatic document processing*, chapter 14, pages 313–323. Prentice Hall, Englewood Cliffs, 1971.

[Rog92]   Andrew W. Rogers. *Textbook of Anatomy*. Churchill Livingstone, Edinburgh, 1992.

[RR96]   Andreas Raab and Michael Rüger. 3D–Zoom: Interactive Visualisation of Structures and Relations in Complex Graphics. In Bernd Girod, Heinrich Niemann, and Hans-Peter Seidel, editors, *3D Image Analysis and Synthesis*, pages 125–132. infix–Verlag, Erlangen, 1996.

[RRD05]   Edward Rosten, Gerhard Reitmayr, and Tom Drummond. Real–Time Video Annotations for Augmented Reality. In *International Symposium on Visual Computing*, pages 294–302, 2005.

[RSHS03a]   Felix Ritter, Henry Sonnet, Knut Hartmann, and Thomas Strothotte. Illustrative Shadows: Integrating 3D and 2D Information Display. In *International Conference on Intelligent User Interfaces*, pages 166–173, 2003.

[RSHS03b]   Felix Ritter, Henry Sonnet, Knut Hartmann, and Thomas Strothotte. Illustrative Shadows: Integrating 3D and 2D Information Display. In *International Conference on Intelligent User Interfaces*, pages 166–173, 2003.

[RSZ94]   Evguenii A. Rakhmanov, Edward B. Saff, and Yong M. Zhou. Minimal Discrete Energy on the Sphere. *Mathematical Research Letters*, 1(6):647–662, 1994.

[RT92]   Kenneth B. Roberts and James D. W. Tomlinson. *The Fabric of the Body: European Traditions of Anatomical Illustration*. Clarendon Press, Oxford, 1992.

[SAB93]   Gerard Salton, James Allan, and Chris Buckley. Approaches to Passage Retrieval in Full Text Information Systems. In *16th Annual International ACM SIGIR Conference on Research and Development in Information Retrieval*, pages 49–58, 1993.

[SABS94]   Gerard Salton, James Allan, Chris Buckley, and Amit Singhal. Automatic Analysis, Theme Generation, and Summarization of Machine–Readable - Texts. *Science*, 264(5164):1421–1426, 1994.

[Sal71]   Gerard Salton. Relevance Feedback and the Optimization of Retrieval Effectiveness. In Gerard Salton, editor, *The SMART retrieval system — experiments in automatic document processing*, chapter 15, pages 324–336. Prentice Hall, Englewood Cliffs, 1971.

[SBGS06]   Martin Spindler, Marco Bubke, Tobias Germer, and Thomas Strothotte. Camera Textures. In *4th International Conference on Computer Graphics and Interactive Techniques in Australasia and Southeast Asia (GRAPHITE '06)*, pages 295–302, 2006.

[Sch94]   Wolfgang Schnotz. *Aufbau von Wissensstrukturen: Untersuchungen zur Ko-
            härenzbildung bei Wissenserwerb mit Texten.* Beltz PsychologieVerlagsUnion,
            Weinheim, 1994.

[Sch06]   Ingo Schmitt. *Ähnlichkeitssuche in Multimedia–Datenbanken: Retrieval, Suchal-
            gorithmen und Anfragebehandlung.* Oldenbourg Wissenschaftsverlag, Mün-
            chen, 2006.

[SCS04]   Henry Sonnet, M. Sheelagh T. Carpendale, and Thomas Strothotte. Inte-
            grating Expanding Annotations with a 3D Explosion Probe. In *International
            Working Conference on Advanced Visual Interfaces*, pages 63–70, 2004.

[SFW82]   Gerard Salton, Edward A. Fox, and Harry Wu. Extended Boolean Informa-
            tion Retrieval. *Communications of the ACM*, 26(11):1022–1036, 1982.

[SGF⁺05]   Alex S. Szalay, Jim Gray, Gyorgy Fekete, Peter Z. Kunszt, Peter Kukol, and
            Ani Thakar. Indexing the Sphere with the Hierarchical Triangular Mesh.
            Technical Report MSR–TR–2005–123, Microsoft Research, 2005.

[SH00]   Lauren F. V. Scharff and Alyson L. Hill. Discriminability Measures for Pre-
            dicting Readability of Text on Textured Backgrounds. *Optics Express*, 6(81–
            91):4, 2000.

[Sim74]   Herbert A. Simon. How Big is a Chunk? *Science*, 183(1):482–488, 1974.

[Sim91]   John A. Simpson, editor. *Oxford English Dictionary. Volume 1: A–Bazouki.*
            Clarendon Press, Oxford, 2nd edition, 1991.

[Sin91]   John M. Sinclair, editor. *Collins English Dictionary.* Harper Collins, Glasgow,
            3rd edition, 1991.

[SL05]   Henry Sonnet and Silvio Lange. Data Storage: Carrier Objects as Illustration
            Watermarks for 3D Polygonal Models. In *Simulation and Visualization*, pages
            305–316, 2005.

[SM00]   Heidrun Schumann and Wolfgang Müller. *Visualisierung: Grundlagen und
            Allgemeine Methoden.* Springer Verlag, Berlin, 2000.

[Son06]   Henry Sonnet. *Embedding Metadata in Computer Graphics for Interaction.* PhD
            thesis, Otto–von–Guericke–Universität Magdeburg, 2006.

[Sou03]   Mario C. Sousa. Scientific Illustration → Part 1: Traditional Techniques and
            NPR Approaches. In *Theory and Practice of Non–Photorealistic Graphics: Algo-
            rithms, Methods, and Production Systems*, chapter 2. 30th Annual Conference
            on Computer Graphics and Interactive Techniques (SIGGRAPH '03), 2003.

[SPP97]   Johannes Sobotta, Reinhard Putz, and Reinhard Pabst, editors. *Sobotta: Atlas
            of Human Anatomy. Volume 2: Thorax, Abdomen, Pelvis, Lower Limb.* Lippincott
            Williams & Wilkins, Baltimure, 12th English edition, 1997.

[SPP01]   Johannes Sobotta, Reinhard Putz, and Reinhard Pabst, editors. *Sobotta: Atlas of Human Anatomy*. Lippincott Williams & Wilkins, Baltimure, 13th edition, 2001.

[SS97]   Christine Strothotte and Thomas Strothotte. *Seeing Between the Pixels: Pictures in Interactive Systems*. Springer, New York, 1997.

[SS99]   Stefan Schlechtweg and Thomas Strothotte. Illustrative Browsing: A New Method of Browsing in Long On–line Texts. In *International Conference on Computer Human Interaction*, pages 466–473, 1999.

[SS02]   Thomas Strothotte and Stefan Schlechtweg. *Non–Photorealistic Computer Graphics: Modeling, Rendering, and Animation*. Morgan Kaufman, Los Altos, 2002.

[SSLR96]   Jutta Schumann, Thomas Strothotte, Stefan Laser, and Andreas Raab. Assessing the Effect of Non–Photorealistic Rendered Images in CAD. In *SIGCHI conference on Human factors in computing systems (CHI '96)*, pages 35–41, 1996.

[ST04]   Robert Strzodka and Alexandru Telea. Generalized Distance Transforms and Skeletons in Graphics Hardware. In *EG/IEEE TCVG Symposium on Visualization (VisSym '04)*, pages 221–230, 2004.

[SUS⁺06]   Henry Sonnet, Andrea Unger, Lothar Schlesier, Thomas Vogel, Tobias Isenberg, and Thomas Strothotte. Interactive Images using Illustration Watermarks: Techniques, Study, and Applications. Technical Report 7, Department of Computer Science, Otto–von–Guericke Universität Magdeburg, 2006.

[Suz01]   Motofumi T. Suzuki. A Web–based Retrieval System for 3D Polygonal Models. *Joint 9th IFSA World Congress and 20th NAFIPS International Conference*, 4(25–28):2271–2276, 2001.

[Swa92]   Julia Swannell, editor. *Oxford Modern English Dictionary*. Clarendon Press, Oxford, 1992.

[SWY75]   Gerard Salton, Benjamin A. Wong, and Changsheng S. Yang. A Vector Space Model for Automatic Indexing. *Communications of the ACM*, 18(11):613–620, 1975.

[Sys]   Systems in Motion. Coin3D. http://www.coin3d.org/, Accessed July 1, 2007.

[TFTN05]   Shigeo Takahashi, Issei Fujishiro, Yuriko Takeshima, and Tomoyuki Nishita. A Feature–Driven Approach to Locating Optimal Viewpoints for Volume Visualization. In *IEEE Visualization*, page 63, 2005.

[TH04]   Vineet Thanedar and Tobias Höllerer. Semi–Automated Placement of Annotations on Videos. Technical Report 2004–11, Department of Computer Science, University of California, Santa Barbara, 2004.

[Tor97]   Gerhard J. Tortora. *Introduction to the Human Body: The Essentials of Anatomy and Physiology*. Benjamin Cummings, Redwood City, 1997.

[Tro]   Trolltech. Qt: Cross–Platform Rich Client Development Framework. http://trolltech.com/products/qt, Accessed July 1, 2007.

[Tuf97]   Edward R. Tufte. *Visual Explanations: Images and Quantitatives, Evidence and Narrative*. Graphics Press, Cheshire, 1997.

[Tuf06]   Edward R. Tufte. *Beautiful Evidence*. Graphics Press, Cheshire, 2006.

[Tur]   David Turner. The FreeType Project. http://www.freetype.org/, Accessed July 1, 2007.

[VFSG06]   Ivan Viola, Miguel Feixas, Mateu Sbert, and Meister E. Gröller. Importance–Driven Focus of Attention. *IEEE Transactions on Visualization and Computer Graphics*, 12(5):933–940, 2006.

[VFSH01]   Pere-Pau Vázquez, Miguel Feixas, Mateu Sbert, and Wolfgang Heidrich. Viewpoint Selection using Viewpoint Entropy. In *Vision Modeling and Visualization Conference*, pages 273–280, 2001.

[VFSL06]   Pere-Pau Vázquez, Miguel Feixas, Mateu Sbert, and Antoni Llobet. Real-time Automatic Selection of Good Molecular Views. *Computers & Graphics*, 30(1):98–110, 2006.

[VKG04]   Ivan Viola, Armin Kanitsar, and Eduard Gröller. Importance–Driven Volume Rendering. In *IEEE Visualization 2004*, pages 139–145, 2004.

[VVAH07]   Ian Vollick, Dan Vogel, Maneesh Agrawala, and Aaron Hertzmann. Specifying Label Layout Styles by Example. In *ACM Symposium on User Interface Software and Technology (UIST'07)*, (to appear) 2007.

[WAF⁺93]   Wolfgang Wahlster, Elisabeth André, Wolfgang Finkler, Hans-Jürgen Profitlich, and Thomas Rist. Plan–Based Integration of Natural Language and Graphics Generation. *Artificial Intelligence*, 63(1–2):387–427, 1993.

[Wei94]   Bernd Weidenmann, editor. *Wissenserwerb mit Bildern: Instruktionale Bilder in Printmedien, Film/Video und Computerprogrammen*. Verlag Hans Huber, Göttingen, 1994.

[Wei95]   Bernd Weidenmann. Multicodierung und Multimodalität im Lernprozeß. In Paul Klimsa and Ludwig J. Issing, editors, *Information und Lernen mit Multimedia*, pages 65–84. Psychologie Verlags Union, Weinheim, 1995.

[WKLH00]   Jian K. Wu, Mohan S. Kankanhalli, Joo-Hwee Lim, and Dezhong Hong. *Perspectives on Content–Based Multimedia Systems*. Kluwer Academic Publishers, Boston, 2000.

[WKLW98] Stuart Weibel, John Kunze, Carl Lagoze, and Misha Wolf. Dublin Core Metadata Element Set, Version 1.0: Reference Description, IETF #2413. Retrieved July 1, 2007, from http://dublincore.org/documents/1998/09/dc-es/, 1998.

[WO90] Colin Ware and Steven Osborne. Exploration and Virtual Camera Control in Virtual Three Dimensional Environments. In *Symposium on Interactive 3D Graphics (SI3D '90)*, pages 175–183, 1990.

[Wyn05] Martin Wynne, editor. *Developing Linguistic Corpora: A Guide to Good Practice*. Oxbow Books, Oxford, 2005.

[YCB05] Yonggao Yang, Jim X. Chen, and Mohsen Beheshti. Nonlinear Perspective Projections and Magic Lenses: 3D View Deformation. *Computer Graphics & Applications*, 25(1):76–84, 2005.

[YDF04] Changbo Yang, Ming Dong, and Farshad Fotouhi. Learning the Semantics in Image Retrieval — A Natural Language Processing Approach. In *Conference on Computer Vision and Pattern Recognition Workshop (CVPRW '04). Volume 9*, page 137, 2004.

[YKCK06] Fei Yan, Alexey Kostin, William Christmas, and Josef Kittler. A Novel Data Association Algorithm for Object Tracking in Clutter with Application to Tennis Video Analysis. In *IEEE Computer Society Conf. on Computer Vision and Pattern Recognition (CVPR)*, pages 634–641, 2006.

[ZC01] Cha Zhang and Tsuhan Chen. An Active Learning Framework for Content Based Information Retrieval. Technical Report AMP01–04, Carnegie Mellon Technical Report, 2001.

List of Figures

Figure Number   Page

1.1   Human inner ear as example for an annotated illustration. (Source: [Tor97])   2

1.2   Combination of continuous text and illustration. (Adapted from [Tor97]) .   3

2.1   Three different options to store the annotations of 3D models.   15

2.2   Abstracted examples of books predominantly consisting of illustrations I
      (left) and conjunctions of expository text T and illustrations (right).   16

2.3   Perspective (left) and orthogonal (right) projection of a cube.   19

2.4   Reference by spatial proximity (left) and reference by figure captions (right). 22

2.5   Reference to illustration parts by verbal description (left) and reference by
      annotations (right).   22

2.6   The layers of illustrations.   23

3.1   Internal annotation styles. (Source: [SPP01, p. 279] and [Gra18, p. 1328]) . .   30

3.2   External annotation layout styles. (Source: [Rog92, p. 191] and [SPP97,
      p. 19])   31

3.3   Annotation boxes styles. (Source: [Tor97, p. 129] and [Lip00, p. 310])   33

3.4   Original figure (left), redrawn figure (right). (Source: [Tuf97, p. 74])   34

3.5   Magnified excerpt of a map with different types of annotations. (Source:
      [Hir94])   36

3.6   Simplified medial axis (dashed line) according Blum [Blu67].   37

3.7   Annotated virtual campus (left) and human model (right).   41

3.8   Multiple annotated buildings with billboarded annotations.   42

3.9   Virtual landscape with annotations communicating depth by font size. . .   43

3.10 Zoom Illustrator interface with annotations in designated areas.   44

3.11 Morphing from internally annotated shadows external annotation.   44

3.12 Annotated explosion diagrams: different external annotation styles.   45

3.13 Multiple internal annotation styles.   46

3.14 Multiple external annotation styles. 47

3.15 External annotation by allowing overlaps with primary object. 47

4.1 Salient point S and $n = 5$ letter centers L. 54

4.2 Anchor A and
$n = 4$ connection points T. 54

4.3 Exemplary pixels covered by secondary elements. 55

4.4 Translation between color-ID (shades of gray) and textual annotation. . . . 58

4.5 Exemplary distance field: banana shaped object with color–ID 1 on its
background with color–ID 0 (left) and its distance field (right). 58

4.6 Color–coded heart indicated by differing shades of gray (left) and its distance field (right). The darker the pixels, the higher the distance values. . 59

4.7 The application's architecture in *layout only mode* ① and *rendering mode* ②. 60

4.8 The numbers refer to the sequence of allocated squares of annotation
boxes (left) and internal annotation candidates (right). Hatched parts denote another color–ID. 61

4.9 Orbit: constant distance to the 3D model's silhouette (left) or bounding
box (right). 62

4.10 Internal letter layout element (left) and its parameters for different text
strokes (right). 64

4.11 Sequential placement of the letters on the distance field. First, the midst
element is placed on a candidate with an initial angle of $\alpha_{init} = 180°$.
Subsequent letters (see ordinal numbers) are placed by $\alpha_{max} = 75°$. 65

4.12 Assignment of the top three candidates (left), simultaneous expansion
(right). 66

4.13 Dashed line: convex hull of anchor points (left), anchors on the convex
hull have to be accommodated on the remaining valid candidates (right). 67

4.14 Agent evaluating neighborhood of P (middle), movement (right). 68

4.15 Annotation–Agents request (middle), and response (right). 68

4.16 Adapting annotation types during user zooms into a heart model. 71

5.1 Only veins are annotated, whilst other parts are deemphasized by semi–
transparency (Source: [SPP01, p. 89]). 74

5.2 Illustration with grouped annotations and colored (shaded) parts (Source:
[Tor97, p. 113]). 75

5.3 Determination of centroid (left), accommodation of external annotations
in the nearest annotation box candidate (right). 77

5.4 Changing between groups (without transparency). 77

5.5 Different exclusively annotated contexts (supported by transparency). . . 78

5.6 The experimental application with the taxonomy editor (left). 79

5.7 Contextual groups of a motor. 80

5.8 10 out of 20 buttons are annotated, find those which are listed on the right. 82

5.9 Grouped annotations without resolving reference line intersections. 83

5.10 Time required to solve the test modes of the user study. 84

6.1 The users are interested in the brightly marked text. They have to find the illustrations' parts which accord with the technical terms. (Adapted from [Tor97, p.127]) 89

6.2 The users are interested in the brightly marked parts of the illustration. They have to find the text segments addressing these parts. (Adapted from [Tor97, p.127]) 89

6.3 The preprocessing step for the creation of the textual descriptor databases. 93

6.4 Both search tasks supported by the approach. 93

6.5 The generation of paragraph descriptors. 94

6.6 Recursive decomposition of the sphere (Levels 1 to 5). (Source: [SGF⁺05]) 95

6.7 The generation of view descriptors. 96

6.8 Centricity measure of 3D parts by concentric ellipses. 99

6.9 According to the cosine measure the document d_2 is most similar to query q. 105

7.1 A text $\mapsto$ view query (left) with its results (right). 112

7.2 A view $\mapsto$ text query (right) and its results (left). 113

7.3 Refinement of a text query. 114

7.4 Refinement of a view query. 115

7.5 Select the alternative (a,b,c) where the green spheres are optimally visible. 116

7.6 Which view (a,b,c) shows the optimal visibility of the *steering wheel*, the *gearshift lever*, and the *center console*? 117

7.7 Which text (a,b,c) describes the visible parts of the illustration most appropriate? 117

7.8 Test results of the measures relative visible size and centricity. 118

7.9 Text$\mapsto$Illustration retrieval results (left) and Illustration$\mapsto$Text retrieval results (right). 119

A.1 Working combustion engine. (Source: [Pie]) 131

A.2 Problems induced by moving secondary elements. 133

A.3 Detection of calm areas. 134

A.4 Annotation of animation paths. 136

A.5 Calm (white) and fluctuating (grey) regions of a motor (animated ventila-
      tor and pistons). 137

A.6 Annotated calm regions. 137

A.7 Annotated animation paths. 138

A.8 Test scene of the user study: Select the corresponding button. 139

A.9 Relative time required for the tasks (normalized by median). 141

D.1 Determination of annotation boxes' and internal annotations' candidates. . 153

D.2 Determination of the best candidate. 154

D.3 Annotation type hysteresis algorithm. 154

D.4 Group annotation layout algorithm. 155

D.5 Algorithm for the selection of the books' specimen. 155

E.1 Exemplary annotation file. 157

E.2 Exemplary taxonomy file. 158

List of Tables

Table Number   Page

3.1   Layout containers share annotation types with equal layout requirements.   28
3.2   Imhof's types of annotations in maps.   37
3.3   Evaluation of the related work according to the specifications.   48

4.1   Distance functions with their graphical representation $(a, b \in \mathbb{N}^2, n = 2)$. .   52

6.1   Evaluation of the retrieval types according to the specifications.   102
6.2   Characteristics of search interaction techniques.   107

A.1   Comparison of two alternative methods for the determination of the mid-
      point of complex–shaped 3D parts.   135
A.2   Comparison of line smoothing methods.   135

B.1   Results of the analysis of the investigated corpus of books.   144

C.1   List of the experts consulted.   149

Index

Symbols

3D Model . . . . 11, *see also* Document
   Animated 132
   Implicit 11
   Procedural 11
   Surface 11
   Voxel 11
3D Parts 11, 57

A

Anchor Point 27, 30, 35, 39
Animations 131
   Calm regions 133, 134
   Path 133, 134
Annotation 12, 57
   Analysis 26
   Approach 40, 57
   Containers 28, 60, 63, 68, 70
   Formal 13
   Function 21
   Guidelines 33–37
   Illustration 21
   Informal 13
   Label 21
   Layout 24
   Metrics 52–57
     Frame Coherence 56, 66, 70
     Legibility 52
     Unambiguity 54
     Visual Occlusion 55
   Path . . . . *see* Text Stroke
   Specifications 38, 40, 132
   Storage 14
   Style 29–32
   Text Stroke 27
   Types 26–28
Applicability . . . . *see* Specifications

B

Book Corpus 26, 143
Boost Function 107

C

Canonical Views 98
Chunking 75
Cognitive Capacity 74
Color–ID 57
COMET 91
Container
   Annotation Box 29
   External 29
   Internal 28
Containers . . . . *see also* Annotation
Context 12
   3D 12
   Text 12
   View 12
Cosine Similarity . . *see* Vector Space Model
Coverage . . . . *see* Specifications

D

Descriptors
   Generation 93
   Indexation 103
   Paragraph Descriptors 92, 93
   View Descriptors 92, 94
Dictionary . . . . *see* Information Retrieval
Distance Functions 52
Document 10
   3D Model 11
   Text 10
Document Vector . . *see* Vector Space Model
Dual use of image space 44

E

Emphasis Techniques 19, 74, 78

Encapsulated Annotation Approach....57
    Adaptivity.........................70
    Agents............................66
    Algorithms 60
    Architecture 59
    Candidates 60
    Initial Layout..................63, 70
    Interfaces 57
    Orbit.............................61
    Weighted Evaluation...............61
Experimental Application 78, 110, 136
Exploration 18
    Eye–in–hand 18, 41
    World–in–hand................19, 43

F

Flexibility .... *see* Specifications
Flocking Behavior.....................68
Frame Coherence .... *see* Specifications, *see*
    Metrics

G

G–buffer
    Distance–buffer...................57
    Frame–buffer 57
    ID–buffer 57
Granularity 92, 93, 120
Guidelines............. *see also* Annotation
    Maps 35
    Scientific Illustrations 33
    Technical Illustrations.............33

H

Hill Climbing 67

I

Illustration...........................15
    Annotated 21
    Computer–based...................18
    Layer Model......................22
    Process 23
    Usage in Textbooks 16
Illustration Background 23

Illustrators Dilemma 74
Importance Values........94, 95, 107, 114
Indexation.......*see* Information Retrieval
Information Retrieval .... *see also* Retrieval
    Dictionary 102
    Indexation.......................102
    Models 102
        Boolean.......................103
        Fuzzy.........................103
        Probabilistic 103
        Vector Space 103, 104
    Query Modification...............106
    Ranking Function.................103
    Relevance Feedback 106
    Stemming 102
    Stopwords.......................102
    Term Weights...........102, 105, 107
Information Visualization 18

L

Layout .... *see also* Annotation
    Exclusive 77
    Grouped 76
Layout Only Mode....................57
Legibility .... *see* Specifications, *see* Metrics

M

Media...................................10
Media capabilities .... *see* Specifications
Metadata..............................11
    Content descriptive 12
    Content independent 11
    Content related 11
Metrics
    Annotation .... *see* Annotation
    Distance 52
Multi–word Terms 120
Multimedia Retrieval........ *see* Retrieval

N

NPR....................... *see* Rendering

O

Orbit . . . . *see* Encapsulated Annotation
    Approach

P

Primary Object 23

Q

Query
    Text↦View 111, 114
    View↦Text 112, 114
Query Modification . . . . *see* Information
    Retrieval

R

Reference Line 27, 30, 35, 39
Referred Part 23
Relevance Feedback . . . . *see* Information
    Retrieval
Rendering 18
    NPR 19
    Projection 18
Rendering Mode 57
Retrieval 100
    Annotation–based 90
    Content–based 90
    Data Retrieval 101
    Information Retrieval 101
    Multimedia 103
    Query 101, 104
    Specifications 100

S

Scalability . . . . *see* Specifications
Search Tasks 88
    Illustration↦Text 89, 91
    Text↦Illustration 88, 91
Search Time 80
Secondary Elements 23
Selectiveness . . . . *see* Specifications
Smallest Effective Difference 33
Specifications . . . . *see* Annotation

Specimen 143
Spring Lens 115
Stemming . . . . *see* Information Retrieval
Stopwords . . . . . . *see* Information Retrieval

T

Taxonomy 75
Term Frequencies . . *see* Vector Space Model
Term Weights . . . . *see* Information Retrieval
Text . . . . 10, *see also* Document
    Expository 10
    Instructive 10
    Narrative 10
Text Illustrator 91
Text Stroke . . . . *see* Annotation
Textual Descriptors . . . . *see* Descriptors
Threshold Value . . . *see* Vector Space Model

U

Unambiguity *see* Specifications, *see* Metrics
User Study 80, 115, 138

V

Vector Space Model . . . *see also* Information
    Retrieval
    Cosine similarity 105
    Dictionary 105
    Document Vector 105
    Term Frequencies 105
    Threshold Value 101, 105
View Management 41
View Selection 94, 96–100, 120
    Informed Methods 98
    Specifications 97
    Uninformed Methods 98
    Viewpoint Entropy 99
Visual Occlusion . . . . . *see* Specifications, *see*
    Metrics

W

WIP 91

Z

Zoom Illustrator 43

www.ingramcontent.com/pod-product-compliance
Lightning Source LLC
LaVergne TN
LVHW062316060326
832902LV00013B/2251